Sea Battles
of the
20th Century

Sea Battles
of the
20th Century

George Bruce

Hamlyn
London·New York·Sydney·Toronto

Published 1975 and
© Copyright 1975 by
The Hamlyn Publishing Group Limited
London · New York · Sydney · Toronto
Astronaut House, Feltham, Middlesex, England

Second impression 1976

ISBN 0 600 38096 3

Printed in Great Britain by
Butler & Tanner Ltd, Frome and London

Contents

Tsushima
May 1905

At dawn on 27 May 1905, the Russian Baltic Fleet steamed slowly through heavy seas in the approaches to the Tsushima Strait, between Korea and Japan. Eight months earlier it had set out from Kronstadt on its epic 18,000-mile voyage round the world, with the express object of destroying Japanese naval power in the Far East. Now that it was within reach of its objective, in the enemy's home waters, almost every one of its officers and men, including the commander-in-chief, Admiral Zinovi Rojdestvensky, hoped and prayed that the fleet would escape battle and, undetected by the Japanese, steam through the Sea of Japan to the Russian base at Vladivostock.

The Russo-Japanese War had its origins in the clash of rival Russian and Japanese imperialism in Manchuria, China and Korea in 1903. Tsar Nicholas II and his Government had repeatedly spurned Japanese offers of conciliation; in February 1904 Japan broke off diplomatic relations and, without a formal declaration of war, attacked and defeated the Russian fleet at Port Arthur. The Japanese then landed troops on the Liao-Tung peninsula, defeated the Russian army there, and by May had occupied Dairen.

In constant naval clashes in the Yellow Sea and the Sea of Japan, Admiral Togo had inflicted loss after loss on the Russians, culminating on 10 August 1904 in the defeat of the Vladivostock squadron, in which five Russian battleships were crippled and the Russian Admiral Vithöft, who was then on his way to aid the Russian army in Port Arthur, was killed. It was a fatal setback for the Russians. On 2 January 1905, after savage fighting, the Russians in Port Arthur surrendered. Just over two months later the important town of Mukden fell, with the loss of 30,000 Russians killed and 90,000 wounded; 40,000 Russians were taken prisoner.

Russia had embarked on a universally unpopular war with Japan at a time of domestic discontent and threatening revolution. And these two factors—political struggles and hatred of the war—had fatal effects upon the quality and the morale of the crews of Admiral Rojdestvensky's Baltic Fleet. Renamed the Second Pacific Squadron, it had been given the unenviable task—after the destruction of Russia's First Pacific Squadron based on Vladivostock—of sailing via the Atlantic, the Indian Ocean and the South China Sea to attack and destroy Admiral Togo's seasoned and victorious fleet in the Far East, with the object of cutting the Japanese army's links with its home bases and rescuing Russia from defeat.

Admiral Rojdestvensky was chosen to achieve this end because he was the Tsar's favourite, though he had never commanded a fleet in battle. Russia's best naval personnel had already gone down with their ships in battles with the Japanese or were languishing in enemy prisoner-of-war camps. Most of the so-called Second Pacific Squadron's new intake were raw recruits dazed by their first experience of warship life, reservists who had not seen the sea for years, or revolutionaries of whom the authorities wished to rid themselves, and who at once set to work to create a mutinous spirit on board the ships of the Squadron.

On the night of 21 October 1904, soon after the Russian fleet sailed from Kronstadt, Rojdestvensky and his officers, all acutely apprehensive of the enemy and his prowess, mistook the British fleet of trawlers from Hull, fishing in the North Sea, for a flotilla of Japanese destroyers. In a wild and confused orgy of gunfire in which discipline vanished like shell smoke, the entire fleet opened fire on the trawlers, sinking one and damaging three of them as well as killing two fishermen and wounding several more. The Russians then failed to stop to give help when they realized that they had made a terrible mistake.

Britain, whose sympathies were firmly with her ally Japan, saw the incident as an outrage and, when there were no suitable public apologies, threatened naval counter-action. With her combined Home and Mediterranean Fleets she played cat-and-mouse with the Russian fleet on its progress south to Spain. Finally,

Opposite: The *Askold,* a ship of the Russian navy's Port Arthur squadron.

at Vigo, four Russian officers were left behind to attend an international court of inquiry in Hull, and for the time being the incident was closed; but it made the progress of the fleet around the world infinitely harder, as many neutral countries firmly refused it harbour facilities for the unending task of coaling.

Rojdestvensky, hailed by the Russian press as a national saviour, spent his days during this long voyage sitting in an armchair on the flagship *Suvaroff*'s bridge, watching to see that the vessels kept line and maintained correct distance from each other. He took little interest in the engine-rooms, gun-turrets or between decks.

However, if a ship got out of line, this tall, grave, imposing admiral, with his penetrating dark eyes and trimmed black beard, completely lost control of himself. Seaman Novikoff-Priboy, an educated rating on board the flagship, wrote later:

He jumped out of his armchair shouting furiously. Sometimes he would fling his cap on the deck, whereupon one of his officers would pick it up and hold it reverently as if it were a holy relic. Panic swept across the bridge. The officers of the watch, the staff, look-out men, orderlies, bluejackets, contemplated the admiral with terror, as though he had been a 15-inch shell about to burst. After a volley of oaths directed at the offending vessel, the order would come: 'Signal that idiot a reprimand!' Or: 'Signal that preposterous almshouse not to lag behind as she is doing.'

In a minute the signal which announced to the entire fleet that a certain warship had blundered was flying and the Admiral would calm down temporarily.

His rear-admirals and captains carefully avoided visiting the *Suvaroff*, except when duty forced them to, for they knew how unpredictable were Rojdestvensky's manners and temper and that an unavoidable meeting might bring a shower of abuse down on their heads in front of subordinates. He referred in public to his officers by the sometimes funny, sometimes offensive nicknames which he had coined. Rear-Admiral Felkersham, a rather portly fellow, he called 'the manure-sack'; Captain Ber, the commander of the *Oslyabya* and a well-known womanizer, he referred to as 'the lascivious carrion'.

In addition to these breaches of naval etiquette, Rojdestvensky kept his commanders completely in the dark about his plans (if he had any) to defeat the enemy. He did nothing about training officers and men to equip them for the trial in seamanship and gunnery which would face them when they met the Japanese. He neither summoned his officers to councils of war nor talked about their troubles and difficulties with them, and went on board the other warships only to hand out reprimands.

Occasionally during the eight-month voyage the fleet carried out simple manoeuvres. Gunnery practice was carried out twice at the Admiral's command, but on both occasions everything went wrong. Ammunition hoists jammed; shells had to be lugged up to the gun turrets by hand; gunners were unable to handle properly the up-to-date new British range-finders or telescopic sights, working out ranges so incorrectly that their marksmanship was wildly inaccurate. In one distressing incident a shell exploded alongside the cruiser *Dmitri Donskoy* and then another, a dud, tore through her bridge, luckily without hitting anyone.

An unprepared and demoralized fleet was thus sailing to battle against a superbly trained enemy, who was confident and ready and whose morale was sustained by a succession of victories. Admiral Togo had commanded the Japanese fleet for eight years, and between him and his officers there flourished an intimate understanding. Five of his vice-admirals and seven of his rear-admirals, either commanding squadrons or ships or serving as junior flag officers, were his old comrades and pupils, having received their naval training under his command.

Togo's career reflected the rebirth and rise of the Japanese navy. Born in 1847, Togo enlisted in the navy in 1863, at the start of its programme of modernization and development. Britain was then the acknowledged

Above: Tsar Nicholas II. He inspected Rojdestvensky's doomed fleet on 9 October 1905, shortly before it sailed.

Opposite, top: Admiral Count Heihachiro Togo, commander-in-chief of the Imperial Navy, deliberately planned to attack the Russian fleet in Japanese home waters, where his men and ships would be at their best. Togo received his naval education at HMS *Worcester* and later studied at the Royal Naval College.

Opposite, bottom: Admiral Zinovi Rojdestvensky, commander-in-chief of the Russian Baltic Fleet, had been assigned the task of defeating the Japanese at sea because he was one of the Tsar's favourites, though he had never seen action before.

Left: Russian battleships of the 1st Pacific Squadron, sunk by Admiral Togo in August 1904, ten months before the battle of Tsushima, lie rusting on their bottoms outside Port Arthur.

9

leading naval power and Togo, already outstanding, was chosen for a naval education on HMS *Worcester*, after which he completed a gunnery course on *Victory* and later studied at the Royal Naval College at Greenwich. Japan was Britain's ally, to whom she turned for instruction in naval techniques and architecture and to whom she entrusted the design and construction of nearly all her warships.

In command of the cruiser *Naniwa* in 1894, Togo played a leading part in the naval actions of the Sino-Japanese war and won a name for himself as a fighting captain and a rigid disciplinarian who drove his men hard but led them to victory. As navy commander-in-chief in the war against Russia he dealt the first devastating blows at Port Arthur that crippled the Russian squadron there. On 13 April 1904 he followed this up by sinking the first-class battleship *Petropavlosk* by mine, and subsequently blockading Port Arthur; in August of that year he inflicted heavy losses on the Vladivostock fleet sailing to relieve the blockaded squadron.

After the fall of Port Arthur on 2 January 1905, the Japanese fleet was withdrawn to Japan for machinery repairs, the replacement of guns, the supply of new, more devastating

Rear-Admiral Nebogatoff became second-in-command of the Russian fleet without knowing it, Rojdestvensky having failed to inform him of the death, shortly before the battle, of Rear-Admiral Felkersham, till then second-in-command. After the destruction of the Russian fleet on the first day of battle, Nebogatoff surrendered the 3rd Division 'to avoid useless bloodshed'.

This still photograph of the mutineers' leaders from the Russian film *Potemkin* illustrates the spirit of mutiny which simmered below the surface on board the Baltic Fleet.

high explosive shells, and also for more intensive training. In April, when Admiral Togo led it to its chosen base in Korea, it was probably the most formidable naval force Japan had ever sent to sea.

On 22 May, Rojdestvensky, still hoping to reach Vladivostock without facing the crash of Togo's shells exploding on the *Suvaroff*'s decks, tried to lure Togo's warships away and out into the Pacific by sending two of his auxiliary cruisers sailing round the east coast of Japan. It was a clever ruse but the auxiliary cruisers were no substitute for a whole fleet, and Togo's scouts were not deceived.

The next day, about three-quarters of the way towards the Straits, Rojdestvensky halted his ships in a calm sea for what he hoped would be their last coaling before reaching Vladivostock. As the black clouds of coal dust rose ominously over his warships, the second-in-command, Admiral Felkersham, died. For his own reasons Rojdestvensky kept the news secret. Felkersham's flag still flew bravely from his flagship although he lay dead in his coffin. Admiral Nebogatoff, now legally second-in-command, was sailing into battle totally ignorant of his new responsibilities, or of the fact that a shell splinter hitting Rojdestvensky

would make him commander-in-chief.

The colliers were ordered to turn and sail for Shanghai on the cold and gloomy morning of 25 May. Officers and men turned their envious glances away from them to the northeast as these grubby vessels vanished in a belt of rain. Everyone was full of inward anguish, noted Seaman Novikoff, for they had only a dreadful end to look forward to. Even the weather seemed ominous. 'The steel hawsers that stayed the masts whistled in the wind. The grey clouds with which the sky was overcast sank lower and lower. Fine rain, falling aslant, troubled the surface of the sea. The

Admiral Rojdestvensky, who was wounded when his flagship *Suvaroff* was crippled by enemy fire, lies in bed, unable to walk, in a Japanese hospital ship.

An artist's impression of the Russian fleet as it set out on its fateful journey from Kronstadt to Tsushima.

皇國興廢在此一戰
各員一層奮勵努力
東郷平八郎書

horizon was wrapped in haze, and waves splashed against the sides of the ironclad.'

Of the two fleets soon to meet in the biggest naval battle since Trafalgar, the Russian fleet had the apparent advantage, with five powerful new battleships and seven old ones against the four effective battleships and eight heavy armoured cruisers of the Japanese fleet. Rojdestvensky's 1st Division comprised his flagship *Suvaroff*, the *Alexander III*, *Borodino* and *Orel*, all with a displacement of 15,000 tons, speeds of up to 18 knots and main armament of four 12-inch guns. Three of Togo's four battleships, the *Mikasa* (his flagship), the *Asahi* and *Shikishima*, had a displacement of some 15,000 tons and the fourth, *Fuji*, a displacement of 12,600 tons; all four had the same speed and main armament as the Russians, whose maximum speed, however, was brought down to a mere 11 knots by the obsolete battleships in the fleet.

The late Admiral Felkersham's flagship, the 12,600-ton *Oslyabya*, led Rojdestvensky's much less formidable 2nd Division. This included the two old and slow battleships, *Sisoy Veliky* and *Navarin*, each with four obsolete 12-inch guns in the main turrets; and the twenty-year-old *Admiral Nakhimoff*, with eight obsolete 8-inch guns. The 3rd Division comprised Nebogatoff's slow flagship *Nicholas I* and three old coastal defence ships, nicknamed 'flat-irons', each with short-range 10-inch guns and maximum speed of about 11 knots.

Admiral Enkvist, on board the *Oleg*, a 23-knot heavy cruiser with twelve 6-inch guns, also commanded the cruisers *Aurora* (eight 6-inch guns), the much smaller *Svetlana* (six 6-inch guns), two obsolete cruisers, *Dmitri Donskoy* and *Vladimir Monomakh* (six 6-inch guns apiece) and three small but fast cruisers, *Zhemchug*, *Izumrud* and *Almaz*, all with smaller armament.

In Togo's fleet, Admiral Kamimura commanded eight fast heavy cruisers mounting eight 8-inch guns, as well as sixteen smaller cruisers with guns varying from 8-inch to 120mm. There were also twenty small destroyers of around 350 tons displacement, each of which was equipped with 77mm and 57mm guns and two torpedo tubes. Rojdestvensky had seven approximately similar destroyers, and both sides also deployed a small number of auxiliary cruisers. Finally, Togo also commanded an important squadron of twenty torpedo-boats which were to play a decisive role in the battle.

In terms of first-line ships, Russia thus mounted twenty-six 12-inch, fourteen 10-inch, four obsolete 9-inch and eight obsolete 8-inch guns; Togo could bring to bear twenty 12-inch, four 10-inch and thirty 8-inch guns. The total weight of a Russian broadside would be greater, but the Japanese total fire would be much more destructive throughout a battle because their training and morale enabled them to aim and reload their guns more quickly.

Rojdestvensky ordered his fleet to adopt a new convoy formation of two columns on the

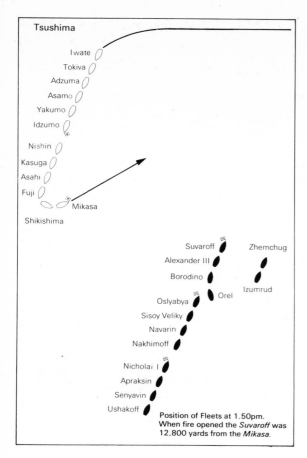

Tsushima

Iwate
Tokiva
Adzuma
Asamo
Yakumo
Idzumo
Nishin
Kasuga
Asahi
Fuji
Mikasa
Shikishima

Suvaroff
Alexander III
Borodino
Orel
Oslyabya
Sisoy Veliky
Navarin
Nakhimoff
Nicholai I
Apraksin
Senyavin
Ushakoff

Zhemchug
Izumrud

Position of Fleets at 1.50pm.
When fire opened the *Suvaroff* was
12,800 yards from the *Mikasa*.

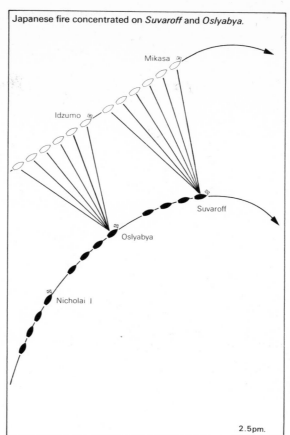

Japanese fire concentrated on *Suvaroff* and *Oslyabya*.

Mikasa
Idzumo
Suvaroff
Oslyabya
Nicholai I

2.5pm.

evening of 25 May, as it steamed into the danger zone through an angry sea and a cold blinding rain. The *Svetlana*, the *Almaz*, and the auxiliary cruiser *Ural* took up position as scouts in wedge formation about two miles ahead. The fleet then formed into two columns: the eight battleships of the 1st and 2nd Divisions to starboard, led by the *Suvaroff*; and to port the 3rd Division and the cruiser squadrons, eight ships in all, led by the *Nicholai* and accompanied by five torpedo-boats. Abreast of the leading ships on each beam were the *Zhemchug* to port and the *Izumrud* to starboard, each supported by two torpedo-boats. Astern of these two columns steamed the line of supply, repair and hospital ships.

When the enemy appeared, the three scouts ahead were to join forces with the cruisers to convoy these transports out of the scene of action. The 1st and 2nd Divisions were to increase speed, steer to port together, take station ahead of the 3rd Division, and then slow down and proceed on the same course so that the three divisions would be in line ahead. *Zhemchug* and *Izumrud* were to station themselves with their torpedo-boats on the far side of the fleet from the enemy's battleships, beyond their gun-range, to stop attacks by enemy torpedo-boats there.

Admiral Togo received the electrifying signal from the *Shinano* that the enemy had been sighted just after 5 am on 27 May 1905, on board his flagship *Mikasa* at Sylvia Basin, in Chinnae Bay, Korea, about 90 miles north of the Russian fleet's position. He at once signalled Imperial Naval Headquarters that he was going out to meet and destroy the enemy. At the same time he gave the signal that sent his battleships and Admiral Kamimura's cruiser squadron steaming out through the quiet seas of Douglas Inlet. 'The flagship *Mikasa* took the lead of the column', noted Captain Togo Kichitaro, Executive Officer of the *Asahi* and Admiral Togo's nephew, 'and our division formed up in the order of the *Shikishima*, *Fuji*, *Asahi*, *Kasuga* and *Nishin*. We proceeded out of port over a tumbling sea, and made for the eastern channel of the Tsushima Straits . . .'

By 6.30 am these two divisions of battleships and armoured cruisers were clear of Douglas Inlet and steaming west through rough seas in the Sea of Japan to intercept the enemy. Vice-Admiral Dewa's fast division of twelve cruisers was racing ahead to join the cruiser *Izumi* which, following an audacious parallel course within range of Rojdestvensky's 12-inch guns, was signalling a stream of information about the enemy fleet. At the same time three divisions of older cruisers which had been awaiting the decisive moment in Osaki Bay, Tsushima Island, also sighted the enemy and thereafter signalled reports of his movements to the commander-in-chief. 'Thus', noted Togo, 'though a heavy fog covered the sea, making it impossible to observe anything at a

In battle formation, Togo's squadron steams out of Chinnae Bay, Korea, soon after 5 am on 27 May 1905, after receiving a message from one of his scouting vessels that the enemy had been sighted 90 miles to the south. A Japanese petty officer stands beside an automatic small-calibre gun.

This contemporary artist's illustration, drawn soon after Tsushima, shows Admiral Togo (centre) on his flagship *Mikasa* at the moment he gave the order for his ships to reverse course in succession, a daring manoeuvre which enabled him to outgun the Russians.

distance of over five miles, all the conditions of the enemy were as clear to us. who were thirty or forty miles distant, as though they had been under our very eyes.'

Unlike Rojdestvensky, at the outset of the battle Togo had a precise operational plan, which had been drawn up well in advance. The first two phases of his seven-point plan were based on a torpedo attack on the enemy battleships in the entrance to Tsushima Strait, but bad weather spared Rojdestvensky this first challenge. Intensive artillery bombardment until darkness comprised the third stage; the fourth was another torpedo-boat assault under the cover of darkness; the fifth, renewed artillery bombardment next day; and for those vessels which still survived, a belt of mines awaited them around the approaches to Vladivostock. When the Russians ran on to the mines, they would be finished off in an attack by torpedo-boats and artillery.

The third phase of this comprehensive plan was about to begin just after 1.30 pm on 27 May 1905, when the Japanese cruiser divisions in the south joined forces with Togo's main battle divisions at a point about ten miles north of Okinoshima island, 40 miles east of Tsushima.

May 27 was the anniversary of the Tsar's coronation, and throughout the Russian fleet bugles sounded for all hands to sing the thanksgiving service, an ironical occasion with death approaching for so many. On board the battleship *Orel*, Seaman Novikoff-Priboy was strangely fascinated by the chaplain's red unkempt beard, 'As tangled as a hayfield that has been trampled by a herd of cattle . . . He gabbled the prayers unceremoniously, his thoughts obviously elsewhere. The men's faces were sour . . . To wind up, they raucously

sang *Long Live The Tsar* and dispersed . . .'

The fleet began to change from convoy to battle formation. The 1st and 2nd Divisions steamed ahead and turned to port to take station in line ahead of the 3rd Division of slow obsolete vessels, while the transports fell back astern and to starboard, protected by cruisers on each beam. Suddenly, without orders, the *Orel* fired a single shot at four enemy cruisers which had shadowed them freely throughout the morning about five miles to starboard. The rest of the fleet joined in. Columns of water arose around the cruisers. The Japanese turned away hastily into the mist while returning the fire, but no hits on either side were registered. 'Ammunition not to be wasted!' signalled Rojdestvensky sternly, and a few minutes later, 'Ships' companies to have dinner'.

So far, having failed to send scouts out, Rojdestvensky had little precise knowledge of the whereabouts of the enemy's main line, although Togo had been informed precisely of the position of the Russian main line. At 1.40 pm Rojdestvensky suddenly signalled to his 1st and 2nd Divisions to turn one after the other, or 'in succession', 90 degrees to starboard and to increase their speed to 11 knots, evidently to threaten additional enemy cruisers which had appeared to starboard. The order was misunderstood, and hopeless confusion followed. The *Suvaroff*, *Borodino*, *Alexander* and *Orel* eventually found themselves in single column in line ahead, separated from the rest of the fleet by some $3\frac{1}{2}$ miles.

Rojdestvensky was now so placed that one column of his fleet could mask the fire of the other, and vice versa. He therefore tried desperately to re-establish a single column, line

The armoured cruiser *Admiral Apraksin* was one of three very slow (11 knots) coastal defence vessels commanded by Admiral Nebogatoff and nicknamed 'flat-irons', owing to their broad beam and squat profile. Their four short-range, 10-inch guns were of little use against Togo's powerful long-range 12-inch guns.

Above: One of the slower Russian torpedo-boats, the *Moonsund*, screening Rojdestvensky's heavier ships during the journey from Kronstadt to Tsushima.

The *Shikishima*, one of Togo's four battleships at Tsushima, was capable of 18 knots, and with her highly drilled gun crews and 12-inch guns she contributed greatly to the destruction of the enemy vessels.

ahead. *Suvaroff* and *Alexander* took station, but left little room for *Borodino* and *Orel*, which forced *Oslyabya* to slow almost to a standstill to avoid a collision. Just at this moment, when their black hulls and bright yellow funnels were sharply etched against the mist, the Japanese emerged through it to the north, seven or eight miles to starboard, a long line of olive-grey hulls merging with the grey-green sea. For Rojdestvensky, it was a potentially disastrous situation.

The most decisive move in the battle now took place. Togo had observed that his enemy was steering a course for Vladivostock, and that to try to force him off this course he must launch his attack from the port side, or westward, farthest from him. Accordingly, he suddenly led his line out of range in a south-west course, at right angles across the enemy's bows, turning southward when the crossing was complete. Soon after completing this manoeuvre, which brought him within range, he signalled his fleet: 'Ships sixteen points (*180 degrees*) to port *in succession*', a daring manoeuvre which, when completed in about fifteen minutes, would place his fleet on a course parallel to and in the same direction as the Russian fleet.

The *Mikasa* put about sharply to complete this U-turn, then steamed on her new course in the opposite direction to the remainder of the fleet. Togo, exposed on the flying bridge, watched with that extraordinary calm for

which he was famous as his flagship offered herself as a target for concentrated enemy fire while masking return fire from his own fleet.

It was a risky manoeuvre, for it gave Rojdestvensky a chance, with rapid, accurate gunfire, to deal a devastating blow against the Japanese ships as they took turns to go about in the identical place on the sea upon which their forerunners had turned. The Russians were astonished at such audacity. 'How rash!' exclaimed Lieutenant Reydkin to Commander Semenoff on board the *Suvaroff*'s afterbridge. 'In a minute we'll be able to roll up the leading ships.'

'Please God, we may', Semenov thought, not very hopefully. 'If we could only put one out of action. Is it possible?' Could the Russian gunners knock out just one of Togo's ships in these fifteen minutes?

Rojdestvensky waited, seemingly for an age, until both the *Mikasa* and the *Shikishima* had finished their U-turns. Then, at a range of about four miles, the *Suvaroff* fired, and the whole fleet, still confused after its recent unsuccessful evolutions, finally opened up. The Russian gunners were not sufficiently well trained to fire the rapid and accurate salvoes that the situation required, but they scored a few hits, several of them on the *Mikasa*, one of which tore away the bridge ladder, leaving Togo himself with a slight flesh wound in the thigh.

The *Asamo* was struck by three shells near

This reconstruction by the artist Matania depicts the scene on board the battleship *Borodino* as she goes down under the weight of Japanese shelling.

the waterline astern, which dislocated her steering and briefly forced her out of the line. A 10-inch shell from one of the enemy's coast defence vessels hit the *Nishin*'s conning tower and wounded Admiral Misu. Two more hit the *Asahi* amidships. 'Fragments of shell splinters flew here and there and the wounded were prostrated amid the havoc', noted Captain Togo Kichitaro. 'The main plates were twisted and bloody hands and feet and mutilated corpses were lying on deck. I went up to the starboard shelter deck and found the shield of the 12-pounder gun had been pierced.'

For some minutes Admiral Togo still held his fire while gradually he shortened the distance between the two fleets as one after the other his ships made the dangerous U-turn. At about 1.55 pm his gunners opened fire, and by the time they had found the range the last ship had rounded the bend and taken station in the new column. A hail of shells exploded on the leading ships of Rojdestvensky's 1st and 2nd Divisions. Togo increased speed and bore down on their van, crossing the Russian 'T' and forcing them to veer to starboard so as to be able to fire their broadsides—for even the *Orel*, fourth in the line, was unable to bring her stern guns to bear. Captain Pakenham, the British naval attaché, who was watching from an exposed position on the *Asahi*'s quarter-deck, his monocle jammed firmly in his right eye, noted that at this moment he could see right down the length of the Russian line.

The *Suvaroff* and the *Oslyabya*, first ship of the 2nd Division, upon which Togo's fire was concentrated, now became infernos swept by blizzards of flame and shell splinters, which tore to pieces the bodies of officers and men exposed at their posts on the decks and the

bridges. 'The shells burst as soon as they touched anything—the moment they encountered the least impediment in their flight', noted Captain Semenoff, on the *Suvaroff*. 'The steel plates and superstructure on the upper deck were torn to pieces, and the splinters caused many casualties. Iron ladders were crumpled up into rings, and guns were literally hurled from their mountings . . . In addition there was the unusual high temperature and liquid flame of the explosions, which seemed to spread over everything.'

In this holocaust a kind of stupor overcame the men on the *Suvaroff*, most of whom were receiving their baptism of fire. Some of them stood staring uncomprehendingly at the flames which leapt up on all sides, holding the hoses in their hands without turning them on. 'Wake up—turn on the water!' Semenov shouted. An enemy shell shattered the foremost funnel, which fell with a crash of steel across the foredeck, and waves of smoke enveloped the ship.

A 12-inch shell struck the armoured shield of one of the main after gun turrets with a mighty explosion, blowing it up into the air and right over the bridges on to the foredeck. In the stiff breeze the fire grew out of control and stopped all communication along the upper deck between stem and stern.

Admiral Rojdestvensky crouched in the cramped conning tower with Captain Ignatzius, Flag Captain Clapier de Colongue, the flag artillery officer, the flag navigating lieutenant and various orderlies, watching the battle through slits in the armour. Shell splinters of white-hot metal hissed through the slits and slammed into rangefinders, chronometers, telephones and men. Rojdestvensky and his staff crouched below the armoured casing for shelter.

Another 12-inch shell burst with a shattering roar close to the entrance. Three seamen were killed and Rojdestvensky's head was torn open by a splinter. At the same time another shell struck the *Suvaroff*'s steering gear, and as she turned wildly out of line a third slammed into the conning tower. Captain Ignatzius fell bleeding from a deep head wound, Rojdestvensky was disabled by a shell splinter in his foot, and several other officers and men were scythed down by shell splinters which ricochetted backwards and forwards inside the conning tower. Every instrument there was smashed and communication with the rest of the ship cut off.

By 2.30 pm the *Suvaroff* was a blazing hulk, her twisted decks littered with dead, her sick bay a shambles of blood and agony, her foremast shot away, both her funnels gone, but her gun crews still serving the few undamaged weapons. The *Alexander*, battered and swept by flames, took the lead of the Russian line

A moment of tense action is caught in this photograph of a Japanese gun crew firing and loading an 8-inch gun while officers record range and hits obtained during the battle. Togo taught his gunners to regard their guns with the same zeal as the old Samurai warriors did their swords.

at about 2.50 pm, drawing the enemy's main fire. Salvo after salvo of shells fell upon her and the *Borodino*, blazing behind her. The *Oslyabya*, the leading battleship of the 2nd Division, which had been forced out of line at the battle's onset through Rojdestvensky's last-moment manoeuvre, had at once become one of the enemy's supplementary targets, more or less stationary as she was.

Several shells struck her port waterline and tore open a huge hole through which sea water poured. In the subsequent hail of shells, her foredeck was shattered, and by 3 pm, with her gun turrets and gun crews smashed to pieces, she ceased firing. Six of Admiral Kamamura's cruisers now moved in through the smoke which hung over the water and shelled her relentlessly at a range of less than a mile. Quite suddenly she went down sharply by the bows, began slowly to capsize and then turned on her side.

Hundreds of sailors scrambled up from below and flung themselves into the water, while many more, trapped behind closed bulkheads in the engine-room and stokehold, were fated to stay there and die. At 3.30 pm the 12,000-ton ship turned turtle and began to go down by the bows, her stern high above the sea and one of her propellers still slowly turning. In a few seconds all that remained was a smoky haze and several hundred men struggling in the water.

Her loss, visible from the decks of her sister ships, became a symbol for the crews of their approaching end, added still more to their terror and left them fighting for mere survival. It also marked an important stage in the development of the battle. 'After the first hour of the action, when the Suvaroff had been disabled and the Oslyabya sunk', commented the British *Official History*, 'all cohesion was lost and the Russian movements can no longer be dignified by the name of tactics: they became nothing more than the efforts of a defeated and disorganized fleet to avoid the overwhelming fire of the enemy and to escape'.

An attempt by the battered *Alexander* and the fire-swept *Borodino* to lead the surviving vessels in a bid to steam to port behind the last ship in the enemy line and make a run for Vladivostock was quickly frustrated. The *Suvaroff*, drifting helplessly between the two fleets, bombarded intermittently by the Japanese and then, in error, by her sister ships, still fired an occasional telling shot at the enemy. Rojdestvensky, who had been wounded three times, was with difficulty transferred with his staff from the *Suvaroff* to the destroyer *Buiny*, which was already overloaded with some 200 sailors picked up from the *Oslyabya*. Since he was barely conscious this was simply an effort to save his life, but the officers and men left aboard his devastated flagship had little hope of survival.

Between 4.30 and 5 pm Togo's warships lost the main Russian line in the heavy smoke and fog drifting over the water. 'Steaming south for about eight miles', Togo reported later, 'we fired leisurely on a second-class enemy cruiser and some special service steamers which we passed on our starboard, and at 5.30 pm our main squadron turned northward again in search of the enemy's principal force, while the armoured cruiser squadron proceeding to the south-west, attacked the enemy cruisers . . .'

He sighted the surviving Russian battleships of the 1st and 2nd Divisions, six altogether, steaming slowly to the north-east; at about 6.30 pm he renewed the fight, gradually

The Japanese torpedo-boat *Niwa*, one of a squadron of 58 of these fast ships. After dark, when Togo's battleships and cruisers temporarily withdrew, the Japanese torpedo boats played a decisive role.

bearing down on their van while hammering them with every gun he had. The battleship *Alexander III*, hit several times below the waterline, capsized and went down with all hands. At about 7pm Togo, surprised to see the *Suvaroff* still afloat after his earlier orders that she should be sunk, instructed the torpedo-boats to finish her off. Two torpedoes on each side of her battered hull blew her to pieces and she vanished into the ocean at 7.20pm. The *Borodino* still survived at the head of the column, but at dusk, just as the Japanese squadron veered off, the *Fuji* hit her with a last carefully aimed 12-inch shell. Pakenham noted: 'Entering the upper part near the foremost broadside turret it burst, and an immense column of smoke, ruddied on its underside by the glare of the explosion and from the fire abaft, spurted to the height of her funnel tops . . .' She went down in seconds and a dense cloud of smoke hung over the water where she had been.

Dusk had fallen and Togo's destroyer and torpedo-boat units were moving in to press home the next phase of operations. 'The main squadron ceased by degrees to press the enemy', he reported, 'and at 7.28 hours when the sun was setting, drew off to the east'. His commanders were ordered to rendezvous at daybreak some 180 miles to the north, leaving the field clear for night attacks by the torpedo-boats.

Rear-Admiral Nebogatoff was leading the Russian line that night on board the *Nicholai I*, followed by the *Orel*, the coastal defence ships *Apraksin* and *Senyavin*, and the remaining older battleships, *Sisoy Veliky*, *Navarin* and *Nakhimov*. Of the cruiser squadron under Admiral Enkvist, which had inflicted on the enemy cruisers as much damage as it had received, only the swift *Izumrud* was present, on the port beam. Enkvist, on board the cruiser flagship *Oleg*, had turned about at dusk that evening and steamed south at top speed, racing through the Straits and making for Manila, 1,500 miles south, where, rather than face the inferno of battle, he had decided to seek internment, despite the protests of a number of his officers.

As night was falling Novikov-Priboy, on the *Orel*, saw the entire enemy torpedo flotilla, some 58 vessels, taking up positions for the attack. 'Compared with the battleships, they looked like innocent toys', he noted. 'Toys though they might seem, we knew that each of them represented a large destructive force . . . Our destruction was imminent'.

Anxious to emulate Togo's victory, the young torpedo-boat and destroyer captains pressed home their attacks with such fierce tenacity, and at such close range, that the Russian gunners were unable to depress their

weapons enough to take aim at them. Torpedoes blasted the *Navarin* apart and she went down with nearly all hands. The *Sisoy Veliky* and the *Admiral Nakhimoff*, hit below the waterline, managed to escape in the darkness and stagger south to Tsushima Island, where the crews opened the sea-cocks and got ashore in rafts and boats.

At daybreak Togo's battle squadron waited after its dash north at a well-chosen point south-west of Matsushima Island; his cruisers were stationed about 150 miles south-west of the Okishima Islands. Together they formed a net from which the survivors of the Russian fleet would find it hard to escape. Nebogatoff's elderly flagship *Nicholai I*, the crippled modern battleship *Orel*, the two coastal defence ships and the fast cruiser *Izumrud* were sighted shortly after dawn steaming north-east at about nine knots. The *Ushakoff*, unable to keep up, wallowed along out of sight astern.

Togo placed himself out of range of all but the *Orel* and opened fire in an accurate, unhurried way. When shells began crashing down on the *Nicholai*'s decks without his having any chance of hitting back, Nebogatoff decided to throw in the towel. Having agreed in council with his officers that not to surrender under these circumstances would simply guarantee the deaths of most of the 3,000 men under his command, he surrendered under a specific article of Russian Naval Instructions 'to avoid useless bloodshed', hoisting the Japanese colours and the international code sign for surrender. Togo ordered a cease-fire

The Japanese 12-inch-gun battleship *Fuji*, 12,600 tons, shown here firing a salute and dressed overall, leaves her home port in Japan early in May 1905. Like most of Japan's warships, she was designed and built in Britain.

and sent officers and men to take over the prize.

The *Izumrud*'s commander, confident of his ship's speed and unwilling to face the disgrace of surrender, made off at top speed and escaped successfully to the north, only to wreck his ship later in a fog in Siberian waters. Near Matsushima the cruiser *Svetlana* encountered the enemy cruisers *Otawa* and *Nitaka* and boldly took on both of them, inflicting heavy damage until their combined fire holed her on the waterline and sank her. The destroyer *Buistri* was also sunk that day, making a total of four such ships lost to the Russians.

The *Ushakoff* sighted her sister ships flying the enemy colours in the afternoon. When the *Iwate* demanded her surrender, she opened fire and was at once subjected to a hail of 8-inch shells from enemy vessels beyond the range of her guns. An hour later, when she was a battered wreck, her captain scuttled her rather than place her in enemy hands. Three hundred survivors were picked up by the Japanese.

No less praiseworthy, in Japanese eyes, was the last engagement in the battle, in which the old cruiser *Dimitri Donskoy* took on six enemy cruisers in the late afternoon. As darkness fell a destroyer flotilla took over from them. The *Dimitri Donskoy* was still afloat and still firing, though a third of her crew were killed or wounded and her captain was dying. During the night of the 28th, she crawled close to the island of Matsushima, to which her crew withdrew. In the morning some of them returned to the ship and scuttled her in deep water.

In the afternoon of the 28th came the event which set the seal upon the close of the battle. The destroyer *Biedovy*, to which Admiral Rojdestvensky had been transferred, was intercepted by two enemy destroyers, and at once hoisted the surrender signal without firing a shot. The Japanese officer who went aboard was astonished by the number of officers aboard emblazoned with the gold braid of senior rank. Still more surprised was he to find that he had captured the Russian admiral himself. Rojdestvensky's chief-of-staff had personally ordered the surrender, to save the life of their commander, who would be an important witness in the inquiry which at some distant date would certainly take place in Russia.

The battle was over. Togo had captured the enemy admiral and had disposed of his fleet in an overwhelming naval victory. Out of thirty-eight ships he had sunk no less than twenty, while six had been captured, two had sunk while escaping, six had been interned, either at Shanghai or Manila, the fate of one was unknown, one had been released after capture and two supply ships had escaped.

The victory had cost the Japanese only 117 dead and less than a thousand wounded, compared with 4,830 Russian dead and 10,000 wounded. Tsushima underlined the vital importance of sea power, for it brought the war to an end on terms favourable to Japan and established her as a major power in the Far East.

The Goeben and the Breslau
August 1914

When war broke out in August 1914, the Royal Navy had not fought a great battle since Trafalgar, and years of peace-time ceremonial had eroded the 'Nelson touch' of personal initiative and daring among most of its officers. The *Goeben* and *Breslau* fiasco was largely the result of this.

In July 1914 Germany had two fast ships well suited to commerce raiding in the Mediterranean: the battle-cruiser *Goeben*, with ten 11-inch guns and a speed of 25 knots; and the *Breslau*, a fast light cruiser with twelve 10.4-inch guns and a speed of 28 knots. They were both under the command of Rear-Admiral Wilhelm Souchon. Britain's Mediterranean Squadron, C-in-C Admiral Sir Berkeley Milne, consisted of three battle-cruisers, *Inflexible*, *Indefatigable* and *Indomitable*, each with eight 12-inch guns and a speed in practice a little less than *Goeben*'s, and four heavy cruisers and four fast light cruisers.

If war broke out, Admiral Milne's task was to protect French troop transports between Toulon and Algiers, to bring the *Goeben* and *Breslau* to action, and to engage Austrian ships in the Adriatic only when Italy's neutrality was certain. Through lack of the Nelson touch he failed to carry out the most important of these—engagement with *Goeben* and *Breslau*. When war seemed certain, Souchon had raced out of the Adriatic, coaled at Brindisi on 31 July and then, so far as Milne was concerned, had vanished. Milne reacted to this alarming news by stationing the light cruiser *Chatham* to watch the Strait of Messina, remaining near Malta himself and placing the rest of his force at the mouth of the Adriatic. In case Souchon was making for the Atlantic, *Indefatigable* and *Indomitable* were later ordered to Gibraltar.

But Souchon had sailed south-west towards Algeria, ready to attack French troopships. At dawn on 4 August 1914, war having started with France, he bombarded two coastal towns, Philippeville and Bona. Then, almost before his gunsmoke had cleared, he received a telegram advising him of an alliance with Turkey and ordering him to sail at once for Constantinople. He turned back to coal at Messina, and now there took place one of the most dramatic events in the war at sea. He passed within 8,000 yards of *Indomitable* and *Indefatigable*. Their sixteen 12-inch guns could swiftly have annihilated his ships, but war between the two nations had not yet begun. The British ships didn't even train their guns on the enemy, but swung round and shadowed them until they lost contact late in the evening.

The German ships stayed coaling at Messina for 36 hours, in disregard of the neutrality laws, until 5pm on 6 August. Milne's three battle-cruisers and two light cruisers were waiting west of Sicily, the light cruiser *Gloucester* to the east. She sighted the enemy at dawn on 7 August as they raced out into the Eastern Mediterranean. Rear-Admiral Troubridge's 1st Cruiser Squadron of four heavy cruisers took up the chase, but at the last moment Troubridge felt that he was outgunned and abandoned the pursuit. *Goeben* and *Breslau* reached Constantinople safely and thus helped Turkey to decide to join forces with Germany. Troubridge, though found not guilty at a naval court martial, never again received a sea command.

3

6

7

1. Rear-Admiral Wilhelm Souchon, commanding the German cruisers *Goeben* and *Breslau*, began his game of hide-and-seek with Admiral Sir Berkeley Milne's battle-cruiser squadron in the Mediterranean before the outbreak of war.

2. The light cruiser *Breslau*, 28.5 knots, twelve 4.1-inch guns, supported her sister ship *Goeben* in her Mediterranean merry-go-round.

3. The battle-cruiser *Inflexible*.

4. The battle-cruiser *Indefatigable*.

5. The *Goeben*, Souchon's flagship, a battle-cruiser with ten 11-inch guns and a top speed of 25.5 knots.

6. The *Goeben* in a Turkish harbour in 1915.

7. Once safely in Constantinople, Admiral Souchon (centre, with Iron Cross) shaved off his moustache, donned the Turkish fez and, together with some of his officers, posed for a photograph with Captain Enver Bei (left), Turkey's chief of naval staff. It was then announced that the two German cruisers had been sold to the Turkish navy, so as to avoid contravening the neutrality laws.

Heligoland Bight
August 1914

The success of torpedo-boats and mines in the Russo-Japanese War had shown conclusively that the battleship was not an all-powerful naval unit, particularly during operations at night. At Tsushima, Japanese torpedo-boats had sunk or crippled three Russian battleships; moreover, prior to Tsushima the sinking by Russian mines of two Japanese battleships in one day at Port Arthur had demonstrated that the approaches to enemy naval bases could be death traps.

Nevertheless, nine years later, on the outbreak of the First World War, what was termed 'the doctrine of battle-fleet supremacy' —that a battle fleet known to be a match for any other combination of battle fleets gave command of the seas—still held good. And this was so despite the introduction of flotillas of submarines charged with much more accurate and destructive torpedoes.

The British Admiralty clung to this view because it had no certain evidence that enemy submarines could operate much beyond the southern areas of the North Sea, a belief which was exploded when a German submarine torpedoed and sank the cruiser *Hawke* in October 1914.

But even in August 1914 anxiety about the submarine menace had led the Admiralty to decide against enforcing a close blockade of Germany's Heligoland Bight as part of its task of protecting Britain from the possibility of invasion. Instead, the Admiralty adopted a policy of sweeping the North Sea, watching for any movement of the German High Seas Fleet out of its bases and, if possible, enticing it to battle. This policy led to the battle of Heligoland Bight, which had its own effects upon the course of naval warfare in the First World War.

Germany had transformed Heligoland into a fortress, bristling with guns for the defence of the Bight—that stretch of sea between Heligoland island and the German coast, in which were located the estuary of the River Ems, Jade Bay and the naval bases of Wilhelmshaven, Emden and the entrance to the Kiel Canal.

Admiral Reinhardt Scheer had established a 'protective zone' for the defence of the Bight consisting of an outermost line of destroyers, flotillas of submarines six nautical miles behind the destroyers, then patrols of mine-sweepers six miles further back, and up to four light cruisers on patrol.

But Scheer, even more than the British, was anxious about the submarine threat to his bigger ships. This, combined with the Great General Staff's very realistic fear of Britain's Grand Fleet, under the command of Admiral (later Lord) Sir John Jellicoe, led to the German policy of prudent inactivity. It involved the failure to challenge the transport across the Channel in August of the British Expeditionary Force; the failure to seize the French coast; and undue reliance on small ships, combined with mine-laying and submarine torpedo attacks. Scheer's strategy in the Bight was to send out destroyer patrols to lure enemy destroyers inside to the south or east and then use his cruisers to try to cut off their retreat and destroy them.

For their part, British cruiser squadrons of Humber Force, destroyers of the Harwich flotilla belonging to Southern Force, and Commodore (later Admiral, Lord) Roger Keyes' 8th Submarine Flotilla, patrolled constantly up to the very margins of the Bight. Keyes, whose submarines had reconnoitred deep into the Bight, had gained and reported a great deal of information about the enemy's defences there. Characteristically he proposed that it afforded the chance of inflicting losses upon the enemy.

'At about 5 or 6pm', he wrote in a letter to the Director of Operations at the Admiralty, 'the destroyers detailed for night work appear to be led to certain points by light cruisers. They then "fan out" and proceed to sea at a good speed—returning at daylight. I would submit that a well-organized drive, commencing before dawn from inshore close to the enemy's coast, should inflict considerable loss on these destroyer patrols . . . The local patrol torpedo-boats off the Ems proceed to sea before dawn and return to harbour at

Opposite: Damage to the German cruiser *Frauenlob* after the action in Heligoland Bight.

daylight. These might be dealt with without any risk.'

Keyes' plan envisaged Commodore (later Admiral Sir Reginald) Tyrwhitt's 1st and 3rd Destroyer Flotillas from Harwich (34 vessels), led by the light cruisers *Arethusa* (flagship) and *Fearless*, making a rendezvous at 3 am south-west of the Horn Reef Lightship; they would then move stealthily into the Bight from the north, stationing themselves between enemy patrols and their bases during the hours of darkness; then, in daylight, drive westwards and attack all enemy vessels that came in view. The submarines were to lurk near the estuaries of the Rivers Ems and Elbe to attack outcoming German cruisers and patrols returning to base.

At a meeting at the Admiralty on 23 August 1914, which was presided over by Winston Churchill, First Lord of the Admiralty, and attended, among others, by Prince Louis of Battenberg, First Sea Lord, Keyes himself and Commodore Tyrwhitt, the plan was approved for 28 August. It was decided to begin the sweep to westward at 8 am, after the enemy night patrols had returned and 'when their day patrols were well out to seaward hunting our submarines, which would do their best to keep them well occupied'.

However, Keyes' request for the support of the Grand Fleet Light Cruiser Squadron and Admiral Sir David Beatty's Battle-Cruiser Squadron (*Lion, Queen Mary, Princess Royal*), in addition to the agreed new battle-cruisers *Invincible* and *New Zealand*, commanded by Admiral Sir Archibald Moore, was opposed. Keyes therefore forgot about Beatty's ships until, incredibly, he found them taking part in the operation on 28 August.

Admiral Jellicoe, C-in-C of the Grand Fleet, was only informed about the operation during the afternoon of 26 August. In the same message came information of the landing that day of 3,000 Marines at Ostend in an attempt to ease the Allied military situation in Belgium; the message added that this might 'cause some movement of the High Seas Fleet'.

It sounded a dangerous and likely possibility. Somewhat concerned, Jellicoe proposed the Grand Fleet's cooperation in the Heligoland venture. The First Lord turned down this proposal, but said that Admiral Beatty's First Battle-Cruiser Squadron could be made available, 'if convenient'. Jellicoe thereupon ordered Beatty and Commodore Goodenough, commanding 1st Light Cruiser Squadron (five ships of 5,500 tons displacement, 25 knots, each with a main armament of eight 6-inch guns) to rendezvous with Sir Archibald Moore and his two battle-cruisers 70 miles north of Heligoland at 5 am on 28 August.

Beatty's three ships, the biggest and newest of their class, each had a displacement of 27,000 tons, 29 knots speed and main armaments of eight 13.5-inch guns; *Invincible* and *New Zealand* were capable of 27 knots and were armed with eight 12-inch guns.

To this force was added the 7th Cruiser Squadron of six older and slower armoured ships and the *Amethyst*, a light cruiser, commanded by Rear-Admiral A. H. Christian. This squadron was not to take part in the drive through the Bight, but was to destroy any enemy vessels that tried to escape west.

Keyes' submarines sailed at midnight on 26 August. Keyes led the way on board the fast destroyer *Lurcher*, which was accompanied by her sister ship, *Firedrake*. Tyrwhitt, on board the new light cruiser *Arethusa* (3,750 tons displacement, 30 knots, two 6-inch, six 4-inch guns), sailed from Harwich at 5 am on 27 August with the two destroyer flotillas, being joined at sea by the *Fearless*, a slightly smaller light cruiser mounting ten 4-inch guns. Beatty's Battle-Cruiser Squadron, Goodenough's 1st Light Cruiser Squadron and the 7th Cruiser Squadron also sailed that day.

From the outset two factors cast the shadow of disaster over the operation. First, the Germans learned exactly what was afoot from radio signals which the British were careless enough to make during their approach. Therefore they made counter-preparations, including the withdrawal of destroyer patrols and the stationing of seven cruisers ready to intercept enemy forces. Secondly, during the night many of the British ships were dangerously handicapped by their ignorance of each other's presence, for Keyes and Tyrwhitt were already at sea, beyond the range of the radio wavelength of the destroyers through which the Admiralty broadcast the news that Beatty's battle-cruisers and Goodenough's light cruisers had joined the operation.

The submarines, therefore, might easily have confused any of these ships with those of the enemy and tried to destroy them with their 18-inch torpedoes. 'Knowing that the only light cruisers we should have in the Heligoland Bight', Keyes wrote later in *Naval Memoirs*, 'would be the new *Arethusa*, with one mast and three funnels, and the *Fearless*, with one mast and four funnels, I made a great point of impressing on the submarine captains that the enemy had no vessels resembling our two cruisers, whose silhouettes they should carefully note. If they sighted light cruisers with two masts and two, three or four funnels, they would be enemy'.

Tyrwhitt's destroyers, as well as the submarines, were thus turned into potential enemies of the light cruisers and battle-cruisers of the Grand Fleet. The first result of this startling situation occurred at 3.30 am. Tyrwhitt's destroyers, following the course of the submarines about 70 miles north of Heli-

goland, saw in the darkness the dim shapes of two cruisers, each with four funnels and two masts. Tyrwhitt concluded that they were the enemy, but to make certain he flashed the 'challenge' to them and learned they were from the 1st Light Cruiser Squadron. 'Beatty is behind us', Goodenough signalled. Saved from what could have been a disastrous confrontation, Tyrwhitt now steamed in a southerly direction, with Goodenough's light cruisers some eight miles behind him. Moore's battle-cruisers and Beatty's battle-cruisers, accompanied by four destroyers, lay about 40 miles north-west. The scene was set for the encounter between submarines and destroyers.

It was a windless day, with a flat calm against which the submarines' periscopes stood out like ducks on a millpond. Now and then the haze over the water, which limited visibility to about two miles, parted to reveal to the south-east the bleak grey cliffs, the forts and houses on the gaunt island of Heligoland.

At 6.52 am Roger Keyes' three foremost submarines, E6, E7, E8, enticed numerous enemy destroyers and torpedo-boats out from behind Heligoland. The first phase of the action was about to begin. When the enemy were firmly on their trail, the British submarines turned back towards the west. Tyrwhitt, on the *Arethusa*, and some of his destroyers then steamed south towards Heligoland at 30 knots with smoke billowing behind them, opened fire on the enemy and gave chase.

The German destroyers, acting as decoys

A German torpedo flotilla photographed in the Kiel Canal in 1914.

Opposite, top: Winston Churchill inspecting harbour works at Dover in 1914 with Prince Louis of Battenberg, First Sea Lord.

Opposite, bottom: Commodore W. R. Goodenough (right), pictured here with Vice-Admiral Robeck.

for their cruisers, turned back to try to lure the British forces into the trap they had set. From about 7.20 am onwards gunners on both sides blazed away in a running fight. Unaware of the trap which he was approaching, Tyrwhitt now altered course eastwards to try to cut the enemy off from their base in Heligoland.

'In squares 142 and 131 (i.e. 20 sea miles north-west of Heligoland) enemy cruisers and destroyers are chasing the 5th Flotilla', the German commander signalled to base.

The waiting German cruisers *Stettin* and *Frauenlob* raced out from Heligoland and for fifteen furious minutes hurled a rain of shells at the newly commissioned *Arethusa*, whose gun crews replied as fast as they could shoot. Soon several of *Arethusa*'s guns were hit or were temporarily out of action. Captain Blunt, on the cruiser *Fearless*, intervened to draw off the enemy fire; then at 8.25 am, at a range of 3,400 yards, a shell from *Arethusa*'s one remaining 6-inch gun shattered the *Frauenlob*'s forebridge, killing some of her officers and seamen and damaging vital controls.

She turned off towards Heligoland, escorted

by the *Stettin*. At the same time, to the east, in the haze which still hung over the water, British destroyers of the 1st Flotilla hit the enemy destroyer V 187 with a shower of shells which shot her masts and funnels away, then holed her below the waterline and left her sinking.

Aware at this point that he had gone dangerously far to the east and could well be cut off, Tyrwhitt ordered his destroyers to reform, turn westward away from Heligoland and reduce speed to 20 knots. Wounded gunners and seamen were carried on stretchers down to the sick-bay, and during this brief lull in the fighting Tyrwhitt ordered speedy repairs to the *Arethusa*'s gun turrets. Soon both of her 6-inch and four of her six 4-inch guns were ready to fire again.

Meanwhile, the Admiralty's failure to ascertain that all those ships involved in the operation were made aware of the identity and positions of others taking part had, in the sober understatement of the official historian, Sir Julian Corbett, caused 'considerable confusion'. Keyes, aboard the destroyer *Lurcher* in company with the *Firedrake*, sighted two cruisers in the morning haze. Unaware of any British cruisers in the area, he assumed them to be German and accordingly warned the battle-cruiser *Invincible*, which was about 30 miles to the west. In fact, these two cruisers were the *Nottingham* and *Lowestoft* from Goodenough's Light Cruiser Squadron.

These ships were now involved in what was almost a comedy of errors, although at any moment it might have become a tragi-comedy. For Commodore Goodenough, in command of the Cruiser Squadron, heard Keyes' signal and led the four remaining cruisers of his squadron to his aid, against the two detached cruisers of his own squadron, *Lowestoft* and *Nottingham*. At 8.53 am Keyes, in the tiny *Lurcher*, was dismayed to observe the big grey shapes of four cruisers approaching him at a distance through the mist; believing them to be another four enemy cruisers, he again signalled to the *Invincible* the presence of four more enemy cruisers, which he would try to entice towards her.

The *Invincible* and the Light Cruiser Squadron were in some danger of a fratricidal battle. Fortunately, at this vital moment Goodenough sensed that 'something was evidently wrong', and just after 9 am he veered off and steered the westerly course that he knew the destroyer flotillas were sailing. This good sense now served to lead him towards greater danger—the outer line of British submarines, whose commanders would certainly assume his vessels were those of the enemy. Worse still, he himself had not been told that British submarines were operating there.

Right: Admiral Sir David Beatty, in command of the Battle-Cruiser Squadron at Heligoland.

Opposite, top: The small destroyer *Lurcher* (35 knots, two 4-inch, two 12-pounder guns), parent ship of the Grand Fleet's submarine flotillas.

Opposite, bottom: Units of Admiral Reinhardt Scheer's High Seas Fleet carry out manoeuvres in Heligoland Bight.

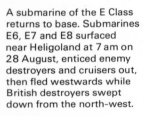

A submarine of the E Class returns to base. Submarines E6, E7 and E8 surfaced near Heligoland at 7 am on 28 August, enticed enemy destroyers and cruisers out, then fled westwards while British destroyers swept down from the north-west.

Just before 9 am Goodenough saw what he took to be an enemy submarine break surface nearby; without hesitation he rang down full speed ahead and ordered the helmsman to ram. In fact, the submarine was the British E6, under Lieutenant-Commander C. P. Talbot, and, as the official historian wrote, 'so close and quick was he [Goodenough] that the submarine only escaped by diving under the flagship, but, thanks to Lieutenant-Commander Talbot's skilful handling, no harm was done, nor did he, being uncertain of his assailant's nationality, make any attempt to attack'.

After this lucky escape Goodenough returned to his westerly course, but the cruisers *Lowestoft* and *Nottingham* sailed off northwest towards Beatty's battle-cruisers' station. Beatty, however, was about to join the drive to the west and he had signalled accordingly, but the *Lowestoft* and *Nottingham* did not receive the signal, continued to the northwest and thus took themselves out of the area of the impending action.

To some extent this dangerous confusion was resolved when Keyes, on the *Lurcher*, challenged by searchlight and was answered by the *Southampton*. As a result he learned that the cruisers he was trying to entice towards the *Invincible* were in fact British. But since it was impossible to signal to the submerged submarines, they remained a menace both to Goodenough's cruisers and to any of Beatty's ships which entered their area of operations.

'I was very much concerned', Keyes recalled later, 'as the submarines had no idea of their presence, and I greatly feared that our ships might be attacked by them, particularly the light cruisers, which resembled the enemy sighted by the submarines on previous occasions. I signalled to this effect to the *Southampton*, who passed my signal on to the *Lion*'.

At this stage in the operation, the results were as follows: one German destroyer had been lost; the cruiser *Frauenlob* had been damaged; the *Arethusa* had been damaged; and our own ships, by a hair's-breadth, had avoided sinking each other. But now, at about 10.30 am, three enemy cruisers, *Strassburg*, *Köln* and *Mainz*, suddenly steamed out and engaged the *Arethusa* and *Fearless*, evidently

The light cruiser *Arethusa* (30 knots, two 6-inch, six 4-inch guns) pursued the German destroyers to within five miles of Heligoland, and at 8 am was suddenly engaged by the waiting enemy cruisers *Stettin* and *Frauenlob*.

believing that there were only destroyers and the two battered light cruisers in these waters.

Before 11 am the cruiser *Stettin*, having escorted the damaged *Frauenlob* back to base, also emerged again. Now there occurred an event that infuriated the British seamen. Boats from two small destroyers, *Defender* and *Goshawk*, had been lowered earlier to pick up survivors from the sunk German destroyer. *Stettin* came up and opened fire on these boats and on the destroyers standing by, which were obliged to move off, leaving the boats unprotected.

Their end, with the German seamen whom they had saved, seemed certain when the submarine E-4, which had been observing the scene through her periscope, surfaced and manoeuvred for a torpedo attack on the *Stettin*, which quickly steamed off. The submarine took on board the destroyers' sailors and directed the enemy seamen in the boats towards nearby Heligoland.

Tyrwhitt's flagship *Arethusa*, whose speed had been lowered to ten knots by enemy gun-fire, now seemed an easy target. Shells fell all around her. The enemy cruiser *Stralsund* also came out from Heligoland and engaged her. *Fearless* and the 1st Flotilla destroyers in their turn opened fire on the *Stralsund*, which turned off into the haze, then emerged on the port quarter and again opened fire; but evidently she had suffered from her enemy's fire,

for she again disengaged and disappeared in the direction of Heligoland.

Fortunately for Tyrwhitt the enemy action was uncoordinated and sporadic, while the mist also split the battle into a number of independent actions. The enemy cruiser *Strassburg* now made his flagship a target for her twelve 4-inch guns, but all her salvoes and two torpedoes failed to find their target, after which the British destroyers made things too dangerous for the *Strassburg* and she disengaged, only to be replaced by the cruiser *Mainz*. Accurate gunnery, however, inflicted severe damage on the *Mainz*, and after 25 minutes she was on fire and down by the stern, but still fighting.

Earlier Tyrwhitt had perceived that the odds were building up against him. Goodenough, alarmed by the danger from British submarines, had withdrawn his cruisers to the north-west and now, at any moment, more and heavier German ships might come out and throw their weight decisively into the fray. It was a prospect that he had to take into account, and at 11 am he called for help from Beatty, whose battle-cruisers were then about 30 miles to the north-west.

Beatty, on receiving Goodenough's signal that the danger from submarines made it advisable for him to withdraw, and learning that no heavier ships were supporting Tyrwhitt, had assumed the responsibility of

ordering Goodenough back to support Tyr-whitt; Goodenough steamed south-east again at full speed. The *Mainz*, already in flames but still a dangerous opponent, now encountered Goodenough's four cruisers. She was over-whelmed by their fire. 'The last I saw of her', wrote Lieutenant Oswald Frewin, on board a destroyer, 'absolutely wrecked alow and aloft, her whole midships a fuming inferno. She had one gun forward and one aft still spitting forth fury and defiance, like a wild cat mad with wounds'.

Despite a threat by one of her officers to open fire, Keyes brought the *Lurcher* along-side, ignoring the danger of explosions, and took off 210 men, 60 of them wounded. 'She had settled considerably by the bows, the after part was crowded with men, many terribly wounded, the battery was a ghastly shambles, amidships she was a smouldering furnace, two of her funnels had collapsed and the wreckage appeared to be red-hot, the heat scorched one's face as far off as the bridge of the *Lurcher* ...' Suddenly, at 1.5 pm, she capsized and sank, her starboard propeller almost hitting the *Lurcher*, which only escaped by going astern at full speed.

Two more enemy cruisers, *Danzig* and *Ari-adne*, had meantime raced at top speed out of Wilhelmshaven, some 25 miles to the south-east, and at about midday had joined the *Stettin* and the *Stralsund* in their attack on the *Arethusa* and the *Fearless*. It looked as if the two British cruisers might be sunk in their turn, but help was on the way, if it could arrive in time.

Between 11.25 and 11.30 am Beatty had received signals for aid both from Tyrwhitt and from Captain Blunt on the *Fearless*. It was the first report he had received about the action which was taking place only 26 miles west of Heligoland and some 25 miles north of Wilhelmshaven, from which port the enemy's biggest ships might at any time emerge. To Beatty, on the bridge of the *Lion* with Captain A. E. Chatfield, his Flag Captain, beside him, the situation seemed 'extremely critical', with 'a possibility of grave disaster'.

Captain (later Admiral of the Fleet Lord) Chatfield noted that on receiving Tyrwhitt's calls for assistance, Beatty asked him: 'What do you think we should do? I ought to go and support Tyrwhitt, but if I lose one of these valuable ships the country will not forgive me.'

Chatfield recalled that his answer was: 'Surely we must go.' Although Goodenough's cruisers were also on their way, Beatty at once decided that this was not enough, that support must be overwhelming, and he steamed south-east at 28 knots. 'He felt him-self justified in risking attack from submarines', said the official report, 'thanks to his speed, and he calculated that he was powerful enough to take on any force which might come out.

German torpedo-boats break through a line of cruisers in the Heligoland Bight during manoeuvres.

The German light cruiser *Frauenlob* (ten 4-inch guns) makes heavy smoke as she races out from Heligoland. At 8.25 am a 6-inch shell from *Arethusa*, at 3,400 yards, crippled her and drove her from the Heligoland action.

wounded, and some 300 prisoners rescued from the sea. The *Arethusa* and the *Fearless* had together borne the brunt of the battle against three enemy cruisers for the best part of an hour.

The moral effect of this defeat upon the German navy was considerable. First, because of the loss of three cruisers; and secondly, due to the sharp rebuke which Kaiser Wilhelm administered to Admiral Tirpitz concerning useless losses and the importance of avoiding actions which could lead to such heavy losses.

The action also led to a hardening of the

Enemy's battleships need not be taken into account, as they would take time to get steam up, locate him, and bring him to action; there again he had the legs of them.'

At 12.30 pm the big grey shapes of these battle-cruisers emerged through the mist to the south-west, 'like elephants walking through a pack of pi-dogs', noted Lieutenant Frewin. The weary and smoke-grimed sailors of the *Arethusa* and the *Fearless*, then engaged with the *Köln*, the *Ariadne*, *Stralsund*, *Danzig* and *Stettin*, raised a cheer at this last-moment reversal of fate. Beatty, on the *Lion*, opened fire at extreme range with four 13.5-inch guns and set the *Köln* on fire with the third salvo. She veered sharply from west to north-east and Beatty set off after her at 27 knots.

The German cruiser *Ariadne* then suddenly emerged ahead. *Lion* fired two accurate salvoes which hit her with terrible effect. In flames and sinking, she turned off southwards into the mist. Beatty decided not to pursue her, having been warned of mines, and instead turned to port in search of the *Köln*. He sighted her at 1.25 pm, steering south for Wilhelmshaven. The *Lion* again opened fire with four 13-inch guns, hit her amidships and tore her apart. She went down at 1.35 pm. British destroyers searched the area but could find no survivors.

The other four enemy cruisers had meantime disengaged and vanished into the mist. At 1.40 pm Beatty turned his battle-cruisers north to cover the retirement of the light forces. When all the destroyers had been accounted for and these as well as the submarines had turned for home, the Light Cruiser Squadron took up a fan-shaped formation ahead of the battle-cruisers in a sweep northward.

By late that night all the British squadrons and flotillas had arrived safely back at their bases. During the day they had destroyed three enemy light cruisers, *Mainz*, *Köln* and *Ariadne*, and one destroyer, without the loss of a single ship. Thirty-five British officers and seamen were killed and some 40 wounded, compared with 700 German dead, many

policy of the German navy's Commander-in-Chief, Admiral von Ingenohl—that of weakening British superiority by mines and submarine attacks until he felt the High Seas Fleet could go into battle against the Grand Fleet on equal terms. Ingenohl kept his battle-ships safe in their bases and as a result something like stalemate between the two battle fleets followed.

Another result of this defeat was Admiral Scheer's radical improvement of the defences of the Heligoland Bight. 'Two large minefields were laid west of Heligoland', he wrote later, 'which increased the danger for the enemy and offered a safe retreat for our patrols when they were hard pressed. The minefields before Heligoland proved effective and in conjunction with progressive defensive measures ... kept the inner area so clear that the danger from submarines came at last to be quite a rare and exceptional possibility.'

The British did not repeat their sortie of 28 August 1914 and venture into the enemy's stronghold again. At this time the question of the whereabouts and intentions of Admiral Count Maximilian von Spee's East Asiatic

The German light cruiser *Mainz* (26 knots, twelve 4.1-inch guns) raced out from her base at Emden to join in the action but was overwhelmed by a storm of shells from Commodore Goodenough's light cruisers.

Squadron bothered the Admiralty. The Admiralty was unaware that a few days earlier, on 22 August, von Spee had left Eniwetok Lagoon, in the German Marshall Islands, after calling there. Five days later, on 27 August 1914, the day Japan declared war on the side of the Allies, he had reached Majuro Atoll, in the south-eastern Marshalls. He was due to arrive at the Chilean coaling port of Coronel on 29 October, and on 1 November he would have his historic encounter with Rear-Admiral Sir Christopher Cradock's armoured cruisers, which was to lead to his downfall a month later in the Battle of the Falkland Isles.

The *Mainz*, with two of her funnels and one of her masts shot away, is watched by a group of sailors, probably on board the destroyer *Lurcher*.

The German light cruiser *Ariadne* (21 knots, ten 4.1-inch guns) was engaged, with three sister ships, in trying to finish off the battle-scarred *Arethusa* and *Fearless* at 12.30 pm. Beatty's flagship, the battle-cruiser *Lion*, emerged through the haze and blasted her with two salvoes at long range which left her afire and sinking.

The *Lion*, flagship of Vice-Admiral Sir David Beatty's 1st Battle-Cruiser Squadron, opened fire with her 13-inch guns on the *Ariadne* and *Köln*, sank both of them within a few minutes, and saved the day.

The Emden
November 1914

Germany's outstanding sea raider of the First World War was the cruiser *Emden*. In the 70 days she spent prowling around the Bay of Bengal, she sank 23 Allied merchant ships, forced all merchant vessels to stay in harbour and compelled troopships to be convoyed from Australasia.

Equipped with a false funnel of canvas to make her look like a four-funnelled British cruiser, the *Emden* was unsuccessfully hunted for days around the Indian Ocean by the cruisers *Hampshire* and *Yarmouth* and the Japanese cruiser *Chikuma*. On 18 September 1914 she shelled the Burmah Oil Company's fuel tanks at Madras and set them afire, then simply by her presence in the area paralysed shipping between Colombo and Singapore.

By the end of October 1914 two more British cruisers from the Mediterranean, a cruiser from East Africa and three Japanese cruisers had joined the hunt for the lone wolf *Emden*.

Then Captain Karl Müller took the fateful step of deciding to destroy the cable and wireless station on Direction Island, one of the remote Cocos Islands in the Indian Ocean. *Emden* arrived off the island at 5.50 am on 9 November and dispatched an armed launch with two boats and 50 men to smash electrical equipment and cut the cable to Australia. However, the wireless officer on the island sent out an urgent call for help, and soon the Australian cruiser *Sydney*, one of a convoy escort happily about 55 miles north, was racing towards the scene.

At 9.15 am the *Sydney* sighted the *Emden* approaching—it had left the landing party behind in its haste—and at 9.40 *Emden* opened fire at 9,500 yards—'very accurate and rapid to begin with', reported Captain John Glossop of *Sydney*. But it was not for long; *Sydney*, faster than the *Emden* and firing 6-inch guns compared with *Emden's* 4-inch ones, stood out of range and hammered her enemy until she was a battered hulk, with her steering gear shattered, her foremast over the side, her three funnels torn apart, her boilers out of action and her guns silent.

Rather than surrender, Captain Müller wrecked his ship on the nearby North Keeling Island reefs—'the decks a litter of tangled ironwork amid which, as in a shambles, lay dead and dying', Glossop reported later. The Kaiser awarded Müller the Iron Cross First Class, but he spent the rest of the war a prisoner in Malta.

7

6

4

1. Captain Karl von Müller was Germany's most successful sea raider—cool and daring in action, while showing consideration towards the crews of his prizes.

2. The German cruiser *Emden* paralysed Allied shipping in and around the Bay of Bengal from August 1914 until 9 November 1914, when the Australian light cruiser *Sydney* shelled her to a standstill.

3. The light cruiser *Sydney*, Royal Australian Navy, on convoy duty near the Cocos Islands on 9 November, raced to intercept the enemy cruiser when a call for help came over the radio.

4. An oil tank blazes in the docks at Madras in September 1914, after close-range shelling from the *Emden*.

5. The German landing party, having destroyed the radio station on Direction Island and cut the cable to Australia, waits in its two ship's boats while the *Emden* engages the *Sydney* in battle.

6. Shells from the *Sydney*'s 6-inch guns raise columns of water around the *Emden*, which is already on fire.

7. Survivors from the battered *Emden* row away to go on board the *Sydney* after Müller had beached *Emden* on a nearby atoll to avoid her seizure.

Coronel and the Falkland Islands

November - December 1914

Admiral Maximilian Graf von Spee, commander of Germany's East Asiatic Squadron, had concentrated his five ships at the secret meeting place of Easter Island from 12–19 October 1914. The squadron consisted of the two armoured cruisers, the *Scharnhorst* (flagship) and *Gneisenau*, and three light cruisers, *Nürnberg*, *Dresden* and *Leipzig*, with their attendant chartered steamers for coaling and supplies.

Von Spee's situation was not an enviable one when war broke out. If he tried to make for Germany, sooner or later his course would become known and the British fleet would concentrate to destroy him. If he had tried to help hold the German colony and base of Tsingtau, in China, he would merely have invited a Japanese blockade and brought to an end his squadron's useful life. His role, therefore, was clear: he was to carry out hit-and-run warfare against enemy merchant ships and neutral vessels carrying enemy supplies, while inflicting any other damage possible upon the British overseas.

It was a role that was bound to end in disaster. Count von Spee, seen in contemporary photographs as tall and burly with a neatly trimmed iron-grey beard and that look of moral earnestness which bespeaks a stern sense of duty, described his situation thus: 'I cannot reach Germany. I must plough the seas of the world doing as much mischief as I can, until my ammunition is exhausted, or a foe far superior in power succeeds in catching me.'

The very mobility of von Spee's squadron was a threat to the Allies, for until it was destroyed he could strike both at merchant shipping in the vital South Atlantic trade routes and vessels sailing across the Indian Ocean with urgently needed food and wool from Australia and New Zealand.

Rear-Admiral Sir George Patey's powerful cruiser squadron on the Australian station was, of course, more than able to deal with the best of Spee's ships. This squadron included the 18,000-ton battle-cruiser *Australia*, with a speed of 25.8 knots and eight 12-inch

guns, as well as the light cruisers *Sydney* and *Melbourne*, and the older *Encounter*, with a speed of 25 knots and eleven 6-inch guns. Unfortunately Patey's squadron was at this time engaged in the seizure of German colonies in the Bismarck Archipelago and Samoa, although this operation, in terms of priorities, should have come second to the destruction of Spee's ships. For Patey had next to make ready for convoying the Australian and New Zealand expeditionary forces to Europe.

When, on 14 September 1914, the Admiralty learned that Spee's squadron had been sighted off Samoa and that the commerce raider *Emden*, the sixth ship of his squadron, was at large in the Indian Ocean, fears for the safety of the Anzac convoy were voiced. Despite the need for these troops to help stem the German drive through France, the sailing of the convoy was delayed until the situation became clearer.

Vice-Admiral Sir Martyn Jerram's China Squadron could also have contributed to the destruction of Spee's force. It consisted of the armoured cruisers *Minotaur* (flagship) and *Hampshire*; the light cruisers *Newcastle* and *Yarmouth*; and at Hongkong, in reserve, the pre-dreadnought battleship *Triumph*. In mid-August a signal to Jerram, evidently sent by the First Lord, instructed him to proceed with the destruction of the *Scharnhorst* and *Gneisenau*, 'as soon as possible', with the *Minotaur*, *Hampshire* and the French cruiser *Dupleix*, although no indication was given as to the enemy's whereabouts.

Jerram believed that interference with British trade in the East Indies was probably the object of the *Scharnhorst* and *Gneisenau*, and for two weeks he carried out an unsuccessful search around the Java Sea. Then, in mid-September, when Spee was off Samoa some 3,000 miles to the west, Jerram signalled that he believed the enemy squadron would next appear off the South American coast. He then proposed that he should establish his flag ashore so as to control his force more effectively, and this he did, at Singapore.

Opposite: Vice-Admiral Sir Doveton Sturdee, the victor of the Falklands. On 11 November 1914 he sailed from Plymouth with the battle-cruisers *Invincible* and *Inflexible* to seek out and destroy von Spee's squadron.

Admiral Maximilian Count von Spee, who commanded Germany's East Asiatic Squadron in August 1914, knew that his chances of returning home to Germany were remote and that he must therefore do as much damage as possible to enemy shipping before his squadron was destroyed by a stronger enemy force.

West Indies and along the South American coast. The *Karlsruhe* escaped east into the Atlantic and for some weeks was not heard of, while the *Dresden* rounded Cape Horn on 16 September 1914, steamed up the coast of Chile, then turned west to join Admiral von Spee at Easter Island on 12 October.

Cradock, who had transferred his flag from the *Suffolk* to the faster armoured cruiser *Good Hope*, sailed south, and at Santa Catarina Island, about 400 miles south-west of Rio de Janeiro, received from the Admiralty these curiously vague instructions:

There is a strong probability of the Scharnhorst *and the* Gneisenau *arriving in Magellan Straits or on west coast of South America. Germans have begun to carry on trade on west coast of South America. Leave sufficient force to deal with* Dresden *and* Karlsruhe. *Concentrate a squadron strong enough to meet* Scharnhorst *and* Gneisenau, *making Falkland Islands your coaling base.* Canopus *is now en route to Abrolhos.* Defence *is joining you from Mediterranean. Until* Defence *joins, keep at least* Canopus *and one County class cruiser with your flagship. As soon as you have superior force, search Magellan Straits, with squadron, being ready to return and cover River Plate, or, according to information, search north as far as Valparaiso, break up the German trade and destroy German cruisers. Anchorage in the vicinity of Golfo Nuevo and Egg Harbour should be searched. Colliers are being ordered to Falkland Islands. Consider whether colliers should be ordered south.*

As if the Navy's most powerful and up-to-date battle cruisers were Cradock's to command, the Admiralty instructions spoke in a matter of fact way of his dealing with *Dresden* and *Karlsruhe*, while at the same time concentrating a squadron 'strong enough to meet *Scharnhorst* and *Gneisenau*', when these last two ships alone were more than a match for his entire squadron. Both of them, launched in 1906, were protected by a belt of 6-inch armour, mounted eight 8.2-inch, six 5.9-inch and eighteen 21-pounder guns, and had a speed of no less than 23 knots.

At this time Cradock's squadron consisted of the obsolete battleship *Canopus*, which had a speed of 12 knots and a main armament of four 12-inch guns of obsolete design; the armoured cruiser *Good Hope*, launched in 1903, with a speed of 23 knots, two 9.2-inch, sixteen 6-inch and twelve 12-pounder guns; the armoured cruiser *Monmouth*, also launched in 1903, with a speed of 22.5 knots and a main armament of fourteen 6-inch guns; the *Glasgow*, a light cruiser launched in 1910, with a speed

Hampshire, originally ordered to reinforce the Anzac convoy soon to sail for Europe, was now ordered to join the search for the brilliantly successful commerce raider *Emden*, with *Yarmouth*, *Dupleix* and the Japanese cruiser *Chikumo*. The *Minotaur* and another Japanese cruiser, *Ibuki*, replaced her in the Anzac convoy. Thus, Jerram's ships seemed to have been fully occupied.

At this point, just before Cradock was set on the course which was to end in his encounter with von Spee, one still marvels, even after the passage of sixty years, at the hopelessly muddled handling of the danger posed by von Spee. Almost from the start there was a failure to establish as overriding priorities the destruction of the enemy's naval forces in the South Pacific and the creation of the kind of force there capable of doing so.

Rear-Admiral Sir Christopher Cradock was in the West Indies when he began to be drawn into the drama which was to end so tragically for him. Perhaps it was a devotion to duty beyond the high sense of it common to nearly all of the Navy's senior officers that led him to assume charge of the entire west coast of South America.

In mid-August two of von Spee's cruisers, *Dresden* and *Karlsruhe*, appeared in the Atlantic. Cradock pursued them through the of 25 knots, two 6-inch, ten 4-inch guns; and the *Otranto*, a merchantman armed with a mere eight 4.7-inch guns. All of these vessels were weak in both armament and speed compared with Admiral von Spee's powerful squadron.

In addition, von Spee was fortunate in having crack crews on his two big armoured cruisers. The *Scharnhorst* had recently won the Battle Practice Cup, for which the entire German Navy competed. Of course, Cradock was promised the armoured cruiser *Defence* which, with four 9.2-inch and ten 7.5-inch guns, would enable him to face the enemy on more equal terms, but the *Canopus*, with its hopelessly slow speed, was in fact a liability.

Cradock was not to know that, owing to the activities of the *Emden*, a proposal to provide an adequate reinforcement of no less than three armoured cruisers had been opposed not only by Prince Louis of Battenberg, the First Sea Lord, but also by Jellicoe, who, obsessed with the apparent threat of an invasion on England's east coast, opposed releasing any Grand Fleet battle-cruisers for the purpose. Churchill lamentably failed to assert his authority on this issue.

By mid-October von Spee had received information about the presence in the South Atlantic of Cradock's flagship, *Good Hope*, *Monmouth* and *Glasgow*. It led to a decisive change in policy, which he outlined to his captains: 'The presence of strong enemy forces on the east coast makes it impossible for the Squadron to carry out its original intention of a war against commerce for the present. This purpose is therefore renounced and the destruction of the enemy forces is substituted for it.'

In early October events began to move towards their conclusion. An Admiralty telegram, sent on 5 October 1914, told Cradock that von Spee's squadron was 'working across to South America.'

The message went on to say that Cradock 'must be prepared to meet them in company. *Canopus* should accompany *Glasgow*, *Monmouth* and *Otranto*, and should search and protect trade in combination'. The telegram meant that these four ships alone were considered strong enough to meet the enemy force and that they were to move north up the west coast of South America as far as Valparaiso, where trade in the area was centred.

Churchill subsequently made it clear that, in his view, Cradock's squadron was perfectly safe as it was accompanied by the *Canopus*. 'The *Scharnhorst* and *Gneisenau* would never have ventured to come within range of her 12-inch guns', he wrote. 'To do so would have been to subject themselves to very serious damage without any prospect of success. The old battleship, with her heavy armour

and artillery, was in fact a citadel around which all our cruisers in those waters could find absolute security.'

It was an opinion founded upon the theoretical situation, not upon the speed and firepower of *Canopus* as she then was, for her 12-inch guns had in fact a few hundred yards less range than the 8.5-inch guns of the two big German cruisers.

Some anxiety over his position now began to appear in Cradock's signals to the Admiralty. In the first of two signals on 8 October, referring to intelligence of the concentration of von Spee's squadron, he said: 'I intend to concentrate at Falkland Islands and avoid division of forces. I have ordered *Canopus* to proceed there, and *Monmouth*, *Glasgow* and *Otranto* not to go farther north than Valparaiso until German cruisers are located again ... When does *Defence* join my command?'

In a second telegram that day, Cradock proposed that it was 'necessary to have a British force on each coast strong enough to bring them into action', in the event of the enemy's heavy cruisers concentrating on the west coast of South America. Cradock was now tactfully informing the Admiralty that he doubted whether his force alone was strong enough to meet the enemy, even with the

Admiral Sir Christopher Cradock, who was in command of the North American station when war broke out, had no illusions about the probable outcome of a battle with von Spee's powerful squadron, for he knew he would be outgunned and overwhelmed.

Defence, which had not yet joined him, and *Canopus*.

On 7 October, *Glasgow*, *Monmouth* and the armed merchant cruiser *Otranto* steamed north up the west coast of South America while *Good Hope* put into the Falklands. Having deliberated on Cradock's telegrams, the Admiralty finally concluded that the destruction of von Spee's force must be the first priority. On 14 October it sent a telegram to Cradock: 'Concur in your concentration of *Canopus*, *Good Hope*, *Glasgow*, *Monmouth*, *Otranto* for combined operation. We have ordered Stoddart in *Carnarvon* to Montevideo as Senior Naval Officer north of that place. Have ordered *Defence* to join *Carnarvon*. He will also have under his orders *Cornwall*, *Bristol*, *Orama* and *Macedonia*.'

Now, for a second time, Cradock expressed his misgivings to the Admiralty: 'I trust circumstances will enable me to force an action, but fear that strategically, owing to *Canopus*, the speed of my squadron cannot exceed 12 knots.'

He was saying that at this speed he could not force an action upon a squadron capable of 21 knots, which could easily escape him if it wished. No less important was the implication that, with its greater speed, the enemy could cross his 'T', or steam across his course at right angles and bring broadsides to bear, while in this situation he could return fire only with his forward guns. Cradock reminded the Admiralty in this telegram that he was likely to face destruction by this classic tactical move.

Fears that von Spee's squadron might now be nearing the west coast of Chile, where his three ships would be at its mercy, now beset Cradock. He waited until *Canopus* arrived on 22 October at Port Stanley, only to be faced with the unwelcome news that her engines needed overhauling. Leaving instructions for the *Canopus* to meet him on the west coast 'by way of the Straits', he steamed off alone to rejoin his four ships, without the 'citadel' the Admiralty believed was the one guarantee of security against the crack enemy squadron.

Good Hope ploughed through the grey seas towards the Horn. Dark storm clouds scudded overhead, the wind tugged at masts and stays. Cradock would have known that, although he was still under orders to bring the enemy to action, he was almost certainly steaming to destruction. On 26 October 1914, after rounding the Horn, in his third and final telegram on the issue, he made a bold move to strengthen his squadron.

'With reference to orders to search for enemy and our great desire for early success, I consider that owing to slow speed of *Canopus* it is impossible to find and destroy enemy's squadron. Have therefore ordered *Defence* to join me after calling for orders at Montevideo. Shall employ *Canopus* on necessary work of convoying colliers.'

Admiral Stoddart at once contended to the Admiralty that he should be given two fast cruisers to replace *Defence*, if this vessel was given to Cradock. The Admiralty accepted Cradock's challenge, countermanded his order and bluntly replied: '*Defence* is to remain on East Coast under orders of Stoddart. This will leave sufficient force on each side in case the hostile cruisers appear there on the trade routes. There is no ship available for the Cape Horn vicinity. Japanese battleship *Hizen*

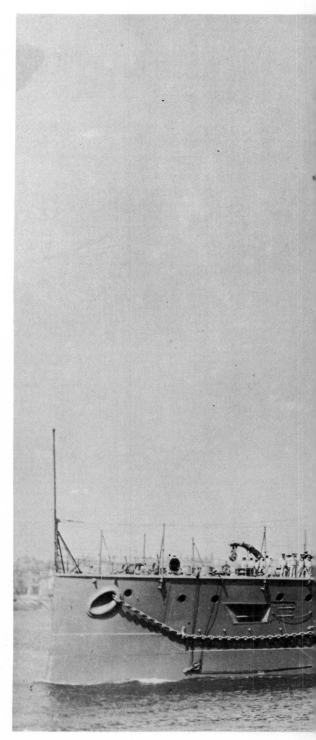

shortly expected on North American coast. She will join with Japanese *Idzumo* and *Newcastle* and move south to Galapagos.'

There is no absolute proof that this telegram reached Cradock. On the other hand, the intelligence officer with the squadron, Lieutenant Lloyd Hirst, who was on board the *Glasgow* at Vallenar on the evening of 27 October, relates that Cradock sent her on ahead to Coronel to collect local intelligence reports and to find out the Admiralty reaction to his bold order for *Defence* to join him. Also, as the *Official History* states: 'He was still hoping, it would seem, to receive a modification of the instructions, which, as he conceived them appeared impracticable . . .'

Hirst boarded the *Monmouth* and *Good Hope* to collect letters from home before leaving for Coronel. 'In the wardroom, a fight within a few days was considered inevitable', he relates, 'but there was not much optimism about the result; two of the Lieutenant-Commanders in *Monmouth*, both old shipmates of mine, took me aside to give me farewell messages to their wives . . .'

On the night of the 20th, as the *Glasgow* steamed towards Coronel, her wireless operator heard the *Leipzig* sending signals less than 150 miles away. Cradock, in *Good Hope*, therefore steamed northwards with *Monmouth*

The 12-year-old battleship *Canopus*, able to steam at barely 12 knots, was regarded by Winston Churchill, First Lord of the Admiralty, as 'a citadel', with her four 12-inch guns, around which Cradock's cruisers would find complete security. In fact she was little more than a liability.

early on 30 October, having ordered *Canopus* to follow. The armed merchantman *Otranto*, which had been seeking information in Puerto Montt, joined Cradock on 31 October. He also ordered Captain Luce of the *Glasgow* to rendezvous with him some 80 miles south-west of Coronel at 1 pm on the following day. Evidently, Luce then brought him the Admiralty's signal countermanding his order for *Defence* to join him. It was decisive.

Cradock was known to be a fearless, even impetuous officer, as well as an experienced one. Three times he had told the Admiralty that his ships were not up to the task of destroying Admiral von Spee's squadron. At last, half an hour after reading his last telegram, he appears to have felt that he had reached the point of no return. He hoisted the fateful signal: 'Spread 20 miles apart and look for the enemy.'

More wireless signals now indicated the presence of a single German ship, the *Leipzig*, to the north. Cradock, believing on the basis of the earlier signals that he was about to meet one ship—an illusion which the enemy had skilfully fostered—ordered his squadron to form a line of search fifteen miles apart north-west by north and to proceed at a speed of ten knots in the order, from east to west,

of *Good Hope, Monmouth, Otranto* and *Glasgow*. But at 4.20 pm, before this manoeuvre was completed, *Glasgow* sighted smoke on her starboard bow and altered course to steam towards it.

Admiral von Spee had taken on coal from the collier *Santa Isabel* some 40 miles off Valparaiso on 31 October and at 2.50 am a German steamer signalled him that the British cruiser *Glasgow* had anchored at Coronel at 7 pm the previous evening. Von Spee, therefore, had formed a line of search and steamed south towards Coronel in the hope of trapping and destroying the cruiser after she had left Coronel.

Thus, as Captain T. G. Frothingham states in *Naval History of The World War*:

The German sweep southward in search of Glasgow, *was thus taking place at the very time the British squadron was sweeping north in its search for the* Leipzig, *which the deceptive German signals had described as being alone. Consequently . . . each squadron was seeking one ship of the other squadron, in belief that it was an isolated enemy ship—and each squadron in ignorance of the fact that finding the enemy single ship would mean finding the whole enemy*

Cradock's flagship, the armoured cruiser *Good Hope*, unable to fire the 6-inch casemate guns seen here below her four funnels, owing to heavy seas, was limited to her two 9.2-inch guns during the battle. Thirty-five 8.2-inch shells from the German cruisers hit her before she sank.

squadron. *This was the strange situation which brought on the Battle of Coronel.*

Not long after altering course to identify the smoke to starboard, the *Glasgow* sighted three ships—one three-funnelled light cruiser and two four-funnelled armoured cruisers. Admiral von Spee's squadron immediately turned in her direction and the *Glasgow* closed at full speed towards the *Good Hope*, signalling at the same time, 'Enemy armoured cruisers in sight'. Soon another cruiser with three funnels joined the enemy ships, which were steaming south in line ahead nearer to the South American coast, which was about twelve miles distant.

During Cradock's search to the north, the *Good Hope* had steamed north-west by north and the other ships north-east by east, so that by 4.20 pm, when the enemy was sighted, Admiral Cradock's flagship was considerably westward of them. At 4.47 pm, after the *Glasgow* had identified the enemy, the *Glasgow*, *Monmouth* and *Otranto* turned west at full speed with the intention of forming line of battle in the following order: *Good Hope*, *Monmouth*, *Glasgow* and *Otranto*.

Inevitably, having regard to the distance, this took time, so the chance was lost of forcing an early action before the enemy squadron was concentrated. It also allowed von Spee more than an hour to get up the necessary steam, for earlier the *Gneisenau* had started to clean two of her boilers and could not approach the 22 knots at which the *Scharnhorst* chased the *Glasgow*.

An hour later, at 5.57 pm, with the enemy approaching about ten miles to the north, Cradock attempted to cross in front of the enemy, but finding this impossible, owing to the low speed of fifteen knots imposed by the *Otranto*, gave this up and altered course in succession to south, with the enemy eastward, on a parallel course.

Lieutenant Hirst, on board the *Glasgow*, noted: 'We then tried by altering slightly towards them to force an immediate action, the conditions being then in our favour, as the setting sun was strong in the enemy's eyes. They declined action, however, by edging away and thus maintained their distance at about 15,000 yards.'

Having failed to win this decisive tactical advantage, Cradock could still avoid action and steam some 250 miles south while awaiting reinforcement by the *Canopus*. In doing so, however, he would run the risk of the enemy escaping him during the darkness or

The *Monmouth*, Cradock's second armoured cruiser, also launched in 1903 and capable of nearly 23 knots, could not fire her 6-inch casemate guns in the heavy sea. She was overwhelmed by a storm of 30 8.2-inch enemy shells and sank soon after the *Good Hope*.

The *Glasgow*, a fast light cruiser capable of 25 knots but armed only with two 6-inch and ten 4-inch guns, was the third warship in Cradock's weak squadron. She escaped after her sister ships had gone down, having been hit only once.

subsequently outstripping the slower, but by now more evenly matched British squadron.

In the light of his orders he chose to engage at once, and at 6.18 pm he signalled *Canopus*: 'I am now going to attack the enemy.' Cradock faced a double handicap, for in these heavy seas his crew of RNR reservists and recruits would encounter special problems in gunlaying, while many of the 6-inch guns on the *Good Hope*'s and *Monmouth*'s main decks would not be fought because their casemates, constructed too near the waterline, could not be opened in this heavy weather.

Shortly before 7 pm the sun dipped below the horizon. Admiral von Spee had succeeded in snatching the tactical advantage from the British. 'We were now silhouetted against the afterglow, with a clear horizon behind to show up splashes from falling shells', Hirst observed, 'while their ships to us were smudged into low black shapes scarcely discernible against the background of gathering night clouds'.

While this significant change was taking place, von Spee gradually closed the range. A minute or two after 7 pm, his squadron— *Scharnhorst*, *Gneisenau*, *Leipzig* and *Dresden* —opened fire at a range of 12,000 yards; *Nürnberg* was still some miles away. All that Cradock had feared, but had felt himself in honour bound not to avoid, now overwhelmed him. From the outset he was faced by twelve of the enemy's 8.2-inch guns, against which

he could at this range pit only the *Good Hope*'s two 9.2-inch guns.

The *Scharnhorst*'s first salvo fell short; her second salvo overshot; but her third knocked out the *Good Hope*'s forward 9.2-inch gun before it had fired a single shell, while at the same time the *Gneisenau* hit the *Monmouth* and set her fore turret afire, which burned furiously despite the waves breaking over her bows. *Good Hope* and *Monmouth* both scored hits on the two heavy enemy cruisers, but none of them caused serious damage.

By now the battle was raging furiously. *Good Hope* was hit amidships time after time, shells twice struck her after turret, and soon flames raging below were licking out through the portholes. More than 30 shells struck the *Monmouth*, too, and suddenly a great column of fire rocketed up on her starboard side. The armed merchant cruiser *Otranto*, whose 4-inch guns were ineffective, had moved out of the action, while the *Glasgow* was dealing effectively with both the *Leipzig* and *Dresden* with her 6-inch guns.

At 7.45 pm Lieutenant Hirst noted that both *Good Hope* and *Monmouth* were in distress. 'Frequently either ship flashed into a vivid orange as a lyddite shell detonated against her upperworks. Ears had become deafened by the roar of our guns and almost insensible to the shriek of fragments flying over head from the shells which burst short.'

Monmouth, by now blazing furiously and

listing, moved out of line to starboard and slowed, forcing the *Glasgow*, which was behind her, to slow down to avoid overtaking her and receiving the stream of shells the *Gneisenau* hurled at her. The flames from the *Good Hope*, now a battered hulk, increased in brilliance, but those few gunners alive still fired as and when they could.

The end of the *Good Hope* came suddenly. 'At 7.50pm', noted Hirst, 'there was a terrific explosion on board between her mainmast and her after-most funnel, and the gush of flames, reaching a height of 'over 200 feet, lighted up a cloud of debris that was flung still higher in the air . . . Her fire then ceased, as did also that of the *Scharnhorst* upon her, and she lay between the lines, a low black hull, gutted of her upperworks, and only lighted by a dull red glare which shortly disappeared'.

The *Glasgow*, firing upon the dim outline of an enemy light cruiser in the half darkness, now received her first hit, on her waterline above the port outer propeller, which made a big dent in her plating but caused no real damage. But now that the *Monmouth* had turned away to the west, where she was busy trying to put out her fires, the *Glasgow* became the new target for both the enemy heavy cruisers. At 8.15pm she stopped firing, so as to avoid drawing the enemy's fire by the flash of her guns.

The enemy vessels now lost contact with both the *Glasgow* and the *Monmouth* in the darkness, with the moon obscured by clouds most of the time. *Glasgow*, recalled Hirst, closed to *Monmouth*'s port quarter and signalled by lamp: 'Are you all right?' *Monmouth* replied: 'I want to get stern to sea. I am making water badly forward.' She was listing to port, down by the bows, and fire glowed from her.

In a flash of moonlight, Captain Luce, on the *Glasgow*, briefly saw the enemy ships approaching some distance away in line abreast. 'Can you steer north-west?' he signalled. 'The enemy are following us astern.'

There was no answer. 'The moon was now clear of the clouds', Hirst observed, 'and it was obvious that *Monmouth* could neither fight nor fly; so our Captain had to decide whether to share her fate, without being able to render any adequate assistance, or to attempt to escape the enemy'. Since it was considered essential that the *Canopus*, approaching the area alone, should be warned, Captain Luce reluctantly turned away at full speed and lost sight of the enemy at about 8.50pm. Afterwards he counted 75 flashes of enemy gunfire upon *Monmouth* before silence, except for wind and sea, returned.

The *Nürnberg*, approaching the scene of the action at high speed, had been ordered to make a torpedo attack. She came upon the fireswept *Monmouth* in the darkness, fired a torpedo which failed to strike home, then opened fire at point-blank range. *Monmouth*

The 8-inch guns of the *Gneisenau* hit *Monmouth*'s fore turret and set it ablaze with her second or third salvo, and although *Monmouth* hit *Gneisenau* three times her shells did scant damage.

seemingly had neither her guns working nor gunners living with which to reply, but she turned as if to ram. The *Nürnberg* let loose a hail of shells and at 9.28 pm the *Monmouth* capsized and went down.

So ended the Battle of Coronel. It had lasted 61 minutes. Admiral von Spee steered north and signalled his squadron: 'With God's help a glorious victory, for which I express my recognition and congratulations to the crews.' His gunners had fired salvoes at fifteen-second intervals, knocking the *Good Hope*'s forward turret out before she had fired a shot. Von Spee noted that the Germans had scored 35 hits on *Good Hope* and that the British ships, handicapped in the heavy sea, were firing one salvo to every three from his squadron.

The Admiralty Staff had sent *Good Hope* and *Monmouth* to an area known for its heavy seas, despite the knowledge that their main deck guns could not be fought in these conditions. Both this and the inexperience of the gunners resulted in the *Good Hope* hitting the *Scharnhorst* only twice; the *Monmouth* hit *Gneisenau* three times, and the *Glasgow* hit her once. As at Heligoland, the poor design of British shells was evident, for the two that struck *Scharnhorst* both failed to explode. In all respects the battle was a disaster for both Britain and her Allies. The prestige of the Royal Navy was questioned as never before and immediate orders were given for a decisive counter-blow.

Admiral Lord Fisher, 'Jacky', the ruthless fighting admiral who had re-fashioned the Royal Navy in the pre-war years, had returned to his post as First Sea Lord on 30 October 1914, two days before the battle, succeeding Prince Louis Battenberg, who was forced to resign owing to his German origin. Winston Churchill recalls in *The World Crisis* how on 3 November the Admiralty received the first certain report that Spee's squadron had been located off the west coast of South America and how in the evening he, Lord Fisher and Admiral Sturdee, Chief of Naval Staff, in a recognition of the realities of Cradock's situation, signalled Admiral Stoddart: '*Defence* to proceed with all possible dispatch to join Admiral Cradock on west coast of America.'

At last, posthumously, Admiral Cradock had been granted decisive reinforcements. But Churchill discovered that no reinforcements could help him now, early on 4 November, when he received a telegram from the British Consul General in Valparaiso telling of the disaster at Coronel. The news was confirmed a few hours later by a message dispatched from Port Stanley by Captain Luce of the *Glasgow*. Occurring as it had done on the same day, 1 November 1914, as the entry of Turkey into the war on Germany's side, it seemed, at the time, an almost equal calamity.

Lord Fisher acted at once with a bold and comprehensive strategical move which totally overshadowed Churchill's tentative proposals. Less than six hours after receiving the news Fisher, risking the narrow supremacy of Jellicoe's Grand Fleet over the German High Seas Fleet, ordered Jellicoe to detach two battlecruisers, *Invincible* and *Inflexible*, for urgent service elsewhere. Admiral Sturdee, whom Fisher had replaced by Admiral Oliver as Chief-of-Staff, was appointed C-in-C South Atlantic and Pacific, a station covering one half of the world's oceans, and the two ships were ordered to coal at once and proceed forthwith to Plymouth to make ready 'with the utmost despatch'. They sailed on their vital mission on 11 November.

Admiral Sturdee's secret instructions were to steam southwards at the maximum economical speed with the *Invincible* and the *Inflexible*, coal at St Vincent, Cape Verde,

and rendezvous with Rear-Admiral Stoddart at Abrolhos Rocks, off the coast of Brazil, with the cruisers *Carnarvon*, *Cornwall* and *Kent*, which had steamed south-west from Sierra Leone, as well as the *Glasgow*, the *Bristol* and the armed merchant cruisers *Macedonia* and *Otranto*.

His task was to seek out and destroy Admiral von Spee's entire squadron. Numerous other dispositions, amounting to 30 vessels, 21 of them armoured cruisers, were made to cover the possible appearance of Spee in the Pacific, or off the west coast of South America or the Cape of Good Hope or, in case he should try to make for home across the South Atlantic, the Cape Verde Islands.

Captain Grant, on the *Canopus*, still beset by boiler troubles, was ordered by Lord Fisher to moor his ship so that the entrance of Stanley Harbour, Falkland Isles—a very likely target for von Spee—was commanded by his guns, if necessary grounding his ship to do so.

He was also instructed to turn his ship into a fort, stimulate the Governor to organize local defence and put guns ashore to help him.

The tabulated list on the following page gives the tonnage, speed, armament and completion date of the British vessels under Admiral Sturdee which were to take part in the intended battle against Admiral von Spee's squadron:

Meanwhile von Spee, putting into Valparaiso with his two heavy cruisers and the *Nürnberg*, had received from the German ambassador there a message that the German Admiralty did not believe cruiser warfare in the Pacific promised good results—despite the *Emden*'s and *Königsberg*'s successes—and that he should try to make his way home. This, apparently, was his ultimate intention. Leaving Valparaiso the next day, he joined up with the rest of his squadron at Mas-a-Fuera, on the same latitude in the South Atlantic, about 350 miles west.

The *Scharnhorst*, von Spee's flagship, mounted eight 8.2-inch guns in her main battery. Her gunners, like those of her sister ship *Gneisenau*, had been champions in their navy's Battle Practice Cup.

He left a single supply ship with orders to give the impression, by constant signalling, that the entire squadron was still there, then steamed south and stayed coaling and carrying out repairs in the hidden anchorage of St Quentin Bay from 21 to 26 November. Then he went south and rounded the Horn on 2 December.

Four days later, at a council of captains, Admiral von Spee decided on a plan to destroy Britain's base in the Falklands, thus disrupting her naval operations in the South Atlantic. Captain Pochhammer of the *Gneisenau* wrote later:

We knew to our cost what it meant to traverse the seas without a refuge, to cruise along interminable coasts without a shelter from the wind, the sea or the enemy, with no other assistance than that of the cargo steamers we had brought with us.

If we succeeded, even temporarily, in rendering useless Stanley Harbour, the chief port, as a revictualling station for the British Fleet, in destroying stocks of coal and provisions and the plant installed for refitting ships, and finally in paralysing the big wireless station which formed part of the network of communications of our enemies, we might acquire by this feat complete freedom of action for our subsequent operations.

A report that the base was undefended because the British warships there had sailed for South Africa was decisive. But von Spee still intended to make for Germany. One of the German Admiralty telegrams which reached him after Coronel asked what his future plans were, and Spee replied, 'A breakthrough by the cruisers to Germany is intended'.

British Forces at the Battle of the Falklands

Ships	Classification	Completed	Displacement	Speed	Armament
Inflexible	Battle-cruiser	1908	17.250	26.5	8 12-in 16 4-in
Invincible	Battle-cruiser	1908	17.250	26.5	8 12-in 16 4-in
Carnarvon	Cruiser	1904	10.850	22.1	4 7.5-in 6 6-in
Cornwall	Cruiser	1904	9.800	24.0	14 6-in
Kent	Cruiser	1903	9.800	24.1	14 6-in
Glasgow	Light Cruiser	1911	4.800	26.0	2 6-in 10 4-in

Thus he made a fatal error of judgement in deciding to launch the Falkland attack. First, because the secrecy of his movements would be lost by warning messages by the Falklands wireless station before its destruction. Secondly, because German occupation of the base would inevitably be of the shortest duration. Third, because the ruse he had successfully used of sending out signals at Mas-a-Fuera to give the impression that he was still on the west coast of South America would be jeopardized, just when it could have been of most use to him in his voyage across the Atlantic from south to north.

National and personal pride had marred Spee's judgement. Having had one great success he now yearned for another, evidently not realizing that to bring his ships safely home across the world would be the greatest triumph, not only because of the new strength it would give the High Seas Fleet, but also because of the problems that seeking him far and wide all that time would mean for the Allies.

Forgetting all secrecy now, von Spee sailed his squadron along the southern coast of Tierra del Fuego, past the straggling coastline of Staaten Island, then 300 miles northeast for the Falklands, whose dark land masses emerged on the northern horizon just before dawn on 8 December 1914. At 5 am *Gneisenau* and *Nürnberg*, with the landing parties, went on fifteen miles ahead so as to reach Cape Pembroke at 8 am, ready for the job of destruction which von Spee had given them. Clearly, his arriving so long after daylight with landing parties, instead of launching a surprise artillery attack at dawn by the

53

whole squadron prior to landing, shows beyond doubt that von Spee was sure he would find the base undefended.

Sturdee, steaming down towards the Falklands, had no precise information as to von Spee's whereabouts. He might be anywhere in the South Atlantic or Pacific. It was, in the words of Lieutenant-Commander Barry Bingham, a gunnery specialist on the *Inflexible*, like 'looking for a needle in five bundles of hay, if the ships had dispersed and were acting independently'.

Lord Fisher's orders of 24 November were that having joined forces with those of Stoddart, Sturdee should 'move south to the Falklands, use this as his base, and then to proceed to the coast of Chile, search the channels and inlets of Tierra del Fuego, while keeping his big ships out of sight.' A message Sturdee had received on 4 December, that the supply ship *Prinz Eitel Friedrich*—which von Spee had left behind on the west coast as a subterfuge—had been sighted off Valparaiso, persuaded him that the whole squadron was likely to be somewhere off the west coast.

Von Spee now departed from his agreed plan to make a dash for home mainly on the strength of an unconfirmed rumour put out by British seamen that the base was undefended. Sturdee, led mainly by the success of von Spee's ruse off the coast of Chile with his supply ship, forgot his earlier uncertainty and put his entire squadron in at the Falklands for coaling before steaming on to the west coast. Misjudgement on both sides thus led to the Battle of the Falkland Isles; and the main source of illusion, which led to the end of von Spee and his squadron, was the presence of the *Prinz Eitel Friedrich*, signalling on the west coast.

Admiral Sturdee's squadron arrived at the Falklands at 10.30 am on 7 December 1914. *Bristol* and *Glasgow* anchored in the inner harbour of Port Stanley and the remainder in Port William, the outer harbour. The *Canopus*, already in position, had done much to organize the defence of the base. The two light cruisers, *Bristol* and *Glasgow*, began coaling almost at once and finished in the evening, a wise decision as it turned out. Coaling all the remaining ships began at dawn next day, and the two battle-cruisers had already taken on 400 tons of coal when, at 7.35 am, came a message from one of the shore look-outs to *Canopus*: 'A four-funnel and a two-funnel man-of-war in sight from Sapper Hill steering northwards.'

Glasgow repeated the message with the signal by flag, 'Enemy in sight'; and to make doubly sure Captain Luce fired a gun. Lieutenant Hirst went up to the *Glasgow's* masthead and swiftly identified the two vessels as *Gneisenau* and *Nürnberg*. Surprised while coaling in harbour, the British squadron was extremely vulnerable to an immediate attack by the German squadron, since most of the ships had colliers alongside. Unfortunately, von Spee had thrown away his chances by arriving at leisure with only two ships. Not until 8.20 am were his other ships seen on the horizon.

And not for some time did the German squadron realize that enemy cruisers were getting up steam behind the high ridge of Cape Pembroke, for they were taken in by the clouds of smoke. 'Here and there behind the dunes', noted Captain Pochhammer, on the *Gneisenau*, 'columns of dark yellow smoke began to ascend, and then coalesced and expanded, as if stores were being destroyed to prevent them from falling into our hands'.

Admiral Sturdee had given his orders at once, the bugles on the British ships had sounded 'Action', the colliers were cast off, coils of smoke poured from the big battle-cruisers' funnels as the stokers fought to get

up steam in time, and by 8.45 am the cruiser *Kent* had taken position at the mile-wide entrance to the great harbour, with orders not to let the enemy out of sight if he chose to move off.

Canopus at last came into her own. Captain Pochhammer had already signalled *Scharnhorst* that he had identified three British cruisers (not *Inflexible* or *Invincible*) and that he was soon going to open fire. Suddenly, at 9.20 am, two shells from the 12-inch guns of the *Canopus* dropped a few hundred yards short, seeming to the Germans to come from a land battery, for the *Canopus* was hidden from seaward by the spit of land leading to Cape Pembroke, her aim being controlled by telephone from a shore observation post. A salvo of three more shells followed, one of which hit the *Gneisenau* by a ricochet.

Von Spee had looked forward to attacking a defenceless base, but to find warships there and to see his own ships shelled by an apparently powerful concealed land battery was too

much. 'He had no desire whatever to engage in a new battle here off the Falkland Islands', declared Pochhammer. Von Spee ordered operations to be suspended and the *Gneisenau* and *Nürnberg* to rejoin the flagship with all speed. The guns of *Canopus* had saved the ships in harbour and the wireless station from a destructive shelling.

Shadowed at 9.45 am by the *Glasgow* and the *Kent*, the enemy squadron made off eastwards at about 21 knots, followed by the rest of the squadron at 10 am. It was a fine clear morning, with a bright sun and almost dead calm. 'So great was the visibility', noted Lieutenant-Commander Bingham, 'that on clearing the entrance of the harbour we were able at once to take the range of the enemy, the tops of whose masts and funnels were just above the horizon. The distance was found to be 38,000 yards, i.e., nineteen miles, or nearly twenty-two sea miles'.

Probably this was an overestimate, for at 10.48 am *Glasgow*, which was three miles

The eight 12-inch guns of *Inflexible* and *Invincible* (seen here), Sturdee's flagship, hammered the *Scharnhorst* and *Gneisenau* at long range until both were blazing hulks. They sank in the late afternoon on 8 December 1914. The British battle-cruisers fired some six hundred 12-inch shells each, but, at a range of about 17,000 yards, only about 60 struck home.

55

ahead, signalled that they were twelve sea miles away. The British ships were steaming at 24 knots and gaining steadily, but making such dense clouds of black smoke that Admiral Sturdee, on board the *Invincible*, could no longer see the enemy. For this reason, and because he was aware that in about two hours he should be able to open fire and that *Carnarvon*, only capable of 20 knots, was dropping far behind, Sturdee signalled to *Inflexible* at 11.26 am that he was reducing speed to 20 knots so that his squadron could keep together.

Captain Fanshawe, commanding the *Bristol*, was now ordered to proceed with the armed merchant cruiser *Macedonia* to attack and destroy two transports then signalled to be approaching the Falklands. They turned out to be the colliers *Santa Isabel* and *Baden*.

At 12.20 pm, when Sturdee's officers and men had finished their midday meal, the *Carnarvon*, then steaming at only 18 knots, was still far behind. Sturdee, realizing that he could wait no longer, decided to press the action and increased speed to 22 knots, and by 12.50 to 25 knots. He then gave the general signal to engage.

Soon after one o'clock, at 16,000 yards, the *Invincible* fired its first sighting shot at the *Leipzig*, last in the enemy's line. It fell short, but the following shots sent great columns of water up all around her, and at 1.20 pm Admiral von Spee signalled to his three light cruisers, 'Turn off, try to escape'. It was an heroic though desperate attempt to save them by drawing on to *Scharnhorst* and *Gneisenau* the fire of the British heavyweights.

But Sturdee, foreseeing just such an eventuality, had earlier instructed his captains that the battle-cruisers would fight the enemy armoured cruisers, leaving the rest of his squadron to pursue and destroy the light cruisers. As the light cruisers *Leipzig*, *Dresden* and *Nürnberg* turned away to the south-west, *Glasgow*, *Kent* and *Cornwall* immediately swung round to the south and took up the chase without Sturdee making any signal.

At the same time, the enemy armoured cruisers turned in succession eight points to port, making right-angled left turns to the north-east, and increased speed to about 23 knots in line ahead, a move which Sturdee followed. Before von Spee had finished his manoeuvre, *Invincible* and *Inflexible* were racing along on his beam at a distance of 16,000 yards.

The battle thus began at 1.20 pm. The *Scharnhorst*, soon followed by *Gneisenau*, opened fire on the *Invincible*, Sturdee's flagship, but their shots fell short. Von Spee shortened the range by turning about 20 degrees to port, then at 13,000 yards opened fire again and hit *Invincible*. Both British ships replied. Sturdee then turned away to port to keep the range beyond the power of the enemy guns, only to obscure both his and the *Inflexible*'s aim by the smoke from his funnels and his guns.

But both enemy ships were already hit, the *Gneisenau* twice, the first shell exploding on the upper deck after grazing the third funnel, badly wounding an officer and three men, killing a stoker and temporarily putting one of her 8-inch guns out of action. The second struck her on the waterline, pierced the armour and lodged in a light ammunition chamber. Fire threatened, but the chamber was flooded at once and the damage limited.

Meanwhile, under cover of the smoke, von Spee turned ten points to starboard, thus altering his course right round to southward and increasing the range to 19,000 yards. A lull in the battle followed as Sturdee followed suit and chased at increased speed, at the same time gradually lessening the range, until at 2.47 pm both British ships again opened fire at 18,000 yards, and as salvo followed salvo the enemy was hit again and again.

Von Spee countered this hail of fire by a sharp turn towards the British line, so as to try to bring his twelve 5.9-inch and sixteen 8.2-inch guns into action, a move calculated to give him an advantage, because the two British battle-cruisers mounted only 4-inch guns as their secondary armament. Soon, in the face of accurate shooting, Sturdee turned away again to stay out of range.

By now the *Gneisenau* was listing, the *Scharnhorst* was on fire forward and her fast rate of fire was falling off. Certain now that he had the enemy mastered, Sturdee swung both his ships in a circle outwards and to windward at 3.15 pm, to get clear of the curtain of smoke obscuring his targets, returning, with the *Inflexible* leading, on the opposite course. According to the British squadron intelligence officer, Lieutenant Hirst, 'the Germans copied this turn, which was completed by 3.25 pm, leaving both sides steering west by south about 12,000 yards apart'.

Frequently now the British 12-inch shells were striking the enemy ships. Soon the *Gneisenau* was in a bad way; Captain Pochhammer noted:

Owing to the great range of the fight, the shells fell aslant and consequently hit the thin armoured deck more often than the strong side plates. Thus they found their way more easily into the ship and wrought considerable destruction, even in the lower compartments . . .

The wireless station was destroyed and a deck officer had his head blown off there. Another shell fell into the after-dressing station, and freed some of the wounded from

their sufferings. The doctor was killed there, and the squadron chaplain ended his life of duty.

Several hits below the waterline had flooded two of *Gneisenau*'s stokeholds, despite all the pumps being in action. Dead, mutilated and wounded men lay in heaps where they had fallen, her speed fell rapidly and she heeled over to starboard, but her gunners fought on with steady and accurate fire.

Meanwhile the *Scharnhorst* had been hit by a hail of 12-inch shells. Pochhammer, 2,000 yards away, observed a large hole forward, another gaping hole where her third funnel had been, smoke, flames and steam rising from her, and flames visible inside her through shell holes in her hull. But still her guns thundered.

At 4 pm, when Admiral Sturdee signalled her to surrender, she made no reply, but signalled *Gneisenau* to try to escape while she endeavoured to turn her bows towards the British ships and launch torpedoes. It was too late. At 4.4 pm she heeled over to port, her bows submerged and her propellers still revolving. A few surviving crew members scrambled from the decks up on to her side. At 4.17 pm she went down bows first; fifteen minutes later, when the *Carnarvon* approached the spot, there was not a single survivor.

Gneisenau, stricken as she was, with her speed down to about 15 knots, now turned towards the two enemy cruisers to try to shorten the range and bring her 5.9-inch guns to bear, but Sturdee countered the move. For nearly two hours *Gneisenau* doggedly fought on against the three British ships from three different bearings at ranges of from 10,000 to 12,000 yards. From time to time dense smoke interrupted their fire, but one after another the *Gneisenau*'s guns were put out of action. Captain Pochhammer recorded:

The armour-plate of the 9-inch casemate was pierced and when the smoke had cleared away, the men were all found dead and the gun out of action. Another shell exploded on the upper deck just above the bed of the 8-inch fore gun. It swept the men away as if they had been bundles of clothes . . . Our ship's resistance capacity was slowly diminishing . . . Debris and corpses were accumulating, icy water dripped in one place and in another gushed in streams through shell-holes. Wherever it was possible to do so efforts were made to man the guns. The after turret had long been jammed, only the fore turret remaining intact and continuing to fire all alone as long as its ammunition lasted.

The last shot the *Gneisenau*'s stubborn gunners, fired in answer to Sturdee's call to

In this picture, taken from the *Invincible* with *Inflexible* in the background, sailors from the sunken *Gneisenau*, many of them wounded, struggle to stay alive in the icy waters of the South Atlantic as British lifeboats rescue them. Some 200 officers and men were picked up out of a crew of 850.

Above and opposite: Otto von Spee and Heinz von Spee, lieutenants in their father's squadron, lost their lives in the battle of the Falkland Isles.

surrender, buried itself deeply in the *Invincible*'s hull. The British ships re-opened fire at 10,000 yards, struck the forward turret with a 12-inch shell which flung it skywards and overboard, and for a further fifteen minutes devastated the *Gneisenau* until she was a floating, blazing hulk, her foremast shot away, the upper deck a shambles of torn steel and blood, and her shattered guns pointing drunkenly in the air.

As she began to go down, survivors among her crew paraded in an orderly manner on deck, gave three cheers for the Kaiser and their ship, then at the order 'All men overboard', jumped into the sea or slithered down the hull and swam clear. The British ships, between five and six miles away, steamed up at full speed as the *Gneisenau* slowly went down stern first, with her bows high. Boats were lowered and some 200 of her crew of 850 were picked up, but many of them died of their wounds during the night. They were buried at sea next day with full military honours.

Admiral Sturdee's tactics had been brilliantly successful, for in this long-range action, although the *Invincible* had been hit about 20 times and *Inflexible* just once or twice, not a single officer or man had been killed and none seriously wounded.

During this ruthless encounter, the three German light cruisers had been fleeing south with a ten miles start over the *Glasgow*, *Cornwall* and *Kent*. The *Dresden*, fastest of the enemy ships, apparently built up to 27 knots and escaped her pursuers to the southwest in the rain squalls that intermittently drove across the sea. Captain Luce, commanding *Glasgow*, therefore joined with Captain Ellerton of *Cornwall* to destroy the *Leipzig*, last ship in the enemy line, while the *Kent* chased eastward after the *Nürnberg*.

At about 4.15 pm the two British cruisers were both hitting the *Leipzig* from about 9,000 yards; later together on the port side to inflict the most damage. The *Leipzig*'s gunners were firing back with their smaller, but accurate and destructive 4.1-inch guns and registering hits.

There were some narrow escapes and some casualties on the *Glasgow*. A dud shell ripped through her foretop and tore off a young signalman's right hand. A minute later, while an officer was applying an emergency dressing to this wound, another dud shell crashed through the foretop, tearing the officer's trousers just above his knee, but barely grazing him. A third shell struck the mast near the top, exploded violently, killed a petty officer standing below and destroyed some electrical circuits.

Captain Ellerton shortened the range so as to inflict more damage with the *Cornwall*'s old 6-inch guns, receiving for his pains ten successive hits, mostly harmlessly on his ship's armour. But the *Leipzig* was hit again and again for more than an hour. Her foremast was shot away and by 6.30 pm she was on fire fore and aft, yet her gunners still fought back, until at 7 pm, when she fired her last shell, she was hardly moving.

Captain Luce signalled her to surrender, circled round and waited, but the surviving Germans, surrounded by fires on board, had no effective means of replying. Unaware of this, and anticipating that her captain might be hoping to sink the *Glasgow* at the last moment by torpedo, the two British ships moved nearer and ruthlessly shelled her until her mainmast and both her funnels were gone and she was a blazing wreck.

Two green signal lights then rose from her, which were accepted as a token of surrender. Luce moved in to within 500 yards of her, then both ships lowered two boats each into the choppy sea to take off survivors. 'Night had closed in rather misty', noted one of the *Glasgow*'s officers.

Two hundred yards ahead was the blazing ship, flames high up on her quarter-deck and shooting out of ports and jagged shell-holes in the side, showing the white-hot furnace within . . . Small explosions would occasionally scatter sparks like a firework— the white steam escaping seemed to complete her national flag—black smoke, white steam and red flames—our searchlights poked hither and thither to assist the cutters in their search for survivors—our guns' crews leaning silently against their guns . . .

The *Leipzig* turned on to her beam ends and went down at 9.23 pm while the flames and red hot metal hissed furiously in the water. Of her complement of over 400, only five officers and thirteen men were lifted from the sea alive. About 230 were alive when she fired her last shot; of these all but 50 were slaughtered in the final shelling and 32 of them either drowned or failed to survive the icy water. The British ships' crews were lucky this time, reversing Coronel. *Cornwall* was hit eighteen times, but not one man was wounded, while two hits on the *Glasgow* had killed one man and wounded four.

Meantime, the cruiser *Kent*, commanded by Captain Allen, had a long chase after the *Nürnberg*. It ended 150 miles south of the Falklands. Burning even every scrap of wood on board to supplement her coal and build up steam, *Kent* came within 11,000 yards of the enemy just after 5 pm. The first two of *Nürnberg*'s salvoes missed, as did the *Kent*'s first; then the *Nürnberg* hit *Kent*'s upper deck and a 6-inch shell from *Kent* penetrated the after steering-flat below the waterline, killing several men.

But it still appeared that the *Nürnberg* might escape before nightfall. Suddenly two of her over-worked boilers exploded, her speed fell to barely 19 knots and she turned to port at 5.45 pm to fight at short range. The *Kent* followed suit, and at 6 pm range was down to 3,000 yards. A shooting match began in which *Kent's* fourteen 6-inch guns struck heavier blows than *Nürnberg's* 4.1-inch guns.

Soon fires blazed on the *Nürnberg* and her topmast was toppling over, but one of her shells penetrated one of *Kent's* 6-inch gun casemates, scattering red hot splinters which killed one and wounded nine of the gun crew. The *Nürnberg* was, by comparison, 'riddled like a watchman's bucket', with only two guns firing on her port side.

She turned as if to try to bring her starboard guns to bear, only to receive two 6-inch shells simultaneously from *Kent*, which knocked out her two forward guns. Captain Allen had the fight all his own way from then on, and by 6.25 pm the *Nürnberg* was down by the stern, blazing fiercely and scarcely moving, although still firing an occasional shot up to 6.35 pm, to which *Kent* replied. *Nürnberg* then fell silent. *Kent* also ceased fire

and waited for the enemy to haul down her colours.

Either the enemy would not, or could not, owing to the fires blazing everywhere, so the *Kent* opened fire again for another five minutes; then at last she surrendered and the only two boats on board *Kent* that would float after the 37 shells that had hit her were lowered to take off survivors. At that very moment, 7.27 pm, the *Nürnberg* turned over on to her starboard side and slipped beneath the waves. While albatrosses circled above, attacking anyone in the water, *Kent's* boats found only twelve men alive out of her crew of 400, five of whom later died. *Kent* had lost four killed and twelve wounded.

Although the fast *Dresden* had for the time being escaped—a matter for which Admiral Sir Doveton Sturdee incurred the First Sea Lord's wrath—Admiral von Spee and his squadron had been eliminated and Allied control of seaborne commerce was now almost complete, for the time being. British sea power was playing a decisive part in the war, but already, as the Battle of the Falkland Isles showed, the destructive power of British shells appeared to be decidedly inferior to that of the enemy's. It was an inferiority that was to show up clearly in the Battle of Jutland.

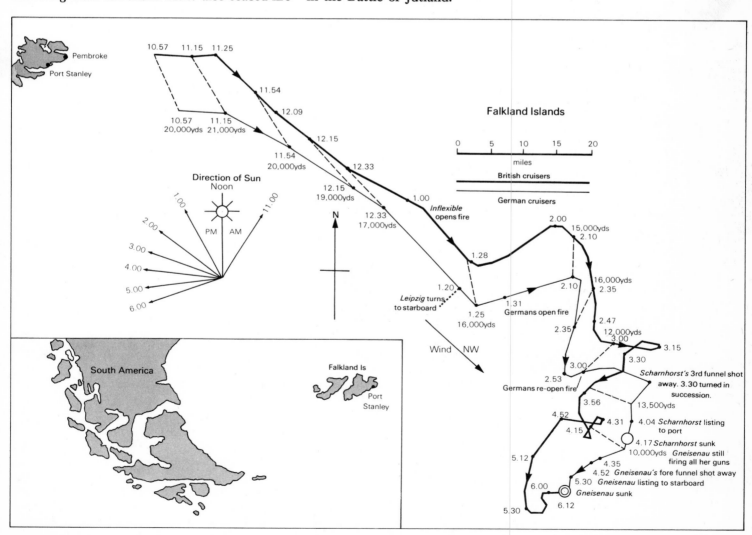

Dogger Bank
January 1915

The Battle of the Dogger Bank, 24 January 1915, demonstrated for the second time in the war the remarkable accuracy of British naval Intelligence, based on intercepted enemy radio messages in a cypher the key to which had been found. When Rear-Admiral Hipper planned, as part of a more aggressive policy, a raid with his 1st and 2nd Battle-Cruiser Scouting Groups to emulate Admiral Funke's earlier bombardment of Scarborough and Hartlepool, the British Admiralty knew of it in advance.

It was therefore able to order Vice-Admiral Sir David Beatty's 1st and 2nd Battle-Cruiser Squadrons of six battle-cruisers, supported by Commodore Goodenough's 1st Light Cruiser Squadron and Commodore Sir Reginald Tyrwhitt's three light cruisers and $2\frac{1}{2}$ destroyer flotillas, to steam to a position near the Dogger Bank which, on 24 January, would place them between the enemy force and its base in the Jade river. And just in case Hipper's squadrons—battle-cruisers *Seydlitz* (flagship), *Moltke*, *Derfflinger* and *Blücher*, six light cruisers and a destroyer flotilla—tried to escape north, Admiral Jellicoe's Battle Fleet put to sea. Barely two hours' steaming north-west of the expected scene of action, two more squadrons of heavy and light cruisers waited. With these dispositions, the imminent destruction of the unsuspecting German force seemed almost certain.

The action began at 7 am on the 24th, when the blanket of darkness over the North Sea was beginning to lift. When the light cruiser *Aurora*, under Captain William Nicholson, sighted the enemy light cruiser *Kolberg*, Nicholson signalled Beatty and opened fire. Hipper at once changed course from north-west to south-east to avoid a possible encounter with enemy battleships and to draw the enemy towards minefields in the Heligoland area. Beatty, in *Lion*, followed by *Tiger*, *Princess Royal*, *New Zealand* and *Indomitable*, set off in pursuit at 29 knots; by 9 am he had cut the range down to $11\frac{1}{2}$ miles from Hipper's last battle-cruiser, the *Blücher*, slowest ship in the enemy line.

Lion hit the *Blücher* at a range of ten miles; as the range fell, *Tiger* and *Lion* both fired on and hit the *Seydlitz*. The *Princess Royal* fired on and hit the *Derfflinger*, while for some minutes the *Moltke*, owing to a misunderstanding of Beatty's signals, escaped being hit. Worse befell the Germans when *Lion* hit *Seydlitz* with a 13-inch shell which put both her forward turrets out of action; but only 30 minutes later *Lion* was in turn hit by shells which slowed her down and then destroyed her entire electrical system. Beatty transferred first to a destroyer then to the *Princess Royal*.

Meanwhile, his second-in-command, Sir Archibald Moore, had taken command. He misread Beatty's contradictory signals and instead of pursuing and destroying the badly damaged ships of the German line, concentrated with the rest of the British squadrons in hammering away at the *Blücher*. She went down after some 70 shells and seven torpedoes had slammed into her. It was small consolation for the escape of *Derfflinger*, *Seydlitz* and *Moltke* and Admiral Moore was removed from his command.

1. The *B6*, one of an early (1911) class of British submarines of only 280 tons displacement, returns to home waters after a routine patrol. This class of submarine, along with other later types, took part in the Dogger Bank operation.

2. The battle-cruiser *Blücher*, with a speed of 25 knots and twelve 8.2-inch guns, was the slowest of Hipper's warships.

3. German sailors scramble desperately down the hull of the stricken *Blücher* as she heels over after being struck by 70 shells and seven torpedoes. British destroyers were able to pick up less than 200 survivors.

Jutland

May 1916

In January 1916 Admiral Reinhardt Scheer's succession as C-in-C of the High Seas Fleet, in place of Admiral Pohl, quickly led to a more aggressive German naval policy. With the exception of the hit-and-run raids in 1914 on Whitby, Scarborough and Hartlepool, when the German battle-cruisers were brought to action without decisive results, and the Dogger Bank engagement on 24 January 1915, when Britain lost another chance of decisively beating the enemy, the German High Seas Fleet had stayed out of harm's way in its safe harbours.

By early 1916, however, as a result of pressure from the military High Command, Scheer had decided to embark on a policy of smashing the Royal Navy's superiority by a combination of ruthless submarine warfare and the well-tried tactic of luring some of the enemy's battle squadrons into a trap and destroying them with overwhelming force. Scheer hoped that after one such successful encounter the High Seas Fleet could challenge the British Grand Fleet on more equal terms.

The first stages of this plan, which was to lead eventually to the Battle of Jutland, went into operation on 25 April 1916, when Scheer's battle-cruisers shelled Yarmouth and Lowestoft. Arthur Balfour, the recently appointed successor to Winston Churchill as First Lord of the Admiralty, gave a public assurance that the Fleet would be redeployed from northern to southern waters off the east coast. Vice-Admiral Bradford's 3rd Battle Squadron came south to a position off the Thames estuary, while at the same time it was decided to move Admiral Jellicoe's Battle Fleet down south, from Scapa and Cromarty to Rosyth, when anti-submarine defences at Rosyth were adequate. Vice-Admiral Sir David Beatty's Battle-Cruiser Fleet was reinforced by the 5th Battle Squadron.

To Admiral Scheer, this first British move —a division of the Grand Fleet—seemed to confirm that his overall plan to lure part of the Grand Fleet to its destruction was feasible. His scheme now crystallized into a decision to try to trap Beatty's battle-cruiser force and

destroy it by a lightning attack with the High Seas Fleet before Jellicoe could move the Grand Fleet down from Scapa. But at the time Jellicoe's staff, on board his flagship *Iron Duke*, were perfecting, in May 1916, the details of 'Operation M', scheduled for 1 June, an almost similar enticement operation by which it was hoped to bring the German High Seas Fleet to battle.

In Scheer's final plan, which was adopted, Admiral Hipper's 1st Scouting Group was to steam north to a position off the Norwegian coast with the battle-cruisers *Lützow, Derfflinger, Seydlitz, Moltke* and *Von der Tann*, aided by four light cruisers. At the same time, 50 miles south, Admiral Scheer himself was to follow with the High Seas Fleet battle squadrons, in the hope that the pro-British Norwegians would signal London about Hipper's squadrons, causing Beatty's battle-cruiser force to race out from Rosyth, only to be trapped and destroyed between steel jaws of Hipper's and Scheer's forces before Jellicoe could steam out to his rescue.

At 3.40pm on 30 May Admiral Scheer ordered the transmission of the vital wireless signal '31 Gg 2490', which would trigger off the operation. It was intercepted by British wireless stations monitoring the enemy wavelengths. The Admiralty was by now in posession of the German secret code and decoding machines—removed by the Russian navy from a German cruiser they had sunk in the Baltic, and passed to Britain—which enabled it to decipher the meaning of the majority of enemy wireless signals. This signal, which meant 'Carry Out Top Secret Instruction 2490 on May 31', was not fully decoded by the Admiralty, but it conveyed the vital fact that an important operation by the High Seas Fleet was afoot.

The Admiralty telegraphed orders to Jellicoe to put to sea with the Grand Fleet and assemble east of the 'Long Forties', which is the area of the North Sea extending for about 110 miles east of Aberdeenshire. The Grand Fleet was then split up among three northern bases as follows:

Opposite: Battleships of Rear-Admiral Mauve's 2nd Battle Squadron—*Hannover, Schlesien* and *Hessen*— steam out of the Kiel Canal for the North Sea.

At Scapa Flow, under Admiral Sir John Jellicoe, Commander-in-Chief:

> The 1st and 4th Battle Squadrons.
> The 3rd Battle-Cruiser Squadron.
> The 2nd Cruiser Squadron.
> The 4th Light Cruiser Squadron, and
> The 4th; part of 11th; and 12th Flotillas of torpedo-boat destroyers.

At Invergordon, under Vice-Admiral Sir Martyn Jerram:

> The 2nd Battle Squadron.
> The 1st Cruiser Squadron and part of the 11th Flotilla of torpedo-boat destroyers.

At Rosyth, under Vice-Admiral Sir David Beatty:

> The 5th Battle Squadron.
> The 1st and 2nd Battle-Cruiser Squadrons.
> The 1st, 2nd and 3rd Light Cruiser Squadrons.
> Part of the 1st; Part of the 9th; Part of the 10th and 13th Flotillas of torpedo-boat destroyers.

Jellicoe acted with commendable speed, and before midnight that day the Grand Fleet was at sea. He instructed Beatty to proceed with the Battle-Cruiser Fleet to about 100 miles north-west of the Horn Reefs, off the Danish coast, by about 2 pm on 31 May, when Jellicoe's fleet would be some 69 miles to the north, on its way to join him. If by then there was no report of the enemy, he was to steam north towards Jellicoe's fleet, 'to get in visual communication'.

Jellicoe stressed later that the distance between his battleships and Beatty's less powerful battle-cruisers, as much as 69 miles, did not seem too great, despite the likely presence of the enemy, because 'this force was far superior in gun-power to the First Scouting Group (which Vice-Admiral Hipper commanded) and the speed of the slowest ships was such as to enable it to keep out of range of superior enemy forces'.

During the night, apart from one or two ineffectual attacks by submarines, no contact with the enemy was made, but at 8.19 am the next day another submarine was sighted and Beatty signalled his squadron to alter course 90 degrees to port for some eighteen minutes, a detour which added several miles to his course. About two hours later, at 10.10 am, Beatty made a curious decision, which was to cost him dear. He instructed his powerful 5th Battle Squadron of 15-inch gun battleships—*Barham*, *Valiant*, *Malaya* and *Warspite*—to station itself five miles to the north-west of his flagship, the *Lion*, while the deployment of the rest of his fleet was founded on the

expectation of a clash with the enemy to the south-east. The guns of the most powerful and the slowest squadron would thus be out of range when the action started.

Meanwhile, Admiral Scheer, in his flagship *Friedrich der Grosse*, preceded by the High Seas Fleet cruisers and battle-cruisers, had left the Jade River by 2.30 am on 31 May and steamed north towards the Norwegian coast. Admiral Hipper's 1st Scouting Group had sailed at 1 am, the first squadrons of a fleet totalling 99 ships and 36,000 officers and men. Reports from his submarines had convinced Scheer that his plan had so far succeeded and that at most he would have to face two squadrons of the Grand Fleet.

It was a very serious underestimation of the massive concentration of naval power now approaching Scheer, and all of his tactical expertise would be needed if he was to escape destruction. The Grand Fleet was at the height of its strength. It comprised 24 battleships with 12-inch and 13.5-inch guns, four battleships with 15-inch guns, nine battle-cruisers, eight heavy cruisers, 26 light cruisers, 77 destroyers, a seaplane carrier and a minelayer. In terms of big guns, this amounted to 24 of 12- to 15-inch and 80 of 12- to 13.5-inch.

Steaming in confident mood towards them was the High Seas Fleet of fifteen dreadnoughts and seven pre-dreadnought battleships, five battle-cruisers, eleven light cruisers and sixty-two torpedo boats. Its battleships mounted a total of two hundred 11- and 12-inch guns and its battle-cruisers forty-four 11- and 12-inch, markedly inferior to the Grand Fleet which, squadron for squadron, was also faster than the High Seas Fleet.

But Jellicoe, as the result of an enemy fleet signal incorrectly interpreted by the Admiralty during the morning of May 31, believed the main elements of the High Seas Fleet had still not left the Jade. Both Admirals were thus sailing towards each other in ignorance of the presence of the other's main forces.

At 2 pm Beatty, in his flagship *Lion*, arrived at the position named by Jellicoe without any sight or news of the enemy. Accordingly he hoisted flags to signal his squadron to turn northward to link up with Jellicoe's battle fleet which, owing to changes of course and other delays, was then some fifteen miles behind its anticipated position. The turn was completed at 2.15 pm, the signal flags were lowered and the force now steamed on a northerly course. The 2nd Battle-Cruiser Squadron was not three miles away to starboard and the 5th Battle Squadron six miles away to port from *Lion*, which was accompanied by the three ships of the 1st Battle-Cruiser Squadron, *Princess Royal*, *Queen Mary* and *Tiger*. Ahead of them were the twelve ships of the three light cruiser squadrons, and darting around the entire fleet, leaving white trails of foam on the calm sea, were the low black shapes of the terrier-like destroyers, all unaware that not far over the horizon to the east were Admiral Hipper's battle-cruisers.

Now there occurred one of those seemingly irrelevant events that can suddenly and unexpectedly affect the course of battle on land or sea. Just as Beatty's fleet had finished its turn, the cruiser *Galatea*, the flagship of Commodore F. S. Alexander-Sinclair, 1st Light Cruiser Squadron, steaming on the north-east wing of the cruiser screen, sighted to the east-south-east first smoke and then the mast of a small steamer, the Danish merchant ship *N.J. Fjord*.

Alexander-Sinclair, accompanied by the cruiser *Phaeton*, at once raced off to investigate. By a curious coincidence, the enemy light cruiser *Elbing*, on the western flank of Hipper's 2nd Scouting Group, sighted the *N.J. Fjord*'s smoke almost simultaneously and altered course to reconnoitre. The British and German cruisers were thus fortuitously brought within sight of each other, both immediately signalling 'Enemy in sight'. Shortening the range, the *Galatea* opened fire at 2.28 pm and the first phase of Jutland began.

At this point luck had decisively favoured von Scheer, for the *N.J. Fjord* had set off the trap before time, thus preventing Hipper's cruisers from leading the High Seas Fleet within range of the concentrated Grand Fleet, still 60 miles away to the north.

Meanwhile, *Galatea*, which had been hit by a dud shell, and *Phaeton* had found that they were outranged by the *Elbing* and altered course to lead the enemy towards Beatty's fleet. At 2.35 pm they sighted heavy smoke on the north-eastern horizon. Hipper's cruisers were racing westwards, eager to deliver their first blow, while at the same time Jellicoe in *Iron Duke* and von Scheer in *Friedrich der Grosse* both increased speed to bring their battle fleets into the area of action as soon as possible.

When Beatty received *Galatea*'s warning message, he at once began to alter course to the south-east, even before the flags signalling the change to his fleet were fully hoisted. Unfortunately, *Barham*, the flagship of the 5th Battle Squadron, could not decipher the message properly at the distance of six miles, and since it was not sent in any other form Admiral Evan-Thomas was unable to perceive that the change in course had been made.

Beatty had also increased speed to 22 knots. Several minutes passed before Evan-Thomas was able to mark Beatty's new course and turn on to it, so he was soon left out of sight beyond the horizon ten miles away. These battleships, which should have been an in-

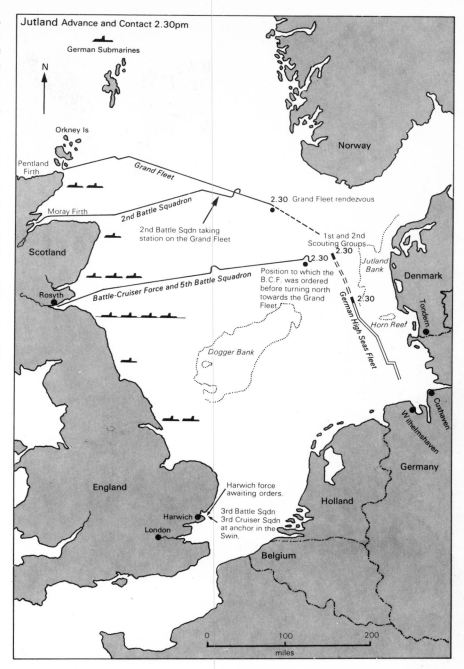

tegral part of Beatty's fleet, would now be unable to bring their powerful guns to bear upon the enemy for some time after the action had begun. Beatty would soon have cause to regret this.

Beatty's and Hipper's fleets were now steaming straight towards each other and at 2.45 pm Beatty ordered the seaplane-carrier *Engadine* to get her aircraft up to reconnoitre the enemy's fleet, but this, the first attempt at aerial reconnaissance, brought no results. The pilot, Flight-Lieutenant Rutland, sighted the Germans and, under fire, had approached to within 1½ miles when a petrol pipe fractured and he was forced down. He was hoisted back on board the *Engadine* when his report was too late to be of use.

By 3.29 pm Admiral Evan-Thomas, realizing the approaching danger, had closed the gap to six miles. Suddenly, five great columns

Admiral Reinhardt Scheer's battle fleet photographed from a German airship as it steams at high speed towards the expected scene of battle on 31 May 1916.

of swirling black smoke from Hipper's ships were sighted to starboard. Hipper's look-outs had sighted the British ships almost ten minutes earlier in the brighter light to the west, identifying them as battle-cruisers.

Hipper, an alert tactician, had promptly increased speed and changed his course from north-west to south-south-east, so as to lure this stronger force approaching him towards Admiral Scheer's High Seas Fleet. At the same time bugles blared, drums beat to quarters, and throughout the fleet ships' companies raced to action stations.

Beatty reacted by changing course at 3.45 pm to east-south-east, so as to converge upon the enemy, but at the same time he was allowing himself to be drawn unwittingly towards the approaching High Seas Fleet, then about 50 miles south. He now formed line of battle in the order of *Lion*, *Princess Royal*, *Queen Mary*, *Tiger*, *New Zealand* and *Indefatigable*, north-west from *Lion*, still steering east-south-east. The sun was behind him, visibility was patchy and the sea was glassy calm.

Soon he recognized the enemy ships, Hipper's flagship *Lützow* leading, followed by the battle-cruisers *Derfflinger*, *Seydlitz*, *Moltke* and *Von der Tann* steering south-south-east. The orange flashes of their first salvoes rippled along the line at 3.48 pm, followed within seconds by the *Lion*'s 13.5-inch guns and those of the rest of the British line, all at a range of about 16,000 yards, with a superiority in Beatty's favour of six to five.

Shells from both sides at first shrieked well above their targets, but gradually they crept closer. Just as a British shell was seen to hit the *Lützow*, the *Lion* was hit twice amidships, two shells slammed into the *Princess Royal*'s range-finder tower and knocked it out, and the *Tiger* was also hit. An eye-witness beside Beatty on the *Lion*'s bridge noted:

We were blissfully ignorant of the fact that two large shells had exploded in the ship: the rush of wind and other noises caused by the high speed at which we were travelling, together with the roar of our own guns as they fired, four at a time, completely drowned the noise of the bursting shell. There was no doubt, however, that we were under heavy fire, because all round us huge columns of water, higher than the funnels, were being thrown up as the enemy shells plunged into the sea.

At 3.55 pm, with the range down to 12,900 yards, the *Queen Mary* slightly evened the blows struck by the Germans by slamming two shells into one of the turrets of the *Seydlitz*, starting a serious cordite fire in the magazine and putting the turret permanently out of action. But this did little to lessen the hail of fire falling on the British ships, and at 3.58 pm Beatty turned away two points, thus steering south, to widen the range again. Hipper also turned away from the fierce British shelling to a course of south-east.

A near-disaster now overtook the *Lion*. At about 4 pm, just as a shell from her again struck the *Lützow*, one of the enemy flagship's shells pierced the *Lion*'s midship turret and burst in the gun house. A minute or two later, a hatless, bloodstained sergeant of Marines stepped up on to the admiral's bridge and told the first officer he saw, Lieutenant W. S. Chalmers: 'Q turret has gone, sir. All the crew are killed, and we have flooded the magazines.' Chalmers looked behind him over the bridge. 'The armoured roof of Q turret', he noted, 'had been folded back like an open sardine tin,

Barham, flagship of Rear-Admiral H. Evan-Thomas and a unit of Beatty's 5th Battle Squadron. Beatty stationed the squadron five miles north-west of his flagship *Lion* and the rest of his fleet. Misunderstandings led to this powerful group being out of range when the action began.

The *Indefatigable*, photographed shortly before she was hit. She blew up and sank at once, only two of her company of nearly 1,000 men surviving.

The battle-cruiser *Von der Tann*, one of Hipper's 1st Scouting Group.

thick yellow smoke was rolling up in clouds from the gaping hole, and the guns were cocked up in the air awkwardly. It was evident that Q turret would take no further part in the battle'.

The explosion had ignited cordite charges in the magazine handling room, but at the very moment when this limited disaster could have spread and destroyed the entire ship, Major F. J. Harvey of the Marines, as he lay dying, gave the order to close the magazine doors, thus confining the danger and saving the ship, although 98 out of the 100 officers and men in Q turret died either in the lethal cordite flash or the first explosion.

But more punishment awaited the British line as the German gunners continued to fire with almost pinpoint accuracy. At 4.2pm a salvo of three shells from the *Von der Tann*, engaged with *Indefatigable* in a murderous shooting match, struck the British battle-cruiser near the mainmast. She lost way and, covered in flame and smoke, moved out of line to starboard, going down by the stern. Two more shells from *Von der Tann* hit her, one on her foredeck and the other on the forward part of her hull. Seconds later a tremendous explosion split the air and a huge sheet of flame and smoke enveloped the *Indefatigable*, which capsized and sank at once. When the haze that hung over the water had cleared away, only two survivors were found out of the 57 officers and 900 men who had gone down in her. Her destruction was the result of an inherent weakness in design.

Indefatigable had been blown apart by the tons of explosive in her magazines, ignited by cordite flash in the gun house, just as the *Lion* would have been had not Major Harvey's last words closed the magazine doors and saved her.

Beatty turned away again and lengthened the range, so as to create a short lull in which the fires on some of his ships could be brought under control. During the shooting, Evan-Thomas had managed to bring the invaluable 5th Squadron within range of the enemy's rear, and at 4.8pm his first two ships opened fire on the *Von der Tann* at 19,000 yards. Even at this long range *Von der Tann* was hit

below the waterline and flooded with 600 tons of water, but owing to her superb construction this barely affected her speed.

Visibility was now decreasing and Beatty turned once more towards the enemy, but another hit on *Lion* destroyed his wireless transmitter, so that thereafter his signals had to be sent visually to *Princess Royal*, next in the line, for transmission by wireless to the fleet and to Jellicoe, an arrangement which inevitably slowed down communication and reaction.

There was no lessening in the kaleidoscope of movement and gunfire. 'A naval battle is a strange experience—almost uncanny', Lieutenant Chalmers reflected later. 'Apart from the noise of gunfire and the shrieking of the wind,

events move so rapidly that the mind seems to lag behind.'

A hail of projectiles from Evan-Thomas' battleships now fell on and around the enemy, most of whose salvoes were aimed at the *Lion*. Both sides ordered their destroyer flotillas to launch diversionary attacks and twelve of the British destroyers raced ahead at their full speed of 35 knots to manoeuvre towards the enemy's bows to launch torpedoes.

At the same time a third disaster overtook the British. Owing to a tactical error, the battle-cruiser *Queen Mary*, whose shooting had inflicted considerable damage on the enemy, was engaged simultaneously by both the *Seydlitz* and the *Derfflinger*. Columns of water rose in the air as their shells burst all

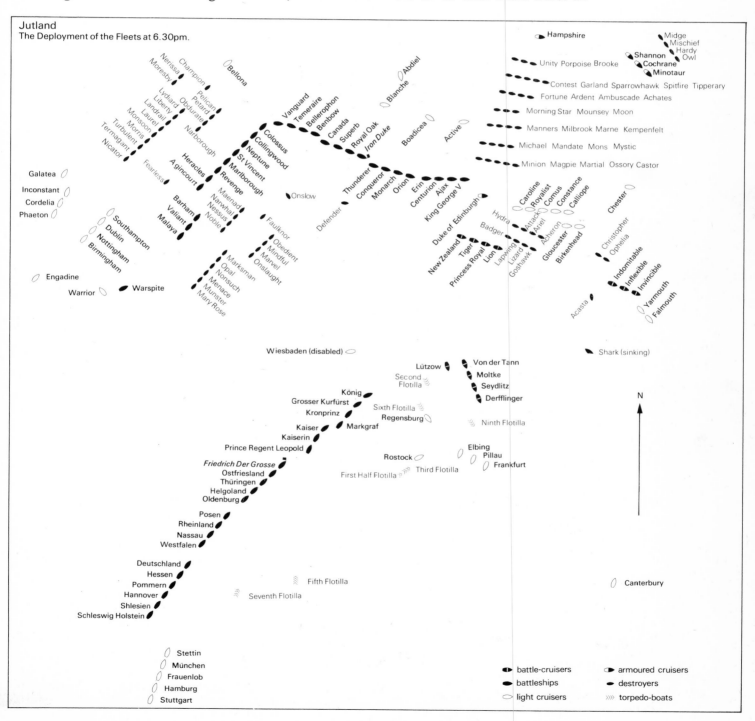

Jutland
The Deployment of the Fleets at 6.30pm.

	battle-cruisers	armoured cruisers
	battleships	destroyers
	light cruisers	torpedo-boats

The battle-cruiser *Queen Mary*, whose accurate shooting had badly damaged Hipper's ships, came under fire—owing to a British tactical error—from two enemy battle-cruisers, *Seydlitz* and *Derfflinger*, at 15,000 yards range. Five shells struck her almost simultaneously at 4.25 pm.

around her. A huge red flame flashed up near her forward turret, followed by first one explosion then another until, enveloped in flame and with a final, deafening explosion, she was torn apart, her masts fell inwards and she went down in a cloud of smoke. Only a few survivors were picked up out of her company of 1,258 officers and men.

Beatty watched this catastrophe with Captain Chatfield from the *Lion*'s bridge. All of Beatty's formidable resilience was reflected in the restraint of his famous understatement as he turned to Captain Chatfield: 'There's something wrong with our bloody ships today, Chatfield.' So indeed there was, not only with the relative lack of armoured protection in the dreadnought type, but also with the British shells, which burst and shattered on impact, without penetrating the German ships' armour; with the signalling from the *Lion* and also, in Beatty's ships, with the gunnery, for the enemy was hit only ten times during the first hour of battle, whereas the Germans scored forty hits during the same period.

During this series of British disasters, the destroyers on both sides had been engaged in a duel. Commander Barry Bingham, leading the British flotillas in *Nestor*, observed fifteen enemy destroyers manoeuvring to launch a torpedo attack on the British squadrons. He opened fire at 10,000 yards and sank two of the enemy. The others fired twelve torpedoes at the 5th Battle Squadron and six at Beatty's force, both of whom evaded being hit by turning away 22 degrees. The enemy turned tail, leaving the British flotilla to pursue them and attack Hipper's squadron with torpedoes.

At the moment *Nestor* fired her third torpedo, she was hit by a shell from a German light cruiser which knocked out two of her boilers and left her stationary on the sea. She was later shelled and sunk by cruisers of the High Seas Fleet, and her crew were taken off by a destroyer. The British torpedo attack was thus frustrated by the counterattack of the enemy's light cruisers.

Both Beatty and Jellicoe, who was about 25 miles to the north-west of the engagement, still believed that they were dealing with only Hipper's squadrons. The sight of them turning off to the east at 4.36 pm to evade the British destroyers' torpedoes, while at the same time seemingly breaking off the action, must have restored some of the confidence lost in the British fleet by the sinking of *Indefatigable* and *Queen Mary*. But Hipper had carried out his task brilliantly, and now that he had lured the enemy right into the path of the High Seas Fleet he had completed half of his mission and could afford temporarily to break off.

At 4.38 pm Commodore Goodenough, reconnoitring to the south in the *Southampton*

The *Queen Mary* blows up. A great column of flame and smoke shoots upward seconds after she is hit. A cordite flash in a gun turret ignited her explosives store and tore her apart. Less than 20 men were saved out of her company of 1,258.

with the 2nd Light Cruiser Squadron, about 5,000 yards ahead of the *Lion* and 13,000 yards from the enemy, suddenly saw a long line of big ships emerge out of the mists gathering on his port bow. Immediately he identified them as enemy ships, and at once sent out the signal: 'Have sighted enemy battle fleet, bearing south-east, course north.' He then pressed on to within about 13,000 yards of them, well within range, turning off and zig-zagging away amid a hail of shells only when he had ascertained clearly the number and type of the approaching enemy fleet for transmission to Beatty and Jellicoe.

For Beatty, who continued on course until he had confirmed with his own eyes this electrifying news, this was a grave setback. His hopes of smashing Hipper's squadrons with the aid of Evan-Thomas' battleships had now vanished. But the situation also held great promise, for Beatty now had it in his power to turn the tables on Hipper and entice the whole German fleet to within range of Jellicoe's mighty force.

Potentially, it was an encounter at sea no less significant and decisive than the German army's move to break through into northern France in the first weeks of the war, for if the enemy now succeeded in crippling the Grand Fleet, the outlook for the smooth and uninterrupted flow of supplies into Britain, of troops over to France and of survival was bleak indeed.

At 4.40 pm, with the long line of von Scheer's battleships appearing on the misty south-eastern horizon about 22,000 yards away, Beatty sent out by flags a general signal for his ships to go about, or turn 180 degrees in succession, a much longer manoeuvre to carry out than a turn together, but this, of course, would have put the *Lion* in the rear instead of the van, where Beatty preferred to be.

Evan-Thomas' 5th Battle Squadron, about seven miles north-west of Beatty's line, was still in action with Hipper's force and the signal by flags to reverse course was not clearly visible on board his flagship *Barham*. So Evan-Thomas decided to continue on course towards the enemy. Beatty now sent another signal to him to reverse course in succession as the two squadrons passed each other in opposite directions.

It was a dangerous manoeuvre to carry out within range of the enemy's guns, and as they turned, one after the other, *Barham*, *Valiant*, *Warspite* and *Malaya* were all hit and damaged. Returning fire, they scored hits on both Hipper's ships and the first battleships of von Scheer's line, *König, Grosser Kurfürst* and *Markgraf*. 'Two of our salvoes hit the leading German battleship', noted an officer on *Warspite*. 'Sheets of flame went right over her

masthead and she looked red fore and aft, like a burning haystack.'

Beatty now increased speed to 25 knots and drew out of range of Hipper's skilful gunners. By 5.30 pm he was far enough ahead to turn gradually from north-west to north-east and to begin to head across the enemy's course. He was trying to deflect Hipper's ships to the east to prevent him sighting Jellicoe's approaching fleet (thus giving von Scheer timely warning) and at the same time attempting to cross Hipper's 'T' and concentrate heavy fire on his leaders.

As a result, Evan-Thomas' slower 5th Battle Squadron was left to face the combined fire of twelve of both Hipper's and von Scheer's heavy ships for some 20 minutes. Fortunately, the most serious damage Evan-Thomas' squadron sustained was two holes in *Malaya*'s hull (on the waterline) and the destruction of one of her 6-inch batteries. At the same time the squadron's steady shooting sent shells crashing into no less than five of the enemy ships, inflicting heavy damage.

By 5.50 pm Beatty, followed by Evan-Thomas, was able, by crossing Hipper's 'T', to bring so concentrated a fire down on to his leading battle-cruisers that Hipper eventually broke away again and turned off in an easterly direction. Beatty had succeeded in his tactical objective of leading Scheer to within range of Jellicoe's guns. A decisive battle was now possible, but only three hours of daylight were left for it.

The approaching Jellicoe was still uncertain as to how he should deploy his fleet, which was steaming towards von Scheer in six columns, each of four ships in line ahead, because Beatty and Evan-Thomas had failed to signal him adequate information as to the enemy's own bearing, course and formation. If he deployed on the basis of guesswork, he was likely to give the enemy a valuable advantage; whereas to wait for the needful facts might lead either to an enemy attack while he was deploying or to failure to deploy at all

before their arrival. He had also to make allowances for differences in position reckoning as between the Grand Fleet and the Battle-Cruiser Fleet in calculating von Scheer's position.

Until he received an informative reply in answer to his repeated signals for information, there was little he could do except signal 'Action Stations', which he had done, and trust his luck. Meanwhile, his 3rd Battle Squadron—*Invincible*, *Indomitable* and *Inflexible* and its cruisers under Rear-Admiral Horace Hood—had steamed ahead south-south-east and eastward of Hipper's squadron, so as to block a possible escape route for von Scheer through the Skagerrak.

Separate individual actions now flared up and died away. The light cruiser *Chester*, about six miles off the *Invincible*'s starboard bow, came under fire from the four light cruisers of Rear-Admiral Boedicker's 2nd Scouting Group. In the space of a few minutes no less than eighteen shells crashed down on her, so that her batteries were demolished and all her gun crews were killed or wounded. Boy 1st Class John Travers Cornwall, aged 16, was badly wounded but, in Beatty's words, he 'remained standing alone at a most exposed post quietly awaiting orders, with the gun's crew dead and wounded all around him', before he too fell. He was awarded the Victoria Cross posthumously and his name became immortal in the Navy's annals.

Hood arrived on the scene in time to save the *Chester*, and his three battle-cruisers inflicted considerable damage on Boedicker's squadron, leaving the *Wiesbaden* a battered wreck. Torpedo-boat and destroyer actions ended this encounter, the last act being the sinking of the destroyer Shark. Commander Loftus Jones, with one leg shot away, floated off as his ship went down and was drowned.

Hipper now turned away southwards to escape more damage, but then, sighting von Scheer's battle squadrons, swung round again to take his station at the head of the column.

Jellicoe was again starved of signalled information about this encounter, while he waited in what must have been a desperate frame of mind for a signal which would give him news of von Scheer's position. At 6 pm he came in sight of the *Lion* and signalled Beatty sharply: 'Where is the enemy's battle fleet?' Impatiently, he waited for several minutes as the British and German forces neared their encounter.

At 6.10 pm he repeated the signal; then at 6.14 pm Beatty at last answered: 'Have sighted enemy's battle fleet bearing south-south-west.' But Beatty omitted to say what course the enemy was steering. Jellicoe could not wait any longer, and a minute later he gave the signal to deploy on his port wing column in

an easterly direction, with the battleship *King George V* leading. Not a second too early, the columns began to swing round to form their battle line.

At this moment the three heavy cruisers of Rear-Admiral Arbuthnot's 1st Cruiser Squadron—*Defence* (flagship), *Warrior* and *Black Prince*—opened fire on the stricken *Wiesbaden*, intending to finish off this seemingly unsinkable ship, already the target of many shells and a torpedo from the destroyer *Onslow*. But while they fired destructive salvoes into her, Rear-Admiral Behncke's 3rd Squadron of seven battleships emerged out of the mist to the south, led by Hipper's now somewhat scarred force. Both squadrons fired at once on the three British cruisers with every gun they had.

Against this hail of 11- and 12-inch shells their 6-inch armour was useless. *Defence* was riddled, her magazine caught fire, a vivid red explosion tore her apart and she went down, leaving only a haze of black smoke and a scum

of floating debris. *Warrior*, hit by fifteen shells, was also set ablaze, but she was able to withdraw and limp westward out of the battle in a cloud of her own smoke.

To the west, after Admiral Evan-Thomas' ships had crossed Hipper's 'T' in Beatty's wake, Hipper sighted the approaching British Grand Fleet, just as Jellicoe had signalled it to deploy at 6.15 pm. Firing on the enemy as and when he could, Evan-Thomas steered to port to take up his alternative station in the rear. There now followed an unexpected setback which nearly ended in disaster for the *Warspite*, one of Evan-Thomas' four ships.

Her helm jammed and she made three complete circles, under heavy fire from all the seven enemy ships in sight, before the trouble was righted sufficiently to make her manageable. However, by then she was so badly damaged that Jellicoe signalled her to withdraw and make for home.

Jellicoe's deployment, a high point in the history of fleet manoeuvre, was carried out

The *Malaya*, a unit of Evan-Thomas' 5th Battle Squadron.

Beatty's flagship *Lion*. She was hit first at about 4.50 pm at a range of 16,000 yards. A few minutes later she was hit again, and her midships gun turret was destroyed with the loss of 98 officers and men. Both shells were from Hipper's flagship *Lützow*.

Iron Duke, Jellicoe's flagship, mounted a main armament of ten 13.5-inch guns and was protected by a 12-inch belt of armour along her sides.

The pre-dreadnought battleship Deutschland, a unit of Rear-Admiral Mauve's 2nd Battle Squadron.

under fire from nearly half the twenty-four ships in the German line and those of his ships in the rear took the first blows at 14,000 yards range. Admiral Burney's flagship *Marlborough*, then opened fire on the enemy at 6.17 pm and the *Revenge* followed suit. The Grand Fleet was now deployed in a single line bearing south-east across the north-east course of the enemy, but Beatty's and Hood's battle-cruisers needed to increase speed to take station at the head of the line, and steaming east to do so about a mile to the south, they inevitably masked the fire of the ships nearest the enemy, preventing Jellicoe from launching an immediate action.

Scheer still steamed north-east. In his flagship *Lützow*, lying thirteenth in the line, he was at this moment still uncertain as to whether or not the Grand Fleet had joined the battle, or whether Beatty had been reinforced. But evidence that Jellicoe had arrived on the scene began to mount.

Beatty's seven battle-cruisers reached their stations at the head of the British line at 6.32 pm and at once concentrated a hail of fire on the flagship *Lützow* and the leading ships of the German line. Soon Hipper, until now steering north-east, was forced by the rain of shells to give ground to the east and lengthen the range to save the *Lützow*. Twelve of Jellicoe's battleships—*Agincourt, Bellero-phon, Conqueror, Thunderer, Hercules, Colossus, Benbow, Iron Duke, Orion, Monarch, Royal Oak* and *Revenge*—were now hitting his leading ships, especially the *König*. Flames sprang up forward on the *König*, she began to list heavily, and her commander, Captain Harder, followed the course of Hipper's cruisers ahead and gave ground to the east to widen the range. Soon Scheer's whole line was bent in the middle around the hail of enemy fire, as the leading ships followed each other in turning away towards the east and the rest continued to steer north-east.

A great weight of metal and explosives descended on Scheer's ships as Jellicoe's 15-inch shells struck home. And now, at 6.30 pm, Scheer received a report at this critical moment that prisoners from an enemy destroyer had stated that 60 British battleships were on the scene. For Scheer, with his 'T' almost fully crossed and disaster staring him in the face, it was too much. He ordered Germany's famous 'battle turn-away' manoeuvre to be carried out. His torpedo-boats raced out to put down a smokescreen and fire torpedoes. During the following twenty minutes, his battleships, steaming in line ahead towards the enemy, made a successful simultaneous turn of 180 degrees to starboard and began to move away to the west through the smoke.

But at the same moment that Scheer

Derfflinger, a battle-cruiser of the High Seas Fleet which was badly damaged in the action, played an important part in the sinking of the *Invincible*.

ordered the turn—*Gefechtskehrtwendung nach Steuerbord!*—the mist and smoke drifted aside. The *Lützow* and *Derfflinger*, at the head of the German line, and the *Invincible*, leading the British line, suddenly faced each other at a range of 10,000 yards.

All three ships opened fire at once. In the ships' conning towers the captains and their staffs peered through slits in the armour and at the periscope eyepieces as the hail of projectiles screamed through the air and the ships shuddered at the kick of the guns. 'Several shells pierced our ship with terrific force and exploded with a tremendous roar which shook every seam and rivet', noted Commander von Hase of the *Derfflinger*.

Admiral Hood observed how *Invincible*'s shells were striking home and shouted through the voice tube to his gunnery officer: 'Your firing is very good. Keep at it as quickly as you can. Every shot is telling.'

Simultaneously, *Lützow* and *Derfflinger* found the range to perfection, and a succession of salvoes struck the British cruiser at a range of 9,000 yards. A sheet of flame wrapped itself round the *Invincible* and a sudden explosion blew her into two pieces. When the smoke cleared, her stem and stern separately pointed up at the smoky sky above the water. Rear-Admiral Hood and all her company of 1,034, except six found clinging to a raft, went down in this magazine explosion —similar to those which had already sunk three ships.

At 6.45 pm Admiral Scheer's High Seas Fleet was retreating west at full speed under cover of its smokescreen, having avoided a calamitous defeat by a hair's-breadth in an action lasting barely twenty minutes. When the thunder of the continuous salvoes had echoed away to silence and once again the slight breeze was heard whistling in the rigging, Jellicoe was already searching for the enemy.

At 6.44 pm Jellicoe altered course to the south-east, so as to place the Grand Fleet between the High Seas Fleet and the Horn Reef, around which the High Seas Fleet might well try to escape home to its base. It was a perceptive move, for Scheer apparently had decided to reverse course to an easterly direction, either to slip astern of the British line and make for home in this way or to renew the action with the light of the setting sun in his favour, having the enemy silhouetted against it in the west, presenting an easy target.

But once again he was foiled. Commodore Goodenough had steamed south with his light cruisers after the enemy turn-about and disappearance in mist and smoke, in an attempt to sight him again. Soon Goodenough sighted Scheer and, zig-zagging to dodge heavy fire, he was rewarded by observing Scheer's line start to change course again at 6.55 pm. At 7.4 pm he signalled Jellicoe that the enemy's new course was east-south-east.

It was encouraging news for Jellicoe, who four minutes later altered the Grand Fleet's course to the south, hoping to close the enemy sooner and cross his 'T' again. He was successful, for moments later the van of the

enemy's fleet loomed out of the mist to the west, led apparently by the *König*. Nearest to him was Admiral Burney's division of eight battleships, which opened fire. During the next six minutes the first three ships fired some 35 to 40 salvoes, and soon the entire British fleet was firing at ranges varying from 8,000 to 14,000 yards. For the second time Scheer faced disaster. The Germans were 'enveloped in a flaming arc of gun flashes, and now they [Jellicoe's ships] were so near that his [Scheer's] predicament was more critical than ever'. *König, Grosser, Kurfurst* and *Derfflinger* were all badly hit. 'The surprise had been complete and realizing at once that his plan for extricating his fleet had been baffled, he saw his only chance of escape was to risk another *Kehrtwendung*, and he immediately (about 7.12) launched his destroyers to attack and raised a smokescreen in order to cover the precarious manoeuvre.'

But Scheer soon realized that even more drastic action than this was needed. He decided to sacrifice his remaining cruisers and hoisted the signal for them to 'Charge the enemy, ram, ships are to attack regardless of consequences'.

These ships were launching a veritable charge into the jaws of death, in an attempt, with the destroyers' aid, to delay Jellicoe's fleet while Scheer's went about and reformed. It would not be too much to call it Jutland's great turning point, for the future of the High Seas Fleet was in the balance as Scheer began his second 'battle turn-away'.

By now Jellicoe had once more formed his fleet into line ahead, while Beatty and the British battle-cruisers were about five miles ahead and to port. When the German cruisers surged in an easterly direction towards them, they drew nearly all the volume of fire on themselves; Captain Hartog's *Derfflinger*, the leading ship, became the target of a hail of shells that blew her turrets apart and started fires fore and aft. George von Hase, her gunnery officer, witnessed the appalling carnage that swiftly followed:

A perfect hail of projectiles beat on us. A fifteen-inch burst in the turret called Caesar. *The flames penetrated to the working chamber, where two other cartridges caught fire; flames leapt out of the turret as high as a house, but they did not explode, as the enemy's cartridge had done. This saved the ship, but the effect was appalling, 73 out of 78 men of the turret crew were killed outright.*

A fifteen-inch shell hit the roof of Dora *turret; again charges were set afire, roaring up into the sky from both after turrets like funeral pyres. The enemy had our range to an inch.*

The *Seydlitz* was heavily down by the bow; the *Lützow* was hidden in the dense smoke of her own fires, and the *Moltke* and *Von der Tann* were both battered. The number of casualties amounted to hundreds; if the cruisers proceeded on their course, they would be blown apart within minutes. But at 7.17 pm, when his fleet was within three minutes of completing its turn and the first

The battle-cruiser *Seydlitz*, one of Germany's finest warships, with eight 12-inch guns, a speed of 27 knots and remarkable buoyancy. She was hit several times around 5.15 pm by the 15-inch guns of *Warspite* and *Malaya*. Four of her gun turrets were put out of action, she was on fire, her forecastle was flooded, her bows were nearly below water, but she was still returning fire.

The pre-dreadnought battleship *Schleswig-Holstein* fired on Beatty's battle-cruisers at dusk when they were pounding the battered *Seydlitz* and *Derfflinger*. This picture shows the *Schleswig-Holstein* in action. She turned away when hit by the more powerful British battle-cruisers.

wave of destroyers was firing its torpedoes, Scheer ordered the cruisers to turn away and saved them from disaster.

By 7.20 pm the battleships had completed their turn in great confusion and were vanishing into the heavy smoke, followed by the cruisers. The first wave of destroyers approached and were met by a heavy curtain of fire, two of them blowing up. They launched eleven torpedoes altogether; then the second wave swept in and loosed another sixteen, before they were driven off by fleet gunfire and by the 4th Light Cruiser Squadron's counterattack.

But not a single torpedo in this all-out attack found a target. Jellicoe evaded them first by turning away $22\frac{1}{2}$ degrees and then still another $22\frac{1}{2}$ degrees. Later, a storm of criticism fell on him for not turning towards the enemy instead, for by turning away he lost visual contact in the swirling smokescreen put down by the destroyers. Unless he was lucky enough to establish contact again in the hour of dusk that remained, his best chance of annihilating the High Seas Fleet had gone.

Brief but costly actions took place as darkness fell. *Calliope*, the flagship of the 4th Light Cruiser Squadron, was hit and damaged badly when the squadron suddenly came within range of the enemy's 3rd Battle Squadron. Rear-Admiral Napier's 3rd Light Cruiser Squadron sighted the five enemy ships of the 4th Scouting Group and opened accurate fire on them, hitting the *München* and causing the enemy to veer away to the west in the twilight. Beatty's squadron once more engaged the battered *Seydlitz* and *Derfflinger*, inflicting further damage before Rear-Admiral Mauve's 2nd Battle Squadron of pre-dreadnoughts intervened to draw off Beatty's cruisers. When the *Pommern*, *Schlesien* and *Schleswig-Holstein* were also hit, Mauve's squadron vanished into the gloom to the west.

At 8.45 pm came the last chance for the British. The light cruisers *Caroline* and *Royalist* sighted three enemy battleships. Commodore Le Mesurier informed Vice-Admiral Jerram, whose 2nd Battle Squadron led the British line to the south, that he was attacking. Jerram first cancelled the attack because he thought the reputed enemy ships were Beatty's cruisers, then authorized Le Mesurier to carry on if he was certain of the ships' identity. While these two light cruisers attacked the enemy, Jerram refused to be convinced and hung back.

A withering hail of fire at a range of 10,000 yards from the *Westfalen* and the *Nassau*, the leading ships of the enemy's 1st Battle Squadron, greeted the *Caroline* and the *Royalist*; lacking support, they were forced to withdraw to avoid destruction. But even now Jerram was unconvinced, and at 9 pm the *Westfalen* led the German line away westwards. Jerram's chance went with it, for at this short range he could have dealt destructive blows against the High Seas Fleet and at the last moment have won the day.

Jellicoe knew nothing of this critical encounter, for neither Jerram nor Le Mesurier

astern, his fleet strung out for almost fifteen miles between Scheer and his home bases. 'Fitfully', records the *Official History*, 'the firing died away; like a Homeric mist the smother of haze and smoke thickened impenetrably between the combatants, and Admiral Scheer, for the time at least, had saved his fleet, but no more.'

Scheer had decided to make for home via the Horn Reef instead of one of the southern routes through the minefields via Heligoland or the Ems, and as early as 9 pm he requested by wireless airship reconnaissance at first light over the Horn Reef. Intercepting his message, the Admiralty deciphered it, but lamentably failed to send it on to Jellicoe. If they had done so, the fate of the High Seas Fleet would have been sealed beyond doubt. Its survival can thus truly be said to have been decided by this gross administrative error.

At 9.10 pm Scheer signalled his fleet: 'Battle Fleet's course SSE$\frac{1}{4}$E', which, later amended to 'SSE$\frac{3}{4}$E', would take his fleet directly to Horn Reef, about 90 miles away. This possibly could bring about a night action, but Scheer was ready for this because his ships, unlike those of the British, were equipped and their companies trained for night fighting.

Jellicoe, however, totally rejected moves which might lead directly to night action, for he believed that they could well lead to disaster for his battle fleet, owing to the difficulty of distinguishing in the dark between friend and foe. He believed that Scheer was now likely to steer south, making for Heligoland. He therefore ordered a southerly course, hoping to envelop Scheer's fleet to the west of Heligoland, so that he would be well placed to renew the engagement early next day. He did not think it likely that the enemy fleet would pass undetected or try to fight its way without his being informed through his light cruiser and destroyer screen astern. But in fact this was soon to happen.

The two fleets were converging on courses

had sent him an appropriate signal, and when he signalled *Comus*, another of Le Mesurier's ships, asking what she was firing at, he received the inadequate answer: 'Enemy battle fleet bearing west.' Beatty's signal, owing to *Lion*'s wireless breakdown, did not reach him until 9.4 pm.

By this time Jellicoe had decided that further action that day was impossible, and since he was unwilling to expose his fleet to the hazards of night action, he signalled for the fleet's course to be altered by divisions to the south. Jerram passively complied and allowed the unidentified ships which had fired so readily on the light cruisers to vanish out of visual contact to the west. With them went the Grand Fleet's last opportunity.

Jellicoe deployed into divisions for night cruising and stationed his destroyer flotillas

This remarkable photograph, taken from the battleship *Benbow* 30 minutes after *Invincible*'s destruction, shows her bow and stern clear of the water while the middle of the ship lies on the bottom, 30 fathoms below. Rear-Admiral Hood, whose flagship she was, and 1,028 officers and men went down with her. Two officers and four men survived, four of whom are on the raft near the approaching destroyer *Badger*. In the background, the battleships *Superb* and *Canada* are seen in action with the enemy.

Iron Duke, Admiral Jellicoe's flagship, fires a broadside with her 13-inch guns. At Jutland, black gunsmoke mixed with mist to hamper accurate sighting.

The German battleship *Prince Regent Leopold*.

80

The battle-cruiser *Moltke*, which took a hammering from battle-cruisers of the British 5th Battle Squadron, but survived to become Admiral Scheer's flagship after the *Lützow* had been crippled and later sunk.

and at speeds which were likely to bring about just such an event. Unless Jellicoe's captains radically improved their signalling and kept him immediately informed of developments, Scheer was fairly sure of being able to extricate his fleet from the danger of destruction at the hands of Jellicoe's greatly superior fleet.

Scheer's destroyers and cruisers began a series of clashes with those astern of the British line as he hauled round to cross to the rear of it. This final struggle in the dark was costly to both sides. At 10.20 pm Goodenough's 2nd Light Cruiser Squadron suddenly sighted four enemy light cruisers, and subsequently two more, at the almost point-blank range of 800 yards. *Southampton* and *Dublin* bore the brunt of an action so savage and destructive that after about fifteen minutes they were compelled to turn away, ablaze fore and aft. As she turned, *Southampton* loosed a torpedo at the fourth ship in the enemy's line, the *Frauenlob*. There was a blinding flash and she went down within a few minutes.

From the *Iron Duke*, where Jellicoe was resting after his long and demanding spell of duty, the brilliant flashes of the action on the dark northern horizon could be seen, but because no significant messages arrived from Goodenough, whose wireless had been destroyed, their meaning was not grasped. Although he was informed that the action was against enemy cruisers, Jellicoe probably assumed that a destroyer attack supported by cruisers was afoot, not that enemy cruisers were scouting ahead of Scheer's van, crossing astern of him.

At 11.5 pm, however, an important Ad-

miralty message reached Jellicoe: 'German battle fleet ordered home at 21.14. Battle-cruisers in rear. Course SSE$\frac{3}{4}$E. Speed 16 knots.' If he accepted this information as correct, Jellicoe would now know that since he was steaming through the night at a speed one knot faster than the enemy on a converging course, the enemy's van was bound sooner or later to pass astern of his rear. Added to the signs of cruiser action he had recently seen, it would call for an immediate change of course and the inevitability of that grimmest of all naval actions, a night battle.

But Jellicoe did not accept the course given in the signal as correct, for he believed he had evidence that, far from being not far astern, the enemy was some distance to the north-west. It was another decisive error by the British, for Jellicoe continued on his course to the south. Thus Scheer's chance of breaking through was better than ever, provided his presence was not reported to the *Iron Duke* within the next two or three hours. By midnight, Scheer was crossing Jellicoe's wake only fifteen minutes behind him in his course to the south-east. From that point onwards their convergence ended and the two fleets began to draw apart.

As Scheer forced his way through the destroyers and cruisers five miles astern of the Grand Fleet, a series of sudden actions erupted in the dark, bringing with them more heavy losses to both sides. Of these desperately fought clashes in which the fate of a ship and its crew was decided in the seconds when searchlights fell upon it, Captain Wintour's 4th Destroyer Flotilla bore the brunt, at one

The battle-cruiser *New Zealand*, whose eight 12-inch guns hit gun turrets on the *Von der Tann* and *Moltke*.

Battered but unbowed, the *Seydlitz* lies at her moorings in dock at Wilhelmshaven.

time challenging the van of the High Seas Fleet's battle line. Two enemy light cruisers went down at the cost of four of the Flotilla's destroyers sunk and three badly damaged. About 2,000 officers and men from both sides were left unavoidably to drown in the icy waters.

No signals about these and similar destroyer actions reached Jellicoe, perhaps as a result of technical or operational problems. But from the *Malaya*, one of the three remaining battleships of the 5th Battle Squadron accompanying the crippled *Marlborough*, British destroyers were actually seen to attack the enemy. *Malaya* noted the leading enemy ship

as a battleship of the *Westfalen* class and her gunnery officer wanted to open fire; but he was refused by her captain because Admiral Evan-Thomas had not previously authorized it. Incredibly, no warning signals were transmitted to Jellicoe.

Other chances occurred, and were missed, until finally, as Scheer held his fleet with such determination to its course, only one British destroyer flotilla lay to the east barring its way to safety. At 1.45 am, just at first light, Captain Stirling, commander of the 12th Flotilla, in the *Faulknor*, saw the long black line of the enemy fleet emerging through the misty grey light. At once he signalled Jellicoe: 'Urgent! Priority! Enemy battleships sighted. My position ten miles behind 1st Battle Squadron.'

Stirling's flotilla then attacked. Six of his destroyers fired seventeen torpedoes before they were driven off by heavy gunfire, but one of them, fired by the *Obedient* at the fourth ship in the enemy line at 2,000 yards range, struck home. The *Pommern*, one of Scheer's pre-dreadnought battleships, was hit amidships. Watchers on board the *Obedient*, who were themselves expecting to be sunk at any moment, saw a dull red glow followed by a heavy detonation as the old ship split into two halves and went down at once with her 844 officers and men.

The last action of the Jutland battle, it could still have led to a renewal of the action near Horn Reef had Jellicoe received Stirling's message, but probably owing to enemy interference it failed to get through, and

Jellicoe continued unknowing on his way south. Jellicoe received the final blow at 4.15 am. An Admiralty message sent at 3.30 am told him that at 2.30 am the High Seas Fleet had been a mere sixteen miles from Horn Reef. By now it had escaped through the minefield to safety, with the exception of the battleship *Ostfriesland*. This vessel had hit a British mine and, although she was not sunk, was badly damaged.

The Grand Fleet set course for home, steaming through the scene of the previous evening's fighting, where the ocean had not yet drawn down into itself the tragic flotsam—hundreds of bodies in British and German uniforms, mingling with brightly coloured signalling flags in a scum of oil and timber.

Apart from the battleship *Pommern*, the Germans had lost the battle-cruiser *Lützow*, the light cruisers *Wiesbaden*, *Rostock*, *Frauen-lob* and *Elbing*, and five destroyers. The battleships *König* and *Grosser Kürfurst*, the battle-cruisers *Seydlitz* and *Derfflinger* were so badly damaged that they were hard put to make home safely.

Total British losses were three battle-cruisers, the *Queen Mary*, *Indefatigable* and *Invincible*; three armoured cruisers, *Defence*, *Warrior* and *Black Prince*, and eight destroyers. Of about 60,000 British officers and men serving at Jutland, 6,097 lost their lives, compared with 2,551 Germans out of 36,000. For complex technical reasons, arising out of poorly designed shells and inadequate flash control in the gun turrets, British losses were greater, but some of her senior commanders heavily contributed to these losses by poor tactics and a total failure to carry out the vital duty of keeping the commander-in-chief informed. Britain's surface fleet confirmed her mastery of the seas (although the U-boat menace remained), for Germany did not dare to challenge it again in the First World War. Jutland therefore marks the end of the naval era in which command of the seas depended mainly upon a battle fleet destroying an opposing fleet in visual contact by superior gunfire. Henceforward, in the battles of the Second World War the aircraft carrier would take over the hitherto dominant role of the battleship.

The German cruiser *Rostock*, which was sunk at Jutland.

A German sailor looks ruefully out of a gaping hole in a shattered gun turret on the *Derfflinger*, safely back home.

River Plate

December 1939

On 13 December 1939, one of the most resolute actions on record was fought in the South Atlantic off Montevideo by the cruiser *Exeter*, with her 8-inch guns, against the pocket battleship *Graf Spee*. *Exeter* was hit by more than 100 shells before she turned away from the action, forcing *Graf Spee*'s captain into taking the fateful step of seeking refuge in Montevideo.

From 23 September to 7 December 1939 Captain Langsdorff of the *Graf Spee*, cruising between the South Atlantic and the Indian Ocean, sank no less than ten cargo ships. From October onwards, nine hunting groups of 23 powerful British warships sought him, making it imperative that the *Graf Spee*, now a heavy strain on naval resources, be destroyed.

Commodore H. Harwood, commanding the heavy cruisers *Cumberland* and *Exeter* and the light cruisers *Ajax* and *Achilles*, foresaw that Langsdorff, re-entering the South Atlantic from the Indian Ocean early in December, would probably descend on the flow of British merchant shipping around the River Plate by 13 December. And just after 6 am on that day *Graf Spee* was sighted in the River Plate region.

Unfortunately, *Cumberland* was then refitting in the Falklands. Harwood, in *Ajax*, therefore deployed his three ships at full speed towards the *Spee* from three different quarters, so as to divide and weaken the enemy's fire. But at 6.17 am Langsdorff concentrated on the *Exeter* alone at 19,400 yards. *Exeter* opened fire three minutes later and both ships hit each other at once.

A hail of 11-inch shells knocked out one of *Exeter*'s gun turrets, killed nearly everyone on the bridge and rendered her almost uncontrollable. But *Exeter*'s shells had damaged the *Spee*, and she was also being hit by the 6-inch guns of *Ajax* and *Achilles*. Briefly, she turned her 11-inch guns on them while *Exeter* made ready to return to the fray. The *Spee* then shelled *Exeter* steadily for half an hour, the *Exeter* replying from her one gun turret. At 7.40 am *Exeter* ceased firing and turned away.

Ajax and *Achilles* both fought on for a while, then put down smoke and disengaged. Langsdorff put in to the neutral port of Montevideo for repairs and to land wounded. Meanwhile, the *Cumberland* returned and other British warships set course for Montevideo, eliminating *Graf Spee*'s chances of a successful breakout and escape. On 17 December, with Hitler's authority, Langsdorff sailed out, blew up his ship and scuttled her. His crew were interned and he shot himself three days later.

Sixty of *Exeter*'s officers and men were killed and 20 wounded in the engagement, while on *Ajax* and *Achilles* casualties were also high. Harwood was promoted to Admiral for having thus helped to free the trade routes.

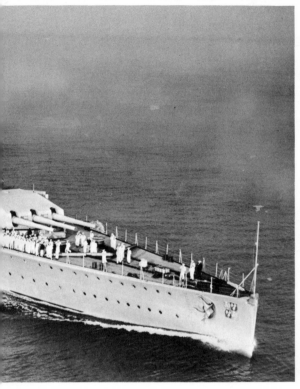

1. The British heavy cruiser *Exeter* bore the brunt of the *Graf Spee*'s big guns and accurate shooting, and after sustaining considerable damage Commander Harwood ordered her to break off and make for the Falklands. Sailors and dockyard workers cheer her as she arrives at Plymouth, 15 February 1940.

2, 3. The two light cruisers, *Ajax* (2) and *Achilles* (3), turned on the enemy battleship like angry terriers and, despite damage to themselves, harried her until she reached the neutral port of Montevideo.

4. The German pocket battleship *Admiral Graf Spee* takes part in manoeuvres in the summer of 1939, shortly before her departure to the mid-Atlantic in August 1939, ready to start commerce raiding when war broke out.

5, 6, 7. Hitler's pride, the *Admiral Graf Spee*, burns furiously in Montevideo Roads on 17 December 1939 after Captain Langsdorff had ordered her to be holed with explosives and scuttled.

3

5

7

Coral Sea
May 1942

Between the Battle of Jutland and the Battle of the Coral Sea, about a quarter of a century later, there was a significant link—the aircraft carrier. At Jutland, the *Engadine*, a Channel steamer converted into a seaplane carrier, was used in a major naval engagement for the first time to carry reconnaissance aircraft in a primitive effort to extend the eyes of the battle fleet.

At Coral Sea in May 1942, the offensive/defensive role of aircraft in sea warfare had become so decisive that it resulted in the first battle to be fought entirely by carrier-borne aircraft. Indeed, in the Second World War, warships without air cover ventured at their peril in daytime into waters within reach of enemy aircraft from land bases or carriers, as was shown by the swift sinking of the British battleship *Prince of Wales* and the battle-cruiser *Repulse* by Japanese bombers in 1942. This development fully justified Japan's extensive reliance on bombers and torpedo-bombers to counter sea power in the war against the Allies she had launched at Pearl Harbor on 8 December 1941.

By early April 1942 success had attended Japan's every move; she had won Hong Kong, Malaya, British Borneo, the Philippines and the Dutch East Indies for her ambitious so-called Greater East Asia Co-prosperity Sphere. Her pride and exultation were unbounded, and what Rear-Admiral Chuichi Hara, who was to command the carrier force at Coral Sea, later called the 'victory disease' so dazzled her naval and military leaders that they either forgot that American inferiority in sea power would be short-lived, or convinced themselves that they would win because the Western democracies were not ready to face a life-and-death struggle.

These false assumptions led to policy changes which resulted in the Japanese over-reaching themselves. Their Basic War Plan, finalized in 1938, was based on the assumption that the conquest of Malaya, the Philippines and the Dutch East Indies would take about six months; but the actual campaign, a combination of surprise, skill and mobility, had in

fast lasted a mere three months. At this point of achievement the original plan had stipulated a pause in offensive operations to allow for the consolidation of Japanese gains; but now pride, ambition and an element of military expediency combined to overcome prudence.

The Emperor and his senior naval and military advisers determined to move without delay to extend the defensive perimeter in the Pacific eastwards from the Kurile Islands, in the north, to the Western Aleutians, Midway Island, Samoa, New Caledonia and Port Moresby, in southern New Guinea.

By this move they hoped to win air mastery of the Coral Sea, to isolate Australia from the United States and to bring to action and destroy the American Pacific Fleet before it could be reinforced by those warships under construction in the USA which would give it overwhelming superiority over the Japanese fleet. The dazzling outcome of victory would be nothing less than freedom for the Japanese to roam at will throughout the Western Pacific, while ferrying to the homeland cargoes of raw materials with which to build up an even more powerful war machine.

The Japanese High Command issued orders for this so-called 'Operation MO' at the end of April 1942. They included the seizure of Tulagi in the southern Solomons, Port Moresby in south-eastern New Guinea, and the occupation of Nauru and Ocean Islands—for their valuable phosphorous mines. The capture of the vital airfield and base at Port Moresby would put an end to the Allied bombing raids launched from it, strengthen the Japanese hold on their nearby base of Rabaul, and provide the means for isolating Australia. Tulagi would provide the Japanese with a base for a subsequent attack on Fiji and New Caledonia.

The Coral Sea, bounded by the Great Barrier Reef in the west, the Solomon Islands and the south-eastern tip of New Guinea in the north and the New Hebrides and New Caledonia in the east, is one of the most inviting stretches of water anywhere in the world. In the graphic words of the American

Opposite: Smoke swirls around the aircraft carrier *Lexington* as internal explosions follow an attack by Japanese torpedo- and dive-bombers, which she survived, during the 19-minute engagement on 8 May 1942. Rear-Admiral Thomas Kinkaid's flagship, the cruiser *Minneapolis*, stands by as a destroyer takes off the stricken carrier's crew.

naval historian Samuel Eliot Morison:

*There is no winter, only a summer that is
never too hot. Almost all the islands on its
eastern and northern edges—New Caledonia,
the New Hebrides, the Louisiades—are lofty,
jungle-clad and ringed with bright coral
beaches and reefs. Here the interplay of
sunlight, pure air, and transparent water
may be seen at its loveliest; peacock-hued
shoals over the coral gardens break off
abruptly from an emerald fringe into deeps
of brilliant amethyst. Even under the rare
overcasts that veil the tropical sun, the
Coral Sea becomes a warm dove-grey in
color in high latitudes. Here too . . . are
some of the last unspoiled island Arcadias,
where a stranded sailor or airman might
believe himself to be back in the Golden Age.*

Or so it was, until the sudden and brutal
advent of mid-twentieth-century naval and
military technology in 1942.

By the end of April both the United States
and Japan had learned, ironically, without the
other knowing it, something of each other's
plans. The Americans, having early in the war
found the keys to the Japanese naval code,
learned by 17 April 1942 that the invasion
group assembled by Admiralissimo Isoroku
Yamamoto was soon to enter the Coral Sea.

The mission assigned to Admiral Chester
Nimitz, C-in-C Pacific (CINPAC), by the US
joint Chiefs of Staff was to hold the lines of
communication between America and Australia; to contain the Japanese in the Pacific;
to support the defence of North America; and
to prepare for major amphibious counter-
offensives in the south and south-western
Pacific.

Nimitz—already short of both available
forces and of time in which to assemble
them—ordered Rear-Admiral Aubrey Fitch,
commanding the heavy carrier *Lexington* and
two cruisers, to rendezvous with Rear-Admiral
Jack Fletcher, commanding Task Force 17
(the carrier *Yorktown* and three heavy cruisers),
on 1 May 1942, at a location west of the New
Hebrides named Point Buttercup. Rear-Admiral Sir John Crace, RN, with two Australian
cruisers and the American cruiser *Chicago*
(Task Force 44), commanded the only other
support available, the overall command of
which was assigned to Fletcher, whose orders
from CINPAC were the essence of simplicity
—to 'operate in the Coral Sea commencing
1 May'.

Japanese Intelligence at this time had
reported the likely presence in the Coral Sea
area of an American naval task force with
one carrier, a move which clearly indicated
a challenge to Japanese invasion plans. Yamamoto, then preparing his Combined Fleet for
the vital Midway challenge to the American
Pacific Fleet, directed Vice-Admiral Takeo
Takagi's 5th Carrier Division of two heavy
aircraft carriers, *Zuikaku* and *Shokaku*, with
125 fighters and torpedo-bombers, two heavy
cruisers and six destroyers—then on its way
home to Japan after operating in the Indian
Ocean—to join the 'MO' Task Force.

This consisted of the Port Moresby Invasion Group of eleven troop transports and
a destroyer squadron; the Tulagi Invasion
Group, consisting of a transport, submarine
chasers, destroyers, minelayers and sweepers;
a Support Group comprising a seaplane
carrier, two light cruisers and three gunboats
for setting up a seaplane base in the Louisiades Islands; and finally, a Covering Group
of one light carrier, the *Shoho*, four heavy
cruisers and six destroyers.

Commanding this formidable array of 70
ships was Vice-Admiral Shigeyoshi Inoue,
then C-in-C of the 4th Fleet in the Central

Pacific; now he was transferred to Rabaul for the operation and was assigned an additional 120 land-based aircraft and six submarines.

On 1 May 1942 the small Australian garrison on Tulagi, informed of the formidable enemy force approaching, saw no point in offering themselves as a sacrifice to the Mikado and made a swift and complete withdrawal. Admiral Fitch's force joined Admiral Fletcher's force that same day and began an unhurried oil-fuelling operation about 95 miles south of Guadalcanal. At this point Intelligence reports reached Fletcher of enemy movements into the Coral Sea and he steamed west with Task Force 17 and the *Yorktown*, leaving orders for Fitch to rendezvous with him on 4 May 1942.

But the first Japanese moves in the battle for the Coral Sea had begun the day before. Admiral Shima's Tulagi Invasion Group had landed on the island unopposed, though two of General MacArthur's reconnaissance aircraft sighted the landings. At 7pm Fletcher received a report on the Japanese landings that spurred him to quicker action. He steamed north at about 24 knots, running the risk of a devastating attack by superior enemy forces, who might, for all he knew, be present in the area. Fitch's Task Force 11, with the *Lexington* and Admiral Crace's cruisers, which had just arrived from Australia, was now 250 miles away to the south.

Within operational reach of Tulagi at 6.30am on 4 May 1942, Fletcher launched twelve torpedo-bombers and 28 dive-bombers for attacks on ships in the harbour, and six *Wildcat* fighters for the defence of the *Yorktown*, holding in reserve another twelve—thus leaving the attacking bombers to defend themselves as best they could with their own

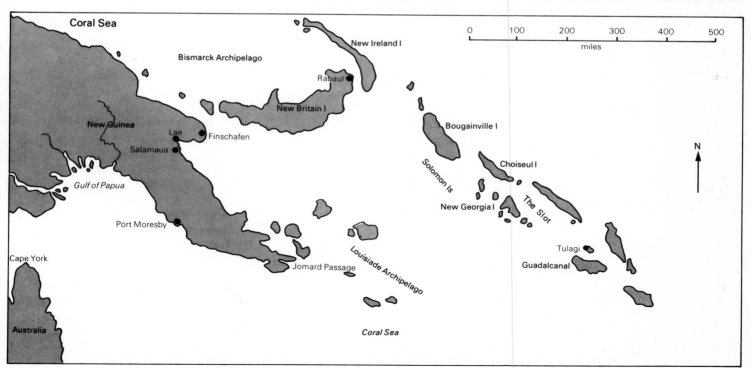

machine-guns, an unenviable task.

It was a risky move, but fortunately the Japanese, overconfident after their long run of success, had withdrawn their carrier covering forces a few hours earlier, when the Tulagi landings were complete. In the face of only heavy anti-aircraft fire, the *Yorktown*'s aircraft made three strikes, dropped a total of twenty-two torpedoes, seventy-six 1,000-lb bombs and fired about 83,000 rounds of ammunition. For this substantial expenditure and the loss of three aircraft, they sunk one destroyer, a few minor vessels and three seaplanes, and slightly damaged another destroyer, which escaped.

It was a feeble opening to America's first big counter to the Japanese onslaught in the Pacific. 'The Tulagi operation was certainly disappointing in terms of ammunition expended to results obtained', commented Admiral Nimitz, with almost saintly forbearance and a call for further target practice. Afterwards Fletcher steamed south to link up with Fitch's and Crace's forces on 5 May 1942, and began a search for the enemy forces.

The Japanese Port Moresby Invasion Group sailed from Rabaul on 4 May 1942 with Admiral Marushige's Support Group. They headed south, to pass through the Jomard Passage in the Louisiade Archipelago, while Admiral Takagi's Carrier Striking Force, with the *Zuikaku* and *Shokaku*, raced south-east, eastward of the Solomons and beyond the range of air reconnaissance, turning westwards into the Coral Sea on 5 May to try to intercept the American force, which they knew had entered the Coral Sea.

Takagi was unlucky, for on 5 May 1942 the *Yorktown*, refuelling within visual contact of Fitch and Crace, would have made an easy target. In the evening Fletcher changed course to north-west, towards New Guinea, directing his search towards the area where the enemy would most likely be found in his course south from Rabaul. By dawn on 6 May he was suitably placed in an area 116 miles south of the Louisiades for an attack on the transports of the Port Moresby Invasion Group when they entered the Jomard Passage, between the Louisiades and the tail of bird-shaped New Guinea.

During the night, Admiral Takagi had approached to within 70 miles of Fletcher's force, and had then to refuel, but neither he nor Fletcher knew how near they were to each other. However, Fletcher's reconnaissance aircraft had earlier sighted the invasion force itself south of Rabaul; by midnight it was nearing the Jomard Passage.

Early on 7 May Admiral Fletcher ordered Admiral Crace's support Task Force, supported by the destroyer *Farragut*, under Commander George P. Hunter, to steam ahead and intercept the enemy invasion force heading for the Jomard Passage. Fletcher later defended this weakening of his force's anti-aircraft screen, and of his power to stop Takagi's force, by contending that he anticipated a carrier battle and therefore needed a separate task force to stop the invasion group. It was hardly a logical argument, for concentration of his strength would have made Takagi's defeat easier, after which the invasion group would have been more easily handled; while if Takagi were to defeat him, it would have been the end of Crace's force too.

While Crace steamed ahead of Fletcher's

Rear-Admiral Frank J. Fletcher, who commanded the vital Task Force 17 which on 7–8 May 1942 halted the Japanese eastward thrust in their attempt to isolate Australia.

The Japanese light carrier *Shoho*, a 12,000-ton converted submarine depot ship which carried approximately 25 torpedo-bombers, became the target of a furious attack by Fletcher's carrier-borne bombers at about 11.15 am on 7 May 1942. Two 1,000-lb bombs and two torpedoes blew her apart. She was abandoned at 11.31 am and sank soon afterwards.

force towards the Louisiades, two smaller craft, the destroyer *Sims*, under Lieutenant-Commander Willford M. Hyman, and the oil tanker *Neosho*, under Captain Phillips, steaming about 400 miles to the south-east towards a fuelling rendezvous, were sighted at about 7.30 am by enemy reconnaissance aircraft, and an over-zealous Japanese pilot reported them as an aircraft carrier and a cruiser.

For Rear-Admiral Tadaichi Hara, commanding the carriers of Vice-Admiral Takagi's Carrier Striking Force, it was good news. He at once met this apparent threat by launching a torpedo and bombing onslaught against the audacious enemy. At 10.38 am, when *Sims* was steaming about a mile forward of the tanker (nicknamed 'Fat Lady'), a squadron of fifteen enemy bombers appeared and dropped their loads from a high altitude, but missed and flew off. Soon afterwards another ten aircraft went into the attack and Commander Hyam swung hard to starboard, dodging nine bombs which flashed past at mast height. But not long afterwards came the end of the *Sims*. Thirty-six bombers came in at low altitude to finish the job. Three bombs hit the *Sims* simultaneously, two of them detonating in the engine room, and within seconds an explosion tore the ship apart. Only fifteen of her company survived.

Seven bombs and a Kamikaze suicide pilot hit the *Neosho* within the next few minutes, but she remained afloat after the enemy had flown off. Surprisingly, she did not explode, but remained a drifting hulk for four days. Finally, she was located by the destroyer *Henley*, and was scuttled after her surviving crew had been taken off. But the loss of these two ships was not altogether in vain, for it was to cause the diversion of Hara's aircraft at a most opportune time for the Americans.

Japanese air reconnaissance pilots were sending in a stream of reports on the movements of Fletcher's carriers and Crace's cruisers, but Admiral Inoue put the safety of his troop transports before all else, and at 9 am, almost within sight of Misima Island, bastion of the Jomard Passage, he ordered the Port Moresby Invasion Group to change from a southerly to a south-westerly course, and thus turn away from its primary objective, until the enemy forces had been destroyed. Here, perhaps, in this poor-spirited commander's over-cautious order, was foreshadowed the approaching Japanese debacle, for this was the nearest the Invasion Group would ever get to Port Moresby.

At dawn Fletcher began a widespread search for the enemy carriers, launching attack groups with scout planes from both of his carriers. Just after 11 am Lieutenant-Commander W. L. Hamilton sighted the carrier *Shoho*, three or four cruisers and some

destroyers; they were not part of the striking force but were the ships of Rear-Admiral Goto's weak group covering the invasion force. Fortunately, most of the aircraft of Takagi's striking force were then engaged locating and bombing the *Sims* and the *Neosho* in the mistaken belief that they were hitting a cruiser and a carrier. Fletcher's onslaught against the *Shoho*—many of whose aircraft were also engaged covering the troop transports—was therefore almost unopposed.

Commander W. B. Ault led the onslaught just after 11 am, and as the waves of dive-bombers and torpedo-bombers roared down to the attack the *Shoho* dodged and weaved in desperate evasive action. But against a concentration of ninety-three bombers it had no chance. Two 1,000-lb bombs struck home, torpedoes tore her apart below decks, and a few minutes after 11.30 am the *Shoho* went down, the first Japanese carrier to be lost.

Lieutenant-Commander R. E. Dixon radioed triumphantly to the anxious Fletcher: 'Dixon to carrier, Scratch one flattop! Scratch one flattop!' Three American aircraft failed to return, but the enemy's Port Moresby Invasion Group now turned away to the north-east, and Admiral Goto hurriedly steamed off on this course with his four cruisers.

Admiral Fletcher had weakened the enemy, but his position was known, and his returning ninety aircraft could not be refuelled and re-armed, so as to be ready for a Japanese counter-attack, until late afternoon. Fortunately, Admiral Takagi's striking force, then about 350 miles to the east, had also to prepare its aircraft after their mistaken flight south to sink the *Neosho* and *Sims*. It was not until 4.30 pm that Lieutenant-Commander Takashashi flew off with a force of twelve dive-bombers and fifteen torpedo-bombers, only to meet squally weather and towering tropical cumulonimbus clouds which frustrated his task of locating and attacking the *Yorktown* and *Lexington*. After sunset, with his pilots exhausted after having been airborne on two separate missions that day, Takashashi reluctantly turned back eastwards to get back on board his own carriers.

But just before twilight Takashashi's aircraft unknowingly passed near to their quarry and were at once detected on American radar screens. Grumman Wildcat F4F fighters flew up to attack, and in the confused aerial dogfight which followed they shot down eight out of fifteen of the enemy Kate torpedo-bombers and one Val dive-bomber for the loss of three Wildcats.

Takashashi's surviving aircraft flew out of their range as fast as possible, but now, in the gathering gloom, they were faced with the problem of locating their mother ships before they ran out of petrol. The overtired pilots

Vice-Admiral Shigeyoshi Inoue, who commanded the Port Moresby Invasion Group which sought to enter the Coral Sea, lacked experience in the vital technique of carrier operations. This, and excessive caution based upon an exaggerated fear of the Emperor's reprimand, contributed to his failure.

A damage control team repairs a corner of the carrier *Lexington*'s aft flight deck, where a Japanese bomb struck a glancing blow and caused minor damage during an early phase of the Coral Sea battle.

to that which on 8 December 1941 had sunk the *Prince of Wales* and the *Repulse*; Crace's escape demonstrated the effectiveness of good evasion tactics.

The air-sea battle of 7 May 1942 in the Coral Sea had resulted in the Americans gaining the upper hand, for neither side was prepared to risk a night attack with cruisers and destroyers. Preparing for battle again next day, the Americans were modestly congratulating themselves at this point; the Japanese, smarting at their defeat, were determined to 'save face', regardless of the cost, by destroying the enemy carriers.

Meanwhile Admiral Inoue had given orders for the landings at Port Moresby to be postponed for two days while his task force

began to suffer from hallucinations, believing that they saw a carrier below which existed only in their imaginations. Finally, they sighted what they took to be their own carrier and swung into their approach and landing pattern.

But at the last moment the leading pilot, going in slowly with flaps down, spotted the Stars and Stripes flag and just in time gunned his engines and sheered off, shouting a warning over the radio to the pilots astern. Strangely enough, the Americans, too, were taken in, for only at the last moment did they open fire and shoot down one enemy plane. But this moment of triumph—the locating of the American carrier—was also one of bitter irony, for the Japanese had jettisoned all their bombs and torpedoes, to save fuel, and were powerless to attack.

Later Admiral Hara ordered the searchlights on the carriers *Shokaku* and *Zuikaku* to be turned on as homing beacons, but several aircraft short of fuel came down in the sea and only about seven of the original twenty-seven homed safely. It had been a bad day for the Japanese.

Meantime adverse flying conditions during the afternoon had dissuaded Fletcher from making another attack, but Crace's force, detected at about 8 am south of the Jomard Passage, had suffered enemy bombardment soon after noon, when a force of 33 bombers and torpedo-bombers escorted by eleven Zeke fighters—not from the carriers, but land-based at Rabaul—appeared in the distance.

Crace's three cruisers and two destroyers were steaming north-west towards Port Moresby at 25 knots in a diamond-shaped anti-aircraft formation. Crace ordered evasion tactics, and as the bombs rained down every ship weaved and twisted, firing with every gun. Good seamanship and good luck won the day, for the Japanese aircraft made off without hitting a single ship or wounding a man. The Japanese force was similar in strength

steamed northwards away from New Guinea, releasing two of its protecting cruisers to Admiral Tagaki's Striking Force.

Scout aircraft roared off the decks of *Zuikaku* and *Shokaku* soon after sunrise; then at 9.15 am Lieutenant-Commander Taka-shashi led off the grey decks of the carriers the biggest Japanese force yet flown in the battle. It consisted of 33 dive-bombers, 18 torpedo-bombers and an escort of 18 fighters. Ten minutes after it had spread into a wide arc to search for the enemy, one of the scout planes reported them 200 miles south of the carrier *Shokaku*. Takashashi ordered the air-craft into attack formation and led them in a sharp turn towards their objective.

A scout aircraft from the *Lexington*, piloted by Lieutenant J. G. Smith, had also spotted the Japanese force and reported its course, estimated speed, location and composition. Soon after receiving Smith's report Fletcher ordered both *Lexington* and *Yorktown* to launch air strikes, and by 9.15 am 82 aircraft were in the air and flying towards the enemy.

Both American and Japanese aircraft were now flying to the attack. The weather above the Japanese force, steaming south-west at 25 knots with the carriers about ten miles apart, sheltered it with cloud, while the Americans, about 300 miles south, were all-too-visible in brilliant sunshine. The Japanese had launched 69 of their 121 aircraft and the Americans 82 out of 122.

Yorktown's aircraft, flying at 17,000 feet,

Officers and men of the *Lexington* take part in an orderly abandonment of the carrier while uncontrollable fires rage below near bomb stores, causing a risk of a final explosion at any minute. The destroyer *Morris* waits behind her and a boat loaded with members of *Lexington*'s crew approaches in the foreground.

sighted the Japanese at about 10.50 am. The carrier *Zuikaku* at once turned into the shelter of a tropical rain storm and cloud, while from the *Shokaku* Zeke fighters took to the air. Lieutenant-Commander Joe Taylor of the 5th Torpedo Squadron led the *Yorktown*'s 39 aircraft into the attack on the *Shokaku*; but either their aiming was inaccurate or the range too great, for despite the great number of torpedoes and bombs dropped only two hits were scored. One hit, scored on the *Shokaku*'s starboard bow, ripped open the flight deck so that she could no longer launch aircraft, and the other exploded more or less harmlessly in a motor repair shop. A fuel store on the foredeck blazed furiously, but without doing any great damage.

Lexington's 43 aircraft had some difficulty in locating the enemy and lost three of their escorting fighters in thick cloud on the way, while the dive-bombers failed altogether to find their target and, running short of fuel, were forced to return. The remaining four dive-bombers, eleven torpedo-bombers and six escorting Wildcat fighters attacked through a gap in the cloud. All of their torpedoes missed, mainly because their slow approach from long range was quickly seen and avoided. One bomb hit the *Shokaku* without inflicting any fatal damage and Zeke fighters downed three Wildcats. Forty men were wounded and more than a hundred killed on the *Shokaku*; she was rendered temporarily unfit for further service, but managed to steam away and return safely to Japan. The *Zuikaku*, sheltering in the rain squall, escaped attack by a single American aircraft.

But during this action the *Yorktown* and *Lexington* suffered a determined Japanese attack, which was pushed home with skill and determination in brilliant sunshine, the best aid in air attack. Before the action Admiral Fletcher had given Rear-Admiral Fitch, an experienced carrier officer aboard the *Lexington*, full tactical command of fighters and of the movements of carriers and attendant warships. At 10.30 am Captain Frederick Sherman of the *Lexington* predicted, on the evidence of overheard enemy radio activity, that the fleet would face an enemy attack from 11 am onwards, and he was right. Blips appeared on the radar screens some 70 miles to the northeast at 10.55; the alarm sounded throughout the ships for action stations, speed was increased to 30 knots and the fleet turned away in a south-westerly direction to reduce the flight duration of the approaching enemy aircraft.

The patrol of eight Wildcats providing aerial cover was increased, and a further nine thundered off the decks to intercept the enemy's greatly superior force. Four of them failed to intercept and returned to the carriers too low in petrol to do anything but put down on the deck. Of the other five, three had not gained enough height to attack the high-flying enemy dive-bombers and the other two, bent on attacking the torpedo-bombers, became involved in a protracted dogfight with the escorting Zekes. Twenty-three American Dauntless dive-bombers sent aloft to attack the Japanese torpedo-bombers were too slow and too poorly armed to undertake the role of fighters.

In the short, sharp combat which followed, the Dauntless dive-bombers managed to knock down four of the slow enemy torpedo-bombers, but the Zekes sent four Dauntlesses spiralling down into the smooth, transparent water.

The carriers were now unprotected and the attack developed into a thunderous tournament between the waves of enemy aircraft and the quick-firing anti-aircraft guns of the fleet of cruisers, carriers and destroyers. 'When we attacked the enemy carriers we ran into a virtual wall of anti-aircraft fire', Lieutenant-Commander Shigekazu Shimazaki, from the carrier *Zuikaku*, reported later.

The carriers and their supporting ships blackened the sky with exploding shells and tracers. It seemed impossible that we could survive our bombing and torpedo runs through such incredible defences. Our Zekes and enemy Wildcats spun, dived and climbed in the midst of our formations. Burning and shattered planes of both sides plunged from the skies. Amidst this fantastic rainfall of anti-aircraft and spinning planes, I dived

almost to the water's surface and sent my torpedo into the Saratoga-*type carrier. I had to fly directly above the waves to escape the enemy shells and tracers. When I turned away, I was so low that I almost struck the bow of the ship, for I was flying below the level of the flight deck. I could see the crewmen on the ship staring at my plane as it rushed by. I don't know that I could ever go through such horrible moments again.*

Amid this hail of bombs and torpedoes, the smaller *Yorktown*'s greater manoeuvrability and speed served her well, so that she had little difficulty, while her quick-firing guns pumped out a stream of shells, in turning away from eight torpedoes darting towards her port bow at 11.8 am. But against the waves of enemy dive-bombers it was not so easy. From the bridge Captain Elliott Buckmaster watched the sky above, shouting change-of-course orders which his helmsman at once

The *Lexington* exploded at about 7.45 pm on 8 May 1942, after the last officer, Captain Sherman, had left the ship and a US destroyer had fired two torpedoes into her to prevent a salvage attempt by the Japanese.

executed to pull the *Yorktown* out of the descending bombs' trajectory. At first he was successful. Then a single 800-lb bomb struck the centre of the *Yorktown*'s flight deck and exploded on the fourth deck, starting a fire and killing or badly wounding 66 men, chiefly by burning, but causing no structural damage or harm to her communication or flight systems. While more bombs cascaded around the *Yorktown*, exploding dangerously near as she weaved and turned, her guns blazing away, the fires on board were put out. Captain Buckmaster avoided another torpedo and the torn bodies of the wounded were rushed off down to the sick bay.

During the *Yorktown*'s fiery ordeal, the *Lexington* suffered much more severe damage. In a new tactic that made turning either away from or into and across the path of the torpedoes almost useless, the Japanese pilots attacked on both port and starboard bows simultaneously from a range of about half a mile and at a height of 100 feet above the sea. Almost at once the first torpedo exploded on the *Lexington*'s port bow with a crash that seemed to rattle her every rivet; then another immediately struck her amidships. While Captain Sherman tried in vain to manoeuvre the *Lexington*'s vast bulk to dodge more torpedoes, a wave of dive-bombers roared down and loosed clusters of 550-lb bombs at 2,500 feet, only two of which hit home, one exploding a case of 5-inch ammunition which lay open beside a gun and the other tearing the smokestack apart.

By 11.40 am, when the enemy aircraft had loosed all their bombs and torpedoes and were climbing once more and flying off north-east towards their carriers, both the *Yorktown* and the *Lexington* were still afloat; none of the cruisers or destroyers had been damaged. The *Lexington* had a seven-degree list, but she continued to launch and recover aircraft, although three fires burned on board and three of her boiler rooms were flooded. Soon the fires were put out and the list was corrected by pumping oil from the port to the starboard tanks. A thrill of pride and satisfaction spread among officers and men that their ship had taken the worst the enemy could hand out and had survived.

Suddenly, at 12.47 am, a tremendous detonation below decks shook the whole ship, filling everyone aboard with dismay. Successive explosions followed below decks. Dense smoke filled hangars, crews' quarters and communication passages. So far, incredibly, neither the fuel system nor the engines were affected, the *Lexington* maintained her 25 knots speed and Captain Sherman's engineers were hopeful that the damage could be contained and the ship manage to reach the nearest base.

Then came an explosion which shattered vital communication systems and destroyed engine-room ventilation. Fire spread, Sherman called for aid from his destroyers and requested the *Yorktown* to receive his incoming aircraft. Soon the blaze was out of control. 'Additional explosions were occurring', Sherman wrote later. 'It was reported the warheads on the hangar deck had been at a temperature of 140 degrees; ready bomb storage was in the vicinity of the fire and I considered there was danger of the ship blowing up at any minute. I had previously directed sick and wounded to be disembarked in our whaleboats and excess squadron personnel had gone on lines to the destroyer alongside.'

A few minutes after 5 pm Captain Sherman gave the order to abandon ship. Officers and men descended by lifeline in disciplined and orderly fashion into the rafts thrown on to the calm water, from which they were picked up without loss by three destroyers. Even Sherman's pet dog was rescued. Together with his executive officer, Commander M. T. Seligman, Captain Sherman was the last to leave the battered and blazing aircraft carrier.

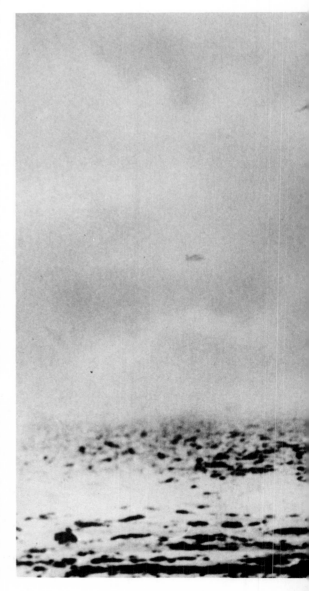

On Admiral Fletcher's orders the destroyer *Phelps* torpedoed and sank the *Lexington* in 2,400 fathoms. Thus, to the 33 aircraft they had lost that day the Americans now had to add the loss of this vital carrier. Moreover, they had to face the chance that the Japanese would launch another attack as soon as possible on the surviving *Yorktown*, leaving the way clear for the Invasion Group to turn about and steam for Port Moresby again. But fortunately this was not to be, for on board the carrier *Zuikaku* there were now only 24 Zekes and 15 bombers which were operational, while the *Shokaku*'s decks were so strewn with the wreckage of smashed aircraft that she was no longer operational.

And now came triumph for the Americans. Once he was fully aware of the situation, Vice-Admiral Inoue postponed the Port Moresby invasion indefinitely, recalling his troop transports, the support groups and the carrier striking force with their cruisers to Rabaul. *Yorktown* thus escaped when perhaps one torpedo could have sunk her.

Once it was clear that the enemy were with-drawing from the Coral Sea and that the invasion had been called off, Admiral Nimitz signalled Admiral Fletcher to withdraw, bearing in mind at this juncture that he needed to conserve his air power for the imminent defence of Midway. The *Yorktown* and two other carriers, *Hornet* and *Enterprise*, which were on their way to join him, now steamed off to Pearl Harbor.

Who won the Battle of Coral Sea? The United States had lost a heavy carrier, a destroyer and an oil tanker; the Japanese had lost a light carrier, one destroyer and several minor vessels, while their two large carriers had been badly damaged. From the less important tactical standpoint it was agreed that the Japanese had won, but the United States had won a strategic victory of far-reaching importance, for the Japanese had been checked in their attempt to extend their defensive perimeter and isolate Australia. And for the first time it had also been demonstrated that the Japanese naval high command lacked the morale and aggressiveness necessary to win a naval war against the Americans.

A last explosion rips through the doomed *Lexington* at 8 pm. Seconds later, America's most admired aircraft carrier went down stern first, through 2,400 fathoms, to the bed of the Coral Sea.

97

Cape Matapan
March 1941

Three Italian 8-inch-gun cruisers and two destroyers were sunk by the Royal Navy during this battle in the Eastern Mediterranean on 27–28 March 1941, at a cost of only two naval aircraft. The action gave Britain undisputed naval supremacy in the Eastern Mediterranean.

Italian Fascist Dictator Benito Mussolini ordered his navy into the Aegean Sea towards the end of March to support Germany's planned invasion of Yugoslavia and Greece by cutting Britain's lines of communication with the troops she had recently landed in Greece.

Admiral Sir Andrew Cunningham, Commander-in-Chief Mediterranean, assembled a force of three 15-inch gun battleships, *Warspite*, *Valiant* and *Barham*, with the carrier *Formidable* and nine destroyers, supported by four cruisers and another nine destroyers under Vice-Admiral Pridham-Whipple.

Cunningham sailed with this force from Alexandria after nightfall on 27 March in the *Warspite*. At dawn next day a reconnaissance aircraft from the carrier reported a force of four Italian cruisers and six destroyers steaming on a south-easterly course into the Aegean. It was a scouting group for Admiral Arturo Riccardi's stronger force, which was made up of the battleship *Vittorio Veneto*, five 8-inch-gun cruisers and five destroyers.

The British cruiser force sighted and engaged the enemy's advance force at 7.45 am. After an engagement lasting half an hour, in which no serious damage was inflicted by the Italian or British ships, which carried 6-inch compared with the Italians' 8-inch guns, the latter turned away and withdrew in a north-westerly direction.

The British cruisers pursued the fast Italian ships for two hours until they were cleverly drawn within range of the *Vittorio Veneto*, which fired her first salvo at the cruiser *Orion* at a range of 16 miles. The *Orion* and her cruisers hastily turned about and made off at full speed to try to draw the enemy battleship inside the range of Cunningham's three battleships, then about 70 miles away and racing towards the scene.

But at the same time aircraft from the *Formidable*, later joined by land-based aircraft from Greece and Crete, attacked the *Vittorio Veneto* with torpedoes and bombs which damaged her and caused her to limp off to the north-west at barely 15 knots. The Italian cruisers formed a protective ring to ward off air attack on the crippled battleship, but the carrier aircraft successfully penetrated this and bombed the cruiser *Pola*. Risking a night engagement, Cunningham sent his battleships into action. The 8-inch-gun cruiser *Fiume* was surprised and sunk by the *Warspite* and *Valiant*'s 15-inch salvoes, and soon after this the cruiser *Zara* was blasted and sunk by all three battleships. Cunningham's destroyers then sank the *Pola* and two destroyers escorting her. The *Vittorio Veneto* escaped. Nine hundred Italian sailors were picked up from the water.

1. Admiral Cunningham, who sailed from Alexandria on 27 March 1941, in the battleship *Warspite*, when a clash with the Italian fleet seemed likely.

2. The Italian cruiser *Zara*.

3. The aircraft carrier *Formidable*, with a Fairey Swordfish torpedo-bomber on the end of her flight deck.

4. The two forward 15-inch turrets of *Warspite*, the veteran of Jutland, refitted and modernized at a cost of £2.5 million.

5, 6. *Valiant* firing a broadside from her 15-inch guns. Her accurate gunnery quickly overwhelmed the Italian 8-inch-gun cruiser *Fiume*.

7. The Italian battleship *Vittorio Veneto*.

8. *Warspite*.

Midway

June 1942

A whirl of air strikes and counter-strikes of devastating power, combined with an intensely dramatic ebb and flow of events, characterize Midway, the most decisive battle of the Second World War, which, in the space of fifteen minutes on 4 June 1942, effectively brought to an end the Japanese mastery of the Pacific. The area of the battle, including the diversionary Aleutian operations, extended for 1,800 miles, from the northern to the central Pacific. On the Japanese side, the battle involved the largest force of men, ships and aircraft up till then assembled. The technique of air-sea warfare, first used at Coral Sea, was advanced by several stages. 'The novel and hitherto utterly unmeasured conditions which air warfare had created made the speed of action and the twists of fortune more intense than has ever been witnessed before', commented Winston Churchill.

The reverse at the Battle of the Coral Sea— the first phase in Japan's revised policy of pressure outwards across the Pacific—had dismayed but not stopped the Japanese. They decided to take Port Moresby later, at their leisure, when they had destroyed American power in the Pacific at the forthcoming battle of Midway, for which Admiral Isoroko Yamamoto, their Commander-in-Chief, had planned unceasingly. Possession of Midway atoll, once described as 'the sentinel of Pearl Harbor', no less than possession of the Western Aleutians, would bring the Japanese several steps nearer their aim of domination of the Pacific.

On 5 May 1942, confident of the outcome of the imminent clash in the Coral Sea, the Japanese Imperial Headquarters in Tokyo issued the appropriate battle order: 'Commander-in-Chief Combined Fleet will, together with the Army, invade and seize strategic points in the Western Aleutians and Midway Island.'

The island of Midway, the farthest west of the Hawaiain Islands and an American possession since 1859, lies about 1,130 miles north-west of Pearl Harbor. The treeless stretches of both atolls housed vast fuel tanks, huge ammunition dumps, a seaplane hangar, a military airport and other vital military and naval stores and buildings.

For his objectives of the seizure of Midway and the Western Aleutians and the destruction of Admiral Nimitz's Pacific Fleet, Yamamoto devised an operational plan of rare complexity: surprise was the essence, diversionary tactics the pivot and, strange as it may sound, the ancient Samurai tactics provided the inspiration.

This involved the division of Yamamoto's forces into no less than five separate and independent operational groups. The first, comprising Admiral Moshiro Hosogaya's Northern Area Force of two carriers, six cruisers, twelve destroyers and the troop transports of occupation forces, was assigned to the diversionary attack on 3 June 1942 against the Aleutians, prior to the big onslaught on Midway. The second group, for the Midway attack, consisted of Vice-Admiral Teruhisa Komatsu's Advance Expeditionary Force of four submarine groups and Vice-Admiral Chuichi Nagumo's Carrier Strike Force, comprising the carriers *Akagi* (flagship), *Hiryu*, *Kaga* and *Soryu*, backed by four cruisers and twelve destroyers. The third group was Vice-Admiral Nobutake Kondo's Midway Occupation Force, made up of a Covering Group, a Close Support Group, Transport Group, Seaplane Group and Minesweeping Group, a total of two seaplane carriers, two battleships, nine cruisers, twenty-one destroyers, twelve transports carrying about 5,200 men, four minesweepers and three submarine chasers; this group was reinforced by Admiral Yamamoto's own group —a light carrier, three battleships, two seaplane carriers and fourteen destroyers. Finally, there was the Aleutian Screen Force of four battleships and two light cruisers, which was to operate half-way between the Aleutians and Midway against enemy ships sailing from either direction.

Yamamoto's overall plan closely resembled a traditional Samurai warrior attack, with its feints, diversions and surprise thrusts. First, as a diversion, the Northern Force carrier aircraft were to launch a bombing onslaught on 3 June 1942 on Dutch Harbor, near the Alaskan Peninsula, to divert the enemy from the main attack on the Eastern Aleutians, which was itself planned as a diversion to draw the Pacific Fleet away from the subsequent attack on Midway. Yamamoto believed that the US had lost the *Yorktown* as well as the *Lexington* in the Coral Sea battle, and also that the carriers *Hornet* and *Enterprise* were still in the South Pacific. Knowing that the US had lost its fast battleships at Pearl Harbor as well, he did not anticipate a serious challenge at Midway.

By the time Admiral Nimitz, whom Yamamoto expected to send a strong force north to deal with the Aleutians attack, could turn back to counterattack in force at Midway, he hoped to have every available aircraft based there, and his own powerful group, which at this point would have taken no part in the operation, would be ready to sweep down with crushing superiority on the US Pacific Fleet.

As in the traditional Samurai plan the success of this operation depended on either passivity or ignorance of battle tactics on the enemy's part, for if Nimitz failed to react as he was expected to, the complex plan would fall apart at the seams.

Fortunately, Nimitz had been informed in advance by American Intelligence of the Japanese key dates and movement orders. He was therefore able to deploy his very much weaker forces where they were most needed. First, however, the damaged *Yorktown* limped into dry dock at Pearl Harbor, where she was repaired and refitted in barely three days by 1,400 highly skilled artisans working long shifts round the clock. By midday on 30 May 1942 she was at sea again. Nimitz was thus able to deploy three fleet carriers, including *Enterprise* and *Hornet*, with 233 aircraft, where Yamamoto believed there would be none.

Little time was available, for the Japanese naval forces began to move towards their battle stations in the last days of May, led by the Northern Force, which was due to attack Dutch Harbor on 3 June 1942. Yamamoto's total force amounted to 280 aircraft and 109 fighting ships, including submarines, compared with Nimitz's 228 aircraft and 59 fighting ships. In combat experience, too, the Japanese added to their great numerical advantage, and their confidence in victory amounted almost to a feeling of elation. Ships' companies and troops shouted war songs together and went through daily exercises on

An American Dauntless dive-bomber soars off the carrier *Enterprise*'s flight deck shortly after 7 am on 4 June in a strike against enemy carriers. In this remarkable split-second photograph, the next aircraft is starting its launch, while gunners and damage control teams wait in readiness at the sides. More than 30 pilots from this carrier failed to return from the Midway combats.

deck in preparation for the battle. However, Yamamoto, who was considered by some to be clairvoyant, was uneasy and in low spirits.

On 2 June 1942 Admiral Raymond A. Spruance's Task Force 16, which included the carriers *Hornet* and *Enterprise*, carried out a rendezvous with Task Force 17 and the *Yorktown*, under Admiral Fletcher who was in overall command, about 325 miles north-east of Midway. By then the Americans were already carrying out air searches, in bad weather, for the approaching Japanese fleet, all the elements of which had sortied from Japan by 27 May. Bombers crammed the airfield at Midway, where the Marines manned the defences in strength and the beaches were mined. During a rehearsal for a destruction plan an enlisted man playfully pulled a switch that exploded 400,000 gallons of aviation fuel and destroyed installations. As a result, during this critical time aircraft had to be refuelled manually from 55-gallon drums.

The Japanese, operating according to an exact schedule, launched the bombing offensive against Dutch Harbor during fog on 3 June 1942. Repeated again next day, it was the feint preceding the main attack on the Western Aleutians which, Yamamoto now expected, would cause Nimitz to order all his available forces the 2,000 miles north to forestall a possible threat to North America.

But Nimitz, certain of the reliability of his Intelligence, knew that the real attack was directed at Midway, and not one American ship was drawn into the trap. Meanwhile, Admiral Fletcher was keeping up intensive air reconnaissance to try to sight and attack the enemy forces as soon as possible. He was rewarded at about 9 am on 3 June 1942 when Ensign Jack Reid, in a Catalina flying-boat based at Midway, sighted a formation of eleven enemy ships steaming eastward at 19 knots some 700 miles west of Midway. Swift action followed Reid's radio report at Midway, and during that same afternoon a force of nine B-17s led by Colonel Sweeney bombed the enemy transports at a point about 580 miles west, reporting hits on a transport and a cruiser (they later turned out to be near-misses). However, in a later night attack a torpedo struck the bows of a tanker. Miraculously it survived, with only slight loss of speed. Unsuccessful though these attacks were, knowledge of the enemy's course towards Midway gave Admiral Fletcher the information which enabled him to move his carriers

Admiral Isoroku Yamamoto, commander-in-chief of the Japanese Combined Fleet.

Pilots aboard the carrier *Enterprise* near Midway observe her sister ship, the carrier *Hornet*, while both vessels steam to the stations north of the atoll assigned to them by Admiral Spruance before the battle on 4 January 1942. *Hornet* lost 32 out of her 79 aircraft during the Midway battles.

Rear-Admiral Raymond A. Spruance, US commander at Midway of Task Force 16, which included the carriers *Hornet* and *Enterprise*, received his post by chance when Admiral Halsey was taken ill. Spruance, a seasoned commander, made no mistakes. After the victory he was made Deputy Commander-in-Chief Pacific, and in time was considered one of the greatest admirals in American history.

The Japanese carrier *Akagi*. As she approached Midway, she was struck amidships by two 1,000-lb bombs released at 1,500 feet by American Dauntless dive-bombers from the carrier *Enterprise*. One bomb detonated a store of torpedoes and the other hit aircraft refuelling and rearming on deck. Fires forced her to be abandoned and the Japanese later torpedoed and sank her.

south-west to within 200 miles north of Midway by first light on 4 June. He was now well placed to swoop on Yamamoto's carrier striking force at the decisive moment.

At 5.45 am scout aircraft from Midway had the good fortune to sight the carrier force as it emerged from fog into sparkling visibility, with its escort of Zeke fighters aloft on dawn patrol and its bombers emerging for launching from the cavernous hangars below the grey decks of the carriers. Lieutenant Howard Ady, the pilot, radioed: 'Many enemy aircraft heading Midway bearing 320 degrees distant 150', followed at just after 6 am by the message: 'Two carriers and battleships bearing 320 degrees, distant 180 miles course 135 degrees, speed 25.'

Ady had sighted and reported only two out of the four enemy carriers and his estimate of their position was some 40 miles out, but Fletcher, Spruance and the Midway command now knew more or less where the enemy was and that his bombers were approaching for their first strike. Later, Ady declared that sighting the enemy carrier force was 'like watching a curtain rise on the biggest show on earth', an apt description for the lightning-swift air-sea drama now about to unfold.

At 6.7 am, when the Japanese fighters and bombers were on their way, hoping to bombard and overwhelm Midway's defences before the invasion force went in, Fletcher instructed Spruance to proceed on a southwesterly course and attack the enemy carriers. Meanwhile, he waited for the return of the reconnaissance mission prior to following Spruance. Barely fifteen minutes earlier Midway radar had located the approaching Japanese strike force of 36 dive-bombers, 36 torpedo-bombers and 36 escorting Zeke fighters. A squadron of 27 Marine Corps fighters took off, climbed high and dived down on the Zekes, which,

outnumbering them with much faster and more manoeuvrable aircraft, engaged them in aerial combat while the bombers flew on towards their target.

At about 6.30 am the first cluster of bombs fell, from a height of 14,000 feet. For the next twenty minutes they rained down on oil tanks, a hospital, supply depots, the seaplane hangar and a powerhouse, but perhaps because they hoped soon to land on the airfield themselves, the enemy neglected the runways—and few of the island's defenders were killed or wounded. Except for two Zekes which made a late attack about 7 am, the main onslaught ended at 6.50 am, and by 7.15 am the survivors of the US fighter force were limping down and slithering in to uncertain landings.

The American fighters had been completely outclassed by the Zekes; no less than seventeen of them—Brewster F2A Buffaloes and Grumman F4F Wildcats—had gone down into the sea, and several of the remainder were badly damaged and their pilots wounded. (Although the Zekes had less armour protection, they could outclimb, easily outmanoeuvre and fly faster than the earlier versions of the American Wildcat. Study of captured Zekes enabled the Americans in due course to produce the much superior Grumman F6F and the Corsair F4U, both of which surpassed the Zeke.)

But while the smoke from the Japanese bombs lay over the tiny atoll and fires still blazed, American carrier aircraft, supported by bombers from Midway which had taken off before the onslaught, launched attacks on the four Japanese carriers. The first ten bombers and torpedo-bombers were manoeuvred into launching positions at about 7 am, but the Zekes were up and waiting for them. Four of them were shot down almost at once, before they could even launch torpedoes or bombs;

anti-aircraft guns knocked down three more, one of which plummetted down on to the *Akagi*'s flight deck and slithered off, wrapped in flame and smoke, into the sea. Only three returned, two of them badly damaged, while such was the impact of the Japanese defence that not one American bomb or torpedo found its target.

More American attacks followed, suffering equally severe losses at the hands of the ubiquitous Zekes and scoring no hits. At 7.55 am sixteen Marine Corps dive-bombers from Midway were led by their commander, Major Lofton Henderson, in a glide-bombing attack which ended in disaster when the Zeke pilots came in behind and above them and shot down seven of them. Having dropped their bombs wide of the target, eight of the dive-bombers managed to get back to Midway, but six of them were so torn by bullets and shell splinters that they were beyond repair. The attack was then pressed home by fifteen Flying Fortresses which dropped heavy loads of bombs from a height of 20,000 feet, only to see them explode harmlessly in the water. They were followed ten minutes later, at 8.10 am, by

eleven slow Vindicator bombers from Midway. Two were shot down by Zekes and the rest veered off to bomb the battleship *Haruna*, again without success, six of them being shot down.

At this point the Japanese had gained the upper hand. They had given Midway a pounding, and the skill of their defending pilots had been too much for the crews of the American land-based aircraft, who were inadequately trained and of poor quality. But now the course of battle was to swing in favour of the Americans, for Admiral Nagumo, commanding the Japanese carriers, was about to face an insoluble problem.

In the early hours, when he launched his attack on Midway, Nagumo still believed that no US carriers were present. Nevertheless, he kept back on board a total of 93 bombers equipped with armour-piercing bombs and torpedoes, just in case any enemy cruisers intervened. Then came a crucial development, upon which hinged a disastrous sequence of events. From Lieutenant Tomonaga, in command of the aircraft which a few minutes earlier had finished pounding Midway, came

A Catalina flying-boat patrols the Midway region during aerial reconnaissance. From this type of aircraft Ensign Jack Reid obtained his legendary sighting of the Japanese 'Midway Occupation Force' about 700 miles from the atoll on 3 June 1942. The Catalina's top speed was barely 200 mph, but it had a range of up to 4,000 miles.

A Japanese Zeke fighter, loaded with a single bomb, roars off a carrier's flight deck during the Midway air battles. Nearly all Admiral Nagumo's Zeke fighters were lost or destroyed at Midway.

Zeke fighters escort Japanese bombers approaching Midway during Admiral Yamamoto's attempted invasion of this vital US base in June 1942. The Zeke had a range of 1,580 miles and a top speed of 328 mph. It was armed with two machine-guns and two 20 mm cannons.

a message to the effect that a second strike would be necessary to subdue the defences before attempting the landing.

It meant that Nagumo's 93 reserve aircraft would need to have their armament changed from torpedoes and armour-piercing bombs to high explosive and fragmentation bombs for a further strike on Midway's defences. A most unwelcome technical decision, it meant that for approximately 60 minutes, until this task was completed and the bombers Nagumo had sent to Midway had touched down on board again and had been refuelled and rearmed, his four

carriers would be exceedingly vulnerable to sudden attack by surface vessels—for at this moment every one of his available Zekes were in the air, fending off the enemy attack from Midway.

Nagumo's reconnaissance aircraft, launched at about 4.30 am, had so far failed to locate Fletcher's force to the north-east; Nagumo decided to take the risk and ordered his 93 aircraft below for rearming for the second contemplated attack on Midway. Upon this fatal decision hinged the entire outcome of the battle, for it was effectively to neutralize the

A Grumman F6F Hellcat fighter, successor to the slower Wildcat, makes an unsuccessful landing attempt as his arrester hook dangles several feet above the arrester cable on the flight deck below. The pilot has gunned his engine and begun to raise his flaps for another try. The Hellcat entered service in the Pacific in 1942.

initial Japanese superiority.

The tide of events now began to flow against Nagumo. At 7.2 am Admiral Spruance, then about 240 miles north-east of the enemy carrier force, began launching torpedo and bomber aircraft from the carriers *Hornet* and *Enterprise* for an all-out attack by 67 Dauntless dive-bombers and 29 Devastator torpedo-bombers, escorted by 20 Wildcats, leaving another 36 Wildcats for a defence patrol flying in rotation above the force. The launchings were complete by 8.06 am, and the 126 planes climbed to 17,000 feet on their epic mission.

Meanwhile, at 7.28 am, an enemy reconnaissance seaplane had caught a first distant sight of Fletcher's force. The pilot reported what he thought were ten enemy ships about 240 miles north-east, giving Nagumo the first pangs of anxiety for his carriers. For fifteen minutes he considered the problem with his staff, then at 7.45 am he sent out the order: 'Prepare to attack enemy fleet units. On those aircraft not yet rearmed with bombs leave torpedoes.' At the same time he ordered the seaplane to inform him what kind of ships he had sighted and to keep them in sight.

Japanese land-based Nell-type bombers, probably from Wake Island, fly on a reconnaissance mission during the preliminaries of the Midway battle. The Nell had a range of 2,240 miles, a top speed of 241 mph and a bomb load of 2,200 lb.

Low-flying Japanese torpedo-bombers from the carrier *Hiryu* press home a daring attack on the *Yorktown* through heavy anti-aircraft fire. Two torpedoes found their target, the Yorktown began sinking and was abandoned. American destroyers took off her crew.

Vice-Admiral Chuichi Nagumo, commander of the Carrier Striking Force attacking Midway, refused to leave the bridge of his flagship, the carrier *Akagi*, when it was bombed and set ablaze. He was dragged off the doomed vessel by his officers.

Smoke billows from installations on Midway Atoll on 5 June 1942, the day after heavy Japanese bombing. Oil tanks, aircraft hangars and petrol installations were among the equipment destroyed. However, few Marine Corps defenders were killed.

At 8.9 the pilot radioed back that there were five cruisers and five destroyers, adding casually about ten minutes later what for Nagumo was the shattering news that there appeared also to be a carrier with the enemy force. The mystery remains as to how this careful scout pilot, flying in perfect visibility, failed to observe the vital fact that aircraft were then taking off from two enemy carriers when he sent his first message. It was a costly omission, for by the time of his last message the American aircraft were winging at 19,000 feet, a quarter of the way towards their objective.

Admiral Fletcher meanwhile prudently waited until reconnaissance had ascertained that no other enemy carriers were present. Then, at 8.38 am, he began launching a force of seventeen bombers, twelve torpedo-bombers and six Wildcats, leaving about the same number ready on deck to launch when called for. Samuel E. Morison vividly recaptures the scene:

Planes swooping in graceful curves over the ship while the group assembles; hand-signalling and waving to your wing-man, whom you may never see again; a long flight over the superb ocean; first sight of your target and the sudden catch at the heart when you know that they see you, from the black puffs of anti-aircraft bursts that suddenly appear in the clear air; the wriggling and squirming of the ships, followed by wakes like the tails of white horses; the dreaded 'Zekes' of combat air patrol swooping down on you apparently out of nothing; and finally, the tight, incredibly swift attack, when you forget everything but the target so rapidly enlarging, and the desperate necessity of choosing the exact moment—the right tenth of a second—to release and pull out.

Yorktown's strike force was aloft and on its way by 9.6 am. From 8.37 am onwards, Nagumo, waiting with overwhelming anxiety after hearing of the presence of an American carrier, watched his aircraft returning from Midway. Soon afterwards he heard the worst —warnings from his reconnaissance planes about the approach of an enemy carrier-based strike force from the north-east, just when his fighters were still being refuelled and his bombers still landing.

For as long as he dared, Nagumo stayed on course towards Midway, in the path of his returning bombers. Then he signalled: 'We plan to contact and destroy the enemy force.' He ordered a 90-degree change of course to east-north-east, and at 9.17 am, when his bombers were all finally aboard, his ships swung round at right angles together, leaving a white pattern on the calm sea which was visible aloft from 50 miles away.

Nagumo's change of course gave him a little extra time before the strike, for one group of dive-bombers missed him altogether. Lieutenant-Commander Mitchell, approaching with 35 dive-bombers, and Lieutenant-Commander John C. Waldron's torpedo-bombers, with their Wildcat escort, lost each other in cloud en route. Mitchell's dive-bombers and the fighters failed to locate the enemy, and flew

on towards Midway, missing the battle entirely, while one by one the fighters flopped down in the sea as they ran out of petrol. It was an ominously ineffective start for the Americans.

Waldron's obsolete torpedo-bombers turned north instead and at 9.25 am sighted the enemy carriers in a box of four. Without the protection of a single fighter, Waldron came down to a low altitude and flew straight for the carrier group, ready to release his torpedoes. Enemy fighters were quickly after them and Captain Marc Mitscher, quoted in Morison's *History*, describes what followed:

Beset on all sides by the deadly Zero fighters, which were doggedly attacking them in force, and faced with a seemingly impenetrable screen of cruisers and destroyers, the squadron drove in valiantly at short range. Aircraft after aircraft was shot down by fighters, anti-aircraft bursts were searing faces and tearing chunks out of fuselage, and still the squadron bored in. Those who were left dropped their torpedoes at short range.

The entire squadron of fifteen aircraft was shot down, some of them before they were even able to release their torpedoes—and none of those launched hit the target. Only one man out of thirty, Ensign George H. Gay, lived to tell the story of this courageous failure by the *Hornet*'s aircraft. From his small rubber life-raft he witnessed much of the subsequent battle and was picked up by a Catalina seaplane next day.

Lieutenant-Commander Eugene E. Lindsey's torpedo squadron from the *Enterprise*, which had also lost its fighter escort, now swooped down in its turn into the arena of death surrounding the four enemy carriers. Again, only three or four aircraft were able to launch their torpedoes, from which the carriers successfully turned away. Once more the Zekes razored in among the cumbersome bombers, shooting down ten out of fourteen.

The massacre was repeated a third time at 10 am, when Lieutenant-Commander Lance E. Massey's torpedo squadron from the *Yorktown*, escorted by six Wildcats, attacked the carrier *Soryu*. Mercilessly harried by numerous darting Zekes, the Wildcats could do nothing to protect the bombers, seven of which spiralled down in flames one after the other, led by Massey's. The five still flying through this hail of bullets launched their torpedoes but failed to strike the target; three of them were then downed and the remaining two limped home riddled with lead.

But even while the Japanese were rejoicing in their victory as they zig-zagged to escape the torpedoes, and their Zekes, flying at low level,

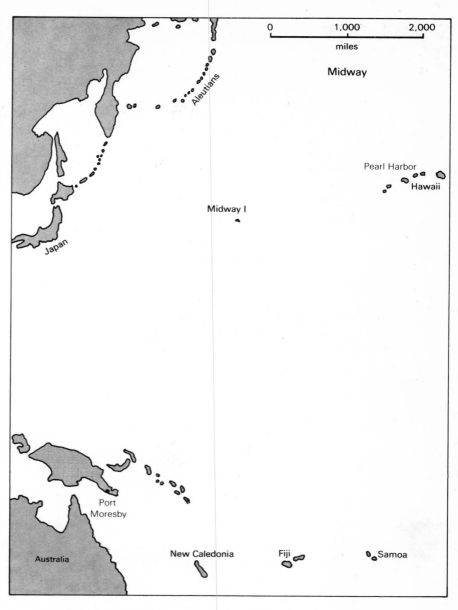

were knocking down the American bombers, Lieutenant-Commander C. W. McClusky, group commander of the carrier *Enterprise*, at last sighted the Japanese carrier force from 19,000 feet with his 37 dive-bombers. The decks of all four carriers were crowded with refuelling aircraft. The *Hiryu* was a mile or two ahead of the *Soryu*, the most easterly, with the *Akagi* on her port beam and the *Kaga* astern between the two.

McClusky's two squadrons attacked the *Kaga* and the *Akagi* first, screaming down in almost vertical 70-degree dives and releasing 1,000-lb and 500-lb bombs at only 1,500 feet. The devastating result is told in the words of two Japanese officers, Masatake Okumiya and Jiro Horikoshi: 'Our carriers were helpless. Bomb after bomb smashed into our ships' vitals, flooding compartments, destroying gun-control systems, knocking out fire-fighting apparatus, setting aflame petrol and oil tanks.'

The *Akagi*, Admiral Nagumo's flagship, was hit by three 1,000-lb bombs in quick succession, one of which exploded among

A Japanese aircraft carrier, the *Soryu*, one of four destroyed during the Midway battle, turns into the wind ready to launch aircraft lined up for take-off on the flight deck. At that moment American bombers hit her with three 1,000-lb bombs in quick succession, crippling her and setting her ablaze. The US submarine *Nautilus* then finished her off with three torpedoes.

aircraft on deck and another in the torpedo store. An uncontrollable fire broke out and soon it was clear that nothing could be done to save the ship, but Nagumo persisted in believing that the situation could be brought under control and, according to Rear-Admiral Kusaka, his chief of staff, quoted in the *United States Strategic Bombing Survey*, would not leave the bridge, even when the ship's captain said the *Akagi* was out of control and should be abandoned. Kusaka wrote later:

I myself tried to convince him that it was

his duty as C-in-C to abandon ship and transfer to some other ship where he could control the actions of the fleet, because it was no longer possible to communicate with other ships by wireless from Akagi, and the signal flags and semaphore weren't sufficient to direct the battle.

Although Admiral Nagumo refused to come down, I finally had the others drag him down by the hand and talk him into leaving the ship, but we couldn't find a way down, everything was so covered with smoke and flame; there was no way of getting down except by rope . . . The deck was on fire and

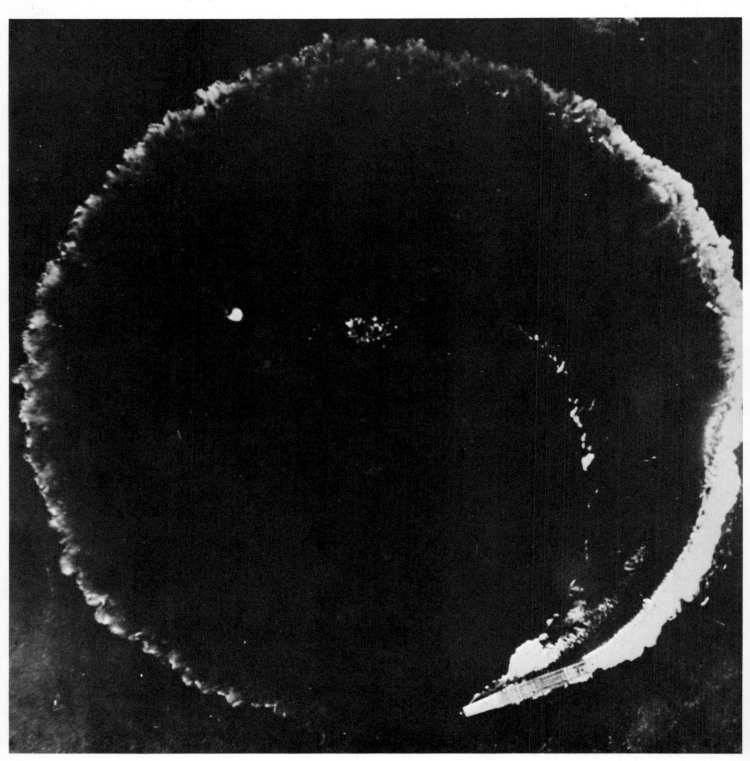

anti-aircraft and machine-guns were firing automatically, having been set off by the fire. Bodies were all over the place, and it wasn't possible to tell what would be shot up next ... We abandoned the Akagi helter-skelter, no order of any kind.

Nagumo transferred his flag to the light cruiser *Nagara*, but more ineffective efforts were made to save the *Akagi* before it was pronounced hopeless. All hands were ordered to abandon ship during the evening and, a floating hulk, the once-proud carrier drifted until she was torpedoed and sunk at dawn by a Japanese destroyer.

During the initial dive-bombing, eight bombs struck home on the *Kaga* while nearly all its aircraft were on deck refuelling. Here, too, petrol and oil ignited in a conflagration that spread from stern to stern, setting aircraft alight and exploding ammunition in a constant roar.

While McClusky's squadron concentrated on the *Akagi* and *Kaga*, Lieutenant-Commander Leslie's squadron of seventeen dive-bombers from *Yorktown*, which had lost no time in locating the enemy, dived down from 14,500 feet on the *Soryu*, releasing at 2,500 feet and hitting the target with three 1,000-lb bombs as she turned into the wind to launch aircraft. Almost at once flames engulfed the *Soryu*. Captain Yanagimoto ordered fire control parties to quell the blaze, but the situation was hopeless, and fifteen minutes later he ordered them to abandon ship. In the afternoon, when she was still afloat, the submarine *Nautilus* hit her with three torpedoes. She sank in the early evening, 30 of her pilots and 700 of her crew being saved. The *Kaga*, none of whose aircraft had taken part in the battle, also sank during the afternoon, with most of them in a tangled mass of wreckage on her deck. Japanese warships saved several hundred of her crew.

The Americans had thus destroyed three of the enemy's best carriers and more than half of his available fighters and bombers in just twelve minutes of fast and furious attack. Altogether, they had lost more than 60 aircraft and over 100 of their best and most courageous aircrew, but for the immense gains they had made it seemed a small price to pay.

Now came a sudden set-back for the US forces. The fourth enemy carrier, the *Hiryu*, had steamed north-west into low visibility, with its air group at full strength, during the strike against her three companion ships. Rear-Admiral Abe, to whom Nagumo had temporarily transferred tactical command of the battle, now received a report of the *Yorktown*'s position and ordered Admiral Yamaguchi, in the *Hiryu*, to send up an air strike against it. The first wave was in the air by 11

A wounded American seaman transfers from a small destroyer, crowded with crew taken off the stricken carrier *Yorktown*, to a nearby cruiser.

am—eighteen dive-bombers and six fighters—expecting to hit the target in about an hour's time.

This time the *Yorktown* had to face a life-and-death challenge. At midday, when Lieutenant-Commander Leslie's dive-bombers were circling above the *Yorktown* with almost empty tanks, awaiting the signal to land after sinking the *Soryu*, fifteen Wildcats were refuelling on deck and a small combat patrol of twelve had just taken the air, the *Yorktown*'s radar screen showed the telltale blips of an estimated 40 aircraft about 45 miles away west-south-west. At once more Wildcats were sent aloft, Leslie's dive-bombers were ordered to make themselves scarce, and Admiral Fletcher ordered a speed of 30 knots, and to follow a zig-zag course when the strike was sighted.

This time the Wildcats pounced on the tight enemy bomber formation and sent eight of them spiralling down in flames. Then anti-aircraft fire from the cruiser screen broke up two more, but eight of them got through and three bombs in quick succession hit the *Yorktown*, starting fires below decks, knocking out five of her six boilers and destroying her radar.

It was a serious, but not fatal attack. Admiral Fletcher transferred his flag to the cruiser *Astoria*, and though at first *Yorktown*'s speed had fallen to six knots, her engine-room staff achieved miracles; four of her boilers were patched up, her speed rose again to 20 knots, fire-control parties controlled the blaze below decks, and refuelling of fighters began for a combat patrol.

Then, at about 2.40 pm, the *Hiryu*'s second strike, ten torpedo-bombers escorted by six Zekes, came in at 7,000 feet. In a daring thrust, almost at water level, four torpedo-bombers released their torpedoes at an estimated 500 yards. *Yorktown* veered wildly away and avoided two of them, but two struck home with fatal effect, tearing a large hole in her port side and jamming the steering gear. Water poured in, making her list so badly that she seemed in danger of capsizing. This time the *Yorktown's* skilled and devoted technicians could do nothing. Her list grew worse and soon she began to settle in the water. Captain Buckmaster gave the order to abandon ship at 3 pm, and four destroyers rushed in to take off and pick up officers and men.

But the *Hiryu's* pilots had little time to give their victory shouts of 'Banzai!' as the surviving aircraft thundered back on to her decks. An American scout plane sighted the carrier at 2.45 pm, and at 3.30 the carrier *Enterprise* launched 24 unescorted dive-bombers, led by the same alert and skilful Lieutenant-Commander McClusky who had spearheaded the victorious morning attack.

McClusky sighted *Hiryu* at 5 pm and once more led his squadron down in an almost vertical dive, releasing bombs a few hundred feet above her as she see-sawed in desperate evasive action, trailing a white wake of foam behind her. Four 1,000-lb bombs crashed into the *Hiryu*, tore her apart below decks and started fires which enveloped her. During the night she was abandoned, but despite Japanese torpedoes she remained afloat, a blazing hulk, until 9 am next day, when she

Pilots and crew of the doomed *Yorktown* slither over the steeply sloping deck as water pours in through the holes torn by the enemy torpedoes below, causing the carrier to list heavily.

The Japanese cruiser *Mogami*.

Below: The cruiser *Mikuma*, blasted by American dive-bombers on 6 June 1942 during the general retirement of the Japanese fleet.

Damage control teams successfully fight fires on the *Yorktown*, ablaze after the first Japanese dive-bomber attack. Prior to the fatal torpedo attack, the dive-bombers hit her with three bombs which set her ablaze below decks, but failed to cripple her.

went down, taking with her Rear-Admiral Yamaguchi.

Thus ended the battle of Midway. Admiral Yamamoto's great armada had been shorn of its four carriers and its fleet of combat aircraft. Without them, while the American force still had two carriers and their aircraft intact, as well as the Midway-based bombers, he was powerless to attack the atoll and in danger of a destructive air strike by the enemy. He had lost command of the sea to the enemy he had set out to challenge and destroy. Those twelve minutes at midday on 4 June, when bombs

rained down on his carriers, saw the turning point in the war in the Pacific.

Doubtless with a sorrowful eye on the Emperor's portrait in his operations room, Yamamoto at first determined to battle on, notwithstanding his vulnerability to air attack, and ordered four heavy cruisers to shell Midway at dawn next day, but the realization that this sortie would be likely to end in another destructive strike by American dive-bombers dictated prudence. At 2.55 am, in agreement with his staff, he conceded defeat and ordered a general withdrawal.

But the last sting in the tail-end of the battle was now ready for him. Two of the cruisers he had ordered to attack Midway collided while avoiding enemy submarine attack, and one of them, the *Mogami*, was badly damaged. Both were left behind in the general retirement. American dive-bombers attacked them on 6 June and sank the *Mikuma*, while the *Mogami* managed to limp back to Japan, remaining out of service for some months.

Twice now in the space of four weeks, at Coral Sea and at Midway, America had defeated her determined and skilful enemy. 'The annals of war at sea present no more intense, heart-shaking shock than these two battles, in which the qualities of the United States Navy and Air Force and of the American race shone forth in splendour', wrote Winston Churchill of these victories. 'But the bravery and self-devotion of the American airmen and sailors and the nerve and skill of their leaders was the foundation of all.'

How true this was the forthcoming battles of Guadalcanal and of Leyte Gulf would prove. The tide had turned against Japan.

The Prince of Wales and the Repulse

December 1941

On 10 December 1941, 100 miles north of Singapore, two of Britain's most powerful battleships, *Prince of Wales* and *Repulse*, were sunk by Japanese bombers in the space of 71 minutes. From that moment Japan established naval supremacy in both the Indian and Pacific Oceans, for there were now no Allied battleships in either ocean to challenge its navy. This sharp reverse underlined the lesson of Pearl Harbor—that even powerful battleships were quite helpless without air cover. It was also a harbinger of the Battle of the Coral Sea.

When the Japanese invasion fleet had been sighted in the Gulf of Siam, Admiral Phillips resolved that rather than remain at anchor in Singapore Roads and be attacked from the air, his two battleships should steam quickly northwards, shoot their way through the force defending the Japanese invasion fleet and destroy it off northern Malaya.

For this purpose he urgently requested air cover from RAF Singapore, but this was denied because of a threatened air attack which never materialized. Phillips was already at sea on 8 December when the RAF refusal reached him. Nevertheless, he resolved that he must act at once, whatever the risks. He hoped that the monsoon storms would temporarily ground the enemy bombers, which were based at Soctrang, near Saigon.

But he was unlucky; Rear-Admiral Sadaichi Matsunaga's 22nd Flotilla of 75 bombers was already out searching for him. At 10 am on 10 December, after a three-day hunt, a force of 35 torpedo-bombers finally located *Prince of Wales* and *Repulse* about 100 miles north of Singapore.

The battleships and their destroyers put up a fierce barrage of anti-aircraft fire, but the first wave of eight bombers flew on through it and hit the *Repulse* amidships, setting her afire. During the next 70 minutes, waves of torpedo-bombers skimmed over the waves to release some 50 torpedoes, eight of them hitting the *Prince of Wales*. She sank at 12.23 pm, about an hour later.

At the same time at least five torpedoes slammed into the *Repulse*. In little more than an hour she had sunk. British destroyers were disregarded by the Japanese bombers while they rescued some 2,000 officers and men out of almost 3,000 from the two ships.

Allied sea power in the Far East was now destroyed and the Japanese invasion of Malaya went on unhindered. It was a turning point in the war because had RAF air cover enabled Phillips' battleships to destroy the invasion fleet, Malaya would probably never have fallen.

1

2

3

1. The battleship *Prince of Wales* shortly before she sailed to her doom in the Far East in December 1941. The lesson of Pearl Harbor, that the most powerful battleships were no longer immune from air attack, had not yet been learned.

2. *Repulse*, carrying out a reversal of course while practising air attack evasion, shows the by no means easy target she made for the Japanese bombers who sank her on 10 December 1941.

3. Survivors scramble off the *Prince of Wales* on to a destroyer just after the fatal Japanese air attack which sent her to the bottom.

Guadalcanal

August - November 1942

The Battle of Savo Island, 7–9 August 1942

The American victory at Midway shook Japan rudely, but Imperial Headquarters in Tokyo reacted quickly with the decision that the centuries-old concept of battleship supremacy was dead. Henceforward, sea power, it was decided, rested not on 18- or 16-inch guns, but on carrier-based aircraft, against which the most powerful battleships were defenceless without air cover.

It was a hard decision to take—and one which the next engagement seemed likely to contradict—for Japan had in hand a programme of battleship construction which was pushing her industrial capacity to the utmost. Nevertheless the edict went out from Imperial Headquarters and the Japanese navy called a halt to the construction of a fast 74,000-ton battleship and two other battleships she had begun early in 1942. A third battleship, the 74,000-ton *Shinano*—destined to be sunk on her maiden voyage by the *Archerfish*, an American submarine—was ordered to be completed as a giant aircraft carrier. And another twenty-one new carriers were ordered.

As a result of this new policy, Admiral Yamamoto gave orders for the Japanese fleet to be reorganized around a nucleus of existing aircraft carriers carrying a total of 1,498 aircraft; henceforward, these were to take over the attack role formerly carried out by surface craft. Simultaneously, Imperial Headquarters changed its recently adopted policy of extended offensive operations in the Pacific to one of defence based on a new line extending from west of the Aleutian Islands to the Marshall Islands, Rabaul, the north-east coast of New Guinea, the Dutch East Indies, Malaya and Burma. Behind this line Japan would remain free to exploit the vast reserves of raw materials for the rebuilding of her war machine.

Yamamoto called his reorganized navy the Combined Fleet, dividing those units of it operating in the vulnerable area north-east of the Solomon Islands into two formations: these were Vice-Admiral Nobutake Kondo's

Vanguard Force of three carriers, two battleships, five heavy cruisers, one light cruiser and twelve destroyers; and Vice-Admiral Chuichi Nagumo's Carrier Task Force of three carriers, two battleships, four heavy cruisers, one light cruiser and sixteen destroyers.

Carrier losses at Midway, and the American use of land-based aircraft for naval operations, convinced the Japanese that they must build airfields in this region, and the army on Guadalcanal began an airfield there shortly after the Midway defeat. Kondo's Vanguard Force supported the army there, while Nagumo's Task Force operated in the seas east of Vanguard Force, ready for likely enemy attacks. The very first naval engagement which arose as a result of this policy was a victorious cruiser action which underlined the vital role of battle-cruisers.

Japanese possession of the southern Solomon Islands, of which Guadalcanal was one, provided springboards first for the seizure of American bases in New Caledonia and the New Hebrides Islands, and subsequently for breaking the line of communications between the United States and Australia and New Zealand. As early as April 1942, before the battles of Coral Sea and Midway, Vice-Admiral Ghormley, commander of the South Pacific Fleet, and his staff had begun working on plans to seize these islands.

On 10 July 1942 Admiral E. J. King, Chief of Naval Staff, received information that the Japanese had reached an advanced stage in the building of an airfield at Guadalcanal. Immediately he issued an order to the effect that the date of the Guadalcanal invasion should be advanced to 1 August 1942 or as soon as possible thereafter. That same day Admiral Nimitz, Commander of the Pacific Fleet, issued his own operational order to Ghormley for the seizure of Guadalcanal, Tulagi and Santa Cruz, the date of which was finally set for 7 August 1942.

It would lead to a gruelling six-month campaign, with ceaseless fighting ashore, and to the six battles at sea collectively known as the Battle of Guadalcanal: Savo Island, Eastern

Opposite: American Mitchell B.25 bombers from Port Moresby attack Japanese bases in the Southern Solomons soon after the Guadalcanal landings on 7 August 1942.

Admiral Ernest J. King, US Chief of Naval Staff, determined to undertake the Guadalcanal invasion on 18 February 1942, about ten weeks before the Battle of the Coral Sea and four days after the fall of Singapore. Part of the plan to drive the enemy out of the Solomons, it was the first action in which the US took the offensive in the Pacific.

The US carrier *Wasp* escorts troop transports to Guadalcanal during the night of 14 September 1942. Two torpedoes from a Japanese submarine hit her fatally and set her ablaze.

Solomons, Cape Esperance, Santa Cruz, Guadalcanal and Tassafaronga.

King's insistence on this early date was to prove invaluable, for it prevented Yamamoto from completing the re-equipping and completion of the 3rd (Air) Fleet which, almost decimated at Midway, was thus kept 'off balance' and forced eventually into a stiff fight with few trained pilots.

Under Ghormley, Vice-Admiral Fletcher commanded a task force of three carriers: *Saratoga* (86 aircraft) under Rear Admiral Leigh Noyes, with two heavy cruisers and five destroyers; *Enterprise* (84 aircraft) under Rear-Admiral Thomas C. Kinkaid, with one battleship, one heavy cruiser, an anti-aircraft light cruiser, five destroyers; *Wasp* (68 aircraft), under Rear-Admiral Boyes, who also commanded the Air Support Force, with two heavy cruisers, six destroyers.

Rear-Admiral Richmond K. Turner's South Pacific Amphibious Force of cruisers, destroyers and transports carried Major-General Alexander A. Vandegrift's Guadalcanal Landing Group and Brigadier General William H. Rupertus' Tulagi Group of 19,000 men of the 1st Marine Division. Rear-Admiral John S. McCain commanded Task Force 63, the land-based Air South Pacific Force of some 229 fighters, bombers and reconnaissance aircraft, including a number from the Royal New Zea-

land Air Force, while General Douglas Mac-Arthur's Allied Air Forces, South-West Pacific, contributed twenty B-17 bombers, two RAF Squadrons with some thirty P-40 fighters, and a number of other fighters, bombers and reconnaissance planes at Port Moresby. Finally, one group of submarines took station near Truk, the enemy advanced naval base, and another six took station at Rabaul.

So tight was Admiral King's schedule for the Guadalcanal operation, and so lacking in experience of amphibious operations were Admiral Turner's Amphibious Force and the Marines, that after sailing from New Zealand a dress rehearsal had to be carried out en route in the Fiji Islands. General Vandegrift was determined that vehicles, gasolene and ammunition should be unloaded first from the nineteen big transports, which were to come in as near as possible to the beaches after a preliminary bombardment by the cruisers and destroyers had swept them clear of defences. At the same time Rear-Admiral Crutchley, RN, deployed the protective screen of cruisers and destroyers against air, submarine and sea attack, backed up by Admiral Fletcher's carrier-borne planes in the air above the Guadalcanal region.

Extreme haste had been the keynote in the assembly of this force and Crutchley did not even have the opportunity of meeting the

cruiser and destroyer captains under his command—a disadvantage of course, but speed is twin to surprise, and surprise on this occasion was complete. Indeed, just after dawn on 7 August 1942, shortly before the operations were due to begin, the Japanese radio station on Tulagi sent out the message: 'A large force of an unknown number of ships and types of ships is entering the Sound. What can these ships be?' The radio operator had good cause to be nervous, for there were only 2,230 Japanese officers and men on Guadalcanal, of whom a mere 530 were infantry, the remainder being made up of airfield construction units.

Tulagi and Guadalcanal are separated by a stretch of about 40 miles of sea which, before the campaign ended, became known as Ironbottom Sound, owing to the numerous ships which bombs, torpedoes and shells sent to the bottom there. The American naval historian Samuel Morison, who was present at Guadalcanal, recalls that between the two the 'serrated cone of Savo Island thrusts up like the crest of a giant dinosaur emerging from the ocean depths', and refers to the sinister and depressing atmosphere of this tropical island, felt nowhere else in the Pacific war region. 'Men who rounded Cape Esperance in the darkness before the dawn of 7 August insist that even then they felt an oppression of spirit', he noted. 'Even the land smell failed to cheer sailors who had been long at sea; a rank heavy stench of mud, slime and jungle arose from the faecaloid island of Guadalcanal.'

Perhaps Admiral Turner, the Amphibious Force commander, also noticed this oppressive atmosphere, for at dawn, shortly before the operations started, he issued an inspiring message which was read over the loud hailer system of every ship as the blacked-out armada moved silently through the water towards its objective:

On August seventh this force will capture Tulagi and Guadalcanal Islands which are now in the hands of the enemy. In this first forward step toward clearing the Japanese out of conquered territory, we have strong support from the Pacific Fleet and from the air, surface and submarine forces in the South Pacific and Australia.

It is significant of victory that we see here shoulder to shoulder the United States Navy, Marines and Army and the Australian and New Zealand Air, Naval and Army services.

I have confidence that all elements of this armada will in skill and courage show themselves fit comrades of those brave men who already have dealt the enemy mighty blows for our great cause. God bless you all!

At 6.13 am the guns of the cruiser *Quincy* smothered the monkey and bird cries of this tropical dawn with a bombardment of a supposed coastal battery, while other cruisers and destroyers concentrated their fire on likely gun emplacements. Then a flight of 44 aircraft from *Enterprise* and *Saratoga* pounded beaches, buildings and the strip of jungle nearest the shore. By 6.47 am the transports were in position, 5,000 yards from the beach, and the first Marines had gone ashore without opposition. By 9 am they had landed two battalions. By midnight some 11,000 Marines were ashore; and at 4 pm on 8 August the enemy's deserted camp was seized and, most important, the air strip too, together with two radio stations, electricity generating plants, a torpedo air-compressing plant and vast quantities of provisions and beer. America's first amphibious combined operation had encountered only a few token small arms shots in opposition and had seized all its objectives.

But at Tulagi a hard fight faced the Marines and, with the defenders foreshadowing their future tactics and fighting until they were killed, the island was not secured until mid-morning on 8 August. Marine casualties were also heavy on the tiny islands of Gavutu—where the enemy's seaplane base was located—and on Tanambogo; these islands were not secured until 10 pm on 8 August. The force of 1,500 enemy were all killed in battles which cost 108 Marines killed and 140 wounded.

The Japanese Admiral Inoue, commander of the South-Eastern Defence Group at Rabaul, reacted swiftly. He ordered Admiral Mikawa, in command of a naval task force, and Rear-Admiral Yamada, commanding the 25th Air Flotilla, to eject the American and Allied force. The Americans had not long to wait. At 1.15 pm on 7 August, 27 of Yamada's bombers, escorted by fighters, made an unsuccessful high-level attack on the transports, followed by another at about 3 pm in which a bomb hit the destroyer *Mugford* and killed 22 men. Wildcat fighters attacking the Japanese bombers were again mauled by the escorting Zekes, but they did manage to shoot down 14 out of the 43 enemy bombers. The next day, in a torpedo attack, seventeen enemy bombers and two Zekes were shot down by accurate anti-aircraft fire. However, a transport was reduced to a burning hulk when an enemy pilot smashed

The cruiser *Vincennes*, seen here with her attendant reconnaissance seaplane, was shelled and sunk with heavy losses during Admiral Mikawa's daring naval counterattack on the American invasion fleet off Guadalcanal on the night of 8 August.

his burning aircraft into it in a suicide dive; fortunately there were few casualties.

For the US Navy, the first of many trials at Guadalcanal was about to start at midnight. Admiral Gunichi Mikawa had sailed from Rabaul with the heavy cruisers *Chokai*, *Kinugasa*, *Furutaka*, *Aoba* and *Kako*, two light cruisers, *Tensyu* and *Yubari*, and a destroyer, the *Yunagi*, with orders to sink or destroy the invading force at all costs. This sortie was to lead to the Savo Island engagement in the six-month struggle for the island known as the battle of Guadalcanal.

Mikawa's cruisers raced south-west between the two parallel chains of the 90-mile-long Solomon Isles during the day and early night of 8 August, hoping to arrive undetected off Guadalcanal during darkness, for the kind of surprise attack which they favoured and for which they were trained. 'Let us attack with certain victory in the traditional night attack of the Imperial Navy. May each one calmly do his utmost', Mikawa signalled his fleet at 4.30 pm. Earlier in the day Australian Air Force pilots had sighted him, but had made reports that failed to give his full strength. Moreover, they had not signalled immediately by radio, but had reported after returning from reconnaissance. Thus Admirals Turner and Crutchley did not receive the report until several hours later, when the enemy was dangerously near and it was too late for MacArthur to lay on a search-and-destroy attack by air.

Worse still, Admiral Fletcher, who was now alarmed for the safety of his two carriers after the loss of *Lexington* and *Yorktown* at Coral Sea and Midway, sent a signal to Admiral Ghormley recommending their immediate withdrawal from their station 120 miles northeast of Savo, and promptly steamed off in a south-easterly direction, out of the region, without even signalling Turner, in charge of the amphibious force, that he was doing so. Fletcher gave a shortage of fuel as the reason for this, but subsequent examination of his ships' logs showed quite adequate reserves and he later came under severe criticism, together with the accusation that his real reason was fear of exposing his carriers to enemy attack.

So Crutchley and Turner found themselves faced with possible attack by an enemy force while they were deprived of air cover and committed to protecting the American transports and cargo vessels still unloading in Lunga Roads, five or six thousand yards from the Guadalcanal beaches. Both knew that in this cramped situation, with lack of seaway, their ships offered an inviting target. It was potentially a disastrous situation.

They regrouped their ships into three forces. The cruisers *Vincennes*, *Quincy* and *Astoria* and two destroyers, *Helm* and *Wilson*, comprised the Northern Force, which was to patrol between Savo and Florida Islands; the cruisers *Australia*, *Canberra* and *Chicago*, with destroyers *Patterson* and *Bagley*, all commanded by Admiral Crutchley, comprised the Southern Force, responsible for holding the stretch of water between Savo Island south to Cape Esperance, on the northern tip of Guadalcanal. Rear-Admiral Norman Scott, with the two light cruisers *San Juan* and *Robart* and the destroyers *Monssen* and *Buchanan*, covered the eastern approaches, some 35 miles to the east.

It was a hot, oppressive night, with low rain clouds drifting overhead; at about 11.45 pm look-outs heard the noise of aircraft engines above, but because their navigation lights were observed they were assumed to be friendly and no action was taken. They were, in fact, Japanese scout planes launched

Japanese torpedoes and gunfire also sunk the cruiser *Astoria* during Mikawa's night attack. Surprise was complete, for none of the American warships was prepared for this assault in the dark.

from their nearby cruisers, which were now sending back over their radios details of the location and movements of the American ships, so that Mikawa's force could enter the Sound and make a lightning attack with deadly precision.

At 1.30 am, undetected in darkness and a heavy raincloud, Mikawa's force entered the Sound between Savo Island and Cape Esperance in line ahead at 25 knots with 1,300 yards between ships. It was the prelude to the most destructive attack ever made upon the US Navy by surface warships unaided by carrier-borne aircraft.

Mikawa ordered 'Independent firing!' at 1.36 am, when the shapes of two cruisers, the *Chicago* and the *Canberra*, and the destroyer *Bagley*, all of Southern Force, loomed up in the darkness ahead. The violent and deadly onslaught of the next 90 minutes, in the darkness fitfully lit by star shell, flares and searchlights, was a tribute to Japanese skill and training in naval warfare at night.

Two or three minutes after orders to start independent firing, Mikawa's flagship *Chokai* launched the first salvoes of torpedoes at 12,000 yards range at *Chicago*, *Canberra* and *Bagley*. Everything now happened at once. At 1.43 am, while the torpedoes sped through the water leaving a telltale wake, the destroyer *Patterson* sighted the enemy warships and radioed an urgent warning – 'Strange ships approaching!' – throughout the fleet – though not with much effect, if the extraordinary lack of subsequent alertness is any criterion.

Simultaneously, an enemy seaplane dropped magnesium flares in which the *Chicago* and *Canberra*, with the torpedoes now only seconds away, were illuminated. Led by the *Chokai*, three Japanese cruisers opened fire with 8½-inch shells at ranges varying from as little as 4,500 yards to 9,000 yards. The attack was brilliantly timed – the first of a hail of 24 shells struck the *Canberra* amidships seconds before two torpedoes tore her hull open.

Fires blazed above and below, her boilers were put out of action, her engines stopped, and as the hail of shells continued she began to list heavily to starboard while her captain,

chief gunnery officer and scores of other officers and men were mown down by shell splinters. Three minutes later, at 1.46 am, the enemy had moved on and the *Chicago* came under fire. A look-out spotted a torpedo's wake to starboard, but it was too late to turn away, for almost at once another torpedo was seen to port. Less than a minute later one of them blew a hole in her bows. *Chicago* turned away and left the action.

At this moment Mikawa's force, still racing through the night at 25 knots, changed course from south-east to north-east and split into two columns as it approached the Northern Force, then about six miles north-east, so that one column went to port and the other to starboard of it. At 1.48, at about 10,000 yards range, the flagship *Chokai* launched four torpedoes at the cruiser *Astoria*. Two minutes later *Chokai* switched on her searchlights and opened fire. Again surprise was complete, despite the *Patterson*'s warning and the flares in the southern sky. Another stream of shells hit their target accurately and flames leaped mast high.

After the initial confusion on *Astoria* had lapsed – it was firmly believed that a friendly ship was hitting her by mistake – she fired back, destroying *Chokai*'s chart room and a forward gun turret; but although the torpedoes had missed, the hail of shells from the entire enemy force to port and starboard tore open *Astoria*'s hull, ripped her turrets apart and left her a blazing hulk.

At the same time the cruiser *Quincy*, under Captain Moore, became the enemy cruiser *Aoba*'s unsuspecting target and then, barely a minute later, the prey of the entire Japanese force as some 50 shells hit her in quick succession, fatally wounding Moore and killing several officers and scores of men. Once again shells tore her heavily armoured gun turrets apart, ripped great holes below her waterline and destroyed her communications and power systems. One of her gunnery officers, according to her *Action Report*, quoted in Morison's *History*, stumbled through the flame and smoke to the bridge for orders. 'I found it a shambles of dead bodies with

The Japanese cruiser *Aoba*, one of Admiral Mikawa's striking force ordered to destroy the US invasion fleet at Guadalcanal.

only three or four people still standing', he reported later:

In the pilothouse itself the only person standing was the signalman at the wheel, who was vainly endeavouring to check the ship's swing to starboard and to bring her to port . . . The Captain, who was at that time lying near the wheel, had instructed him to beach the ship and he was trying to head the ship for Savo Island, distant some four miles on the port quarter. I stepped to the port side of the pilothouse, looked out to find the island and noted that the ship was heeling rapidly to port, sinking by the bow. At that instant the Captain straightened up and fell back, apparently dead, without having uttered any sound other than a moan.

Minutes later, Lieutenant-Commander Heeneberger, her chief gunnery officer and now the senior officer, gave the order to abandon ship; rafts were flung out and survivors floated off just before she sank; later they were picked up.

But at 1.50 am, before this occurred, Mikawa's non-stop onslaught was transferred to the cruiser *Vincennes*, under Captain Riefkohl. Despite warnings, flares and explosions in the distance, only an order for extreme vigilance—not yet for battle stations—had gone out on the *Vincennes*. The order for battle stations had followed only when flares from an enemy seaplane suddenly lit up the night around her. As these faded, searchlights flashed through the darkness and a salvo from the cruiser *Kako* fell 500 yards away.

At 1.53 am the *Vincennes* fired back with a salvo which hit the cruiser *Kinugasa*, but at once she was struck by a hail of enemy shells which set the aircraft amidships on their catapults ablaze, giving the enemy gunners a fine target. White-hot shell splinters tore through armour and cut officers and men down in swathes while inflicting the same material damage as on the other ships.

Three of *Chokai*'s expertly fired torpedoes slammed into her boiler-rooms at 1.55 am, another joined the shells which slammed into her eight minutes later, and soon this fifth cruiser began settling in the water—only fifteen minutes after Mikawa had given his first orders to open fire. But the *Vincennes* refused to sink, though every gun turret was smashed and torn to ribbons, her boiler-rooms and engines were destroyed, and her hull was taking water rapidly.

Mikawa finally ordered a cease-fire at 2.15 am, and now there followed a curious error in his triumphant assault. Minutes later, instead of exploiting the destruction he had inflicted upon the unsuspecting American cruisers and winning another easy victory over the transports and supply ships nearby, he ordered a general withdrawal, and by 2.20 am he was leading his force at full speed on a course to the north-west.

The final, totally unexpected action came when the destroyer *Ralph Talbot* sighted them and, disdaining flight, opened fire and drew down upon herself a lightning bombardment which left her aflame and listing heavily.

In less than half an hour Mikawa had sunk the cruisers *Quincy* and *Vincennes*, had so damaged the cruiser *Astoria* that she sank

An American B-17 Flying Fortress, so-called owing to its armament of eleven or more 5-mm machine-guns, prepares for take-off from Henderson Field on a high-level bombing raid on Japanese bases in the Solomons. Henderson Field was the key to possession of Guadalcanal, and the Japanese tried hard to eject the Americans from it, but without success.

next day after strenuous efforts to save her, and had crippled the Australian cruiser *Canberra*, which, unable to be salvaged, was sunk next day by torpedo. The *Chicago*, in which only two men were killed and 21 wounded, was saved, as was the *Ralph Talbot*, with 11 killed and 11 wounded. The *Australia*, with Admiral Crutchley on board, had taken him to a conference held some distance eastward in the Sound by Admiral Turner before the start of the battle. Afterwards, owing to various delays, *Australia* patrolled the area near the transports in readiness for an enemy attack and so took no further part in the battle.

Mikawa had achieved a destructive non-stop raid of tremendous audacity and skill, but with his main target, the transports and supply ships, within his grasp, he allowed fears of a daylight air strike to persuade him to turn away. He had failed in his main objective; the unloading at Guadalcanal went on, ensuring that the Marines had the equipment and supplies they needed to stem the Japanese onslaught both there and at Tulagi.

Yet it was a serious and alarming defeat for the United States Navy, which lost 1,023 men killed and 709 wounded. An official enquiry later recorded inadequate preparedness, disregard of unidentified aircraft, and failures in communications as the reasons for defeat. In Nimitz's words, the force was not sufficiently 'battle-minded'.

In a final incident, one small, old submarine hurt the enemy, who had lost only 58 men killed and 53 wounded, more than did this entire battle. Lieutenant-Commander John R. Moore's S-44 fired four torpedoes into the cruiser *Kako* and sunk it in five minutes while Mikawa's force was racing back to Rabaul. However, this was but small compensation for the terrible battering the Americans had received at the hands of the Japanese.

The Battle of the Eastern Solomons, 23–25 August 1942

Both sides tried to strengthen their forces in Guadalcanal after the battle of Savo Island; but for two weeks naval action died down. General Harukichi Hyakutake, 17th Army Commander at Rabaul, believed that only 2,000 Americans had got ashore at Guadalcanal, instead of the 17,000 who had landed there, and in an effort to retake the island he landed a mere 900 troops, under Colonel Kiyo Ichiki, on the night of 18 August 1942.

In the battle of Tenaru River they were wiped out by two battalions of Marines under Lieutenant-Colonels Pollock and Cresswell, but the Japanese army, unlike their navy, was still not yet committed to a major effort.

While American air strength was rapidly built up at Henderson Field, the Japanese planned another landing for 24 August 1942, assembling a powerful naval supporting force: two battleships, *Kirishima* and *Hiei*, three heavy cruisers, one light cruiser and ten destroyers; two carriers, *Zuikaku* and *Shokaku*, carrying aircraft of the 3rd (Air) Fleet; the light carrier *Jintsu* and four transports carrying a mere 1,500 men supported by a diversionary group of the light carrier *Ryujo*, a heavy cruiser and eleven destroyers.

The extraordinary imbalance between this tiny force, which was based on a refusal to believe that the enemy had managed to land more than a handful of troops on Guadalcanal, and a naval force amounting to most of the Combined Fleet can be accounted for only by a possible decision to try once more to break the power of the United States Navy in the area.

American reconnaissance aircraft soon detected these preparations and Admiral Ghormley set up three task forces to meet the threat based on his three carriers, two of

which took part in the subsequent battle. They were Admiral Fletcher's Task Force F, which included the carrier *Saratoga*, cruisers *Minneapolis* and *New Orleans* and five destroyers; and Rear-Admiral Thomas C. Kinkaid's Task Force K—the carrier *Enterprise*, the battleship *North Carolina*, the cruisers *Atlanta* and *Portland* and five destroyers. Admiral Leigh Noyes' Task Force N, with the carrier *Wasp*, was ordered south by Admiral Fletcher to refuel and was too distant to participate. Land-based aircraft and submarines on both sides were ready. Kinkaid's *Enterprise* Force and Fletcher's *Saratoga* operated some ten miles apart, each surrounded by a warship screen with a radius of one mile. Fighter aircraft direction was controlled from the *Enterprise*.

Yamamoto's operational plan involved a

Above: The American cruiser *Quincy*, which sank in Ironbottom Sound on 8 August 1942 after the surprise Japanese night attack.

Opposite, top: The Japanese battleship *Kirishima*, flagship of Vice-Admiral Kondo, became the target of a storm of 16-inch shells from the *Washington* during the night of 14–15 November 1942. Her engines and boilers were knocked out and fire spread from stem to stern. She was abandoned and scuttled in the early hours of the morning.

Opposite, bottom: US Marines patrol ground surrounding Henderson Field, the vital Guadalcanal airstrip.

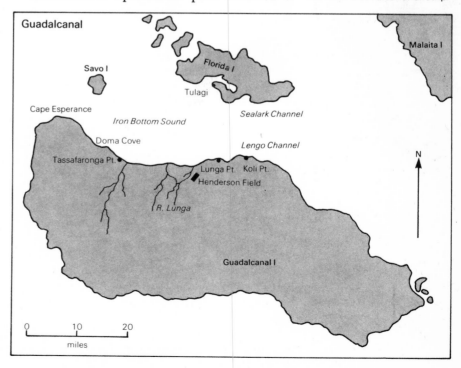

feint attack by Rear-Admiral Tadaichi Hara's Diversionary Group—the light carrier *Ryujo* with 27 aircraft, the cruiser *Tone* and two destroyers—which was intended to draw off the aircraft from the enemy carriers while those from the *Zuikaku* and *Shokaku* hit the *Enterprise* and *Saratoga* during a first cruiser bombardment. This was to be followed by an attack on Henderson Field by Hara's 1,500 troops from the transports.

It was a good plan, which almost succeeded. An American reconnaissance aircraft sighted the enemy transports and their protective cruisers and destroyers about 350 miles north on a course for Guadalcanal at 9.50 am on 23 August, when Fletcher's task forces were about 145 miles east-north-east of Guadalcanal. A force of 37 aircraft took off from *Saratoga* at 2.45 pm, followed an hour later by 23 of the Marines' aircraft from Guadalcanal. After several hours' search through holes in the rain clouds, all the aircraft returned without having had as much as a glimpse of Tanaka's force—in fact he had reversed course to the north-west and taken himself out of range of enemy bombers.

At dawn next day the *Ryujo* diversionary group, stationed far ahead of the rest of the Combined Fleet, led it towards Guadalcanal, and shortly after 9 am a Wildcat pilot reported it 280 miles north-west of Fletcher's force. When enemy aircraft from the *Ryujo* made an ineffective attack on Henderson Field, Fletcher committed most of his air strength against this carrier, only to receive reports soon after of the main enemy force with its two carriers.

Poor communications prevented Fletcher's attempt to divert the strike from the *Ryujo* to the main force. He therefore prepared his remaining 54 Wildcats, some aloft on combat air patrol and the remainder on deck fuelled and ready.

Meanwhile, two search aircraft from *Enterrise* had attacked the *Shokaku* at 3.15 pm, but inflicted only minor damage. Then half an hour later the main strike hit the *Ryujo* with bombs and torpedoes, setting her aflame and causing her to be abandoned. She sank later, but the Japanese had succeeded in their strategy of drawing Fletcher's air strength away from the main force.

A powerful strike force had left the grey decks of *Shokaku* and *Zuikaku* nearly an hour before the attack on *Ryujo*, and at 4.25 pm Fletcher's radar located a force of 36 bombers at 12,000 feet. In less than five minutes the bombs began to shower down around the carrier *Enterprise* despite a powerful anti-aircraft barrage put up by the battleship *North Carolina*, the cruisers and destroyers.

During the fifteen-minute attack three bombs hit the *Enterprise*, killing 74 men, wounding 95, wrecking her 5-inch guns, holing her flight deck and setting her afire; but the damage was not serious and in less than an hour the flames were under control. Then, just as the enemy's second strike was expected, her steering-engines failed, her rudder jammed and for half an hour, until nearly 6 pm, when the trouble was repaired, she swung round in a circle. Fortunately, the enemy strike failed to locate her and in due course the aircraft returned to their carriers. Soon the *Enterprise*'s deck was repaired, and she was able to launch aircraft and steam at 24 knots. Meanwhile, dive-bombers from *Saratoga* hit and damaged an enemy seaplane carrier.

Now that *Enterprise* was operational again, Fletcher—with that eagerness to safeguard his carriers for which he was known—decided to steam south out of the area to refuel and let the action go for the rest of the day. The *Ryujo* was most likely sunk and more than a hundred enemy aircraft had been shot down for the loss of only 17 of his own. Prudently, he had no wish to involve his force in a night battle with Nagumo's more powerful force of battleships and cruisers.

At 4.30 pm Nagumo's second-in-command, Vice-Admiral Kondo, had led his Advance Force and the Vanguard Group, making a powerful force of two battleships, ten cruisers and a number of destroyers, on a course at high speed for Fletcher's position. But at 11.30 pm, after searching in line abreast with ships some ten kilometres apart and seaplanes ahead, no sighting had been made—Fletcher's

force was by then far to the south—and Kondo called the search off and turned north.

Only the enemy Transport Group, with the tenacious Rear-Admiral Tanaka in the light cruiser *Jintsu*, pushed on defiantly through the night towards Guadalcanal and the landing which should have been a walkover, if all had gone according to plan. But at 9.35 pm the Transport Group was sighted about 135 miles north of the island by Lieutenant-Colonel Mangrum's eight dive-bombers from Henderson Field. They hit the *Jintsu* and set the transport *Kinryu Maru* ablaze; later, B-17 bombers sank the destroyer *Mutsuki*.

This brought an end to the battle of the Eastern Solomons, with an enemy failure to retake Guadalcanal and losses of aircraft and pilots so heavy that until reinforcements were received more big attacks there were impossible.

The Battle of Cape Esperance, 11–12 October 1942

The indecisive Eastern Solomons battle simply confirmed the tactical situation in the seas around Guadalcanal: the Americans' air strength gave them sea mastery in daylight, when they could land men, supplies and weapons; after dark Japanese cruiser strength and their night-fighting ability came into its own and gave them supremacy, which they then used to build up their forces and supply dumps by sea.

It was stalemate which neither side desired.

Continual skirmishing between the Marines and enemy infantry for domination of the island now went on, as the Japanese tried to drive towards the vital Henderson Field. This culminated in the Battle of Bloody Ridge on 12–14 September, when after a heavy attack on American positions near the airfield, the Japanese were driven back with nearly 1,500 killed.

During this period the Japanese gained the upper hand in the naval struggle. On 14 September, when the carrier *Wasp*, and the new battleship *North Carolina*, with attendant cruisers and destroyers, were escorting transports bringing in the 7th Marine Regiment to Guadalcanal, enemy submarines torpedoed the *Wasp*, and then hit the *North Carolina* and a destroyer. The transports turned off to the north and got out of the danger area, but flames swept the *Wasp* and soon afterwards she was abandoned, having lost heavily in killed and wounded. The *North Carolina* was easily able to absorb the damage inflicted upon her, while the destroyer was saved and the Marines were safely landed on Guadalcanal four days later. The Japanese navy seemed more aggressive than their army.

Then, on 9 October, General Hyakutake landed on the island with orders to step up the fighting. Two days later a force of converted destroyers bringing in troops, heavy guns and ammunition entered the 'Slot'—the narrow inside channel between the Western and Eastern Solomons—escorted by a force of heavy cruisers. This latter force comprised a

Flames from the US Navy transport *John Penn*, disembarking reinforcements, light up the horizon off Lunga Beach, Guadalcanal, after a Japanese torpedo hit her amidships during a night attack.

bombardment group of three heavy cruisers and two destroyers, with a reinforcement group of two seaplane carriers and six destroyers carrying men and guns; they were under the command of Rear-Admiral Arimoto Goto.

Rear-Admiral Norman Scott's Task Force 64—two heavy cruisers, two light cruisers and five destroyers—was patrolling the waters between Tulagi and Guadalcanal as the enemy force approached on 11 October. A night battle now became inevitable; Scott was prepared for it and determined to try to end the enemy's long-established night-time freedom of the seas in the area.

At 10.28 pm Goto's force was about 50 miles north-west of Savo Island, approaching at about 26 knots on a smooth sea in a dark night with slightly overcast sky and new moon. Goto, in his flagship *Aoba*, led the cruisers in a 'T' formation, with a destroyer on each beam. At this time Scott was steaming around the western coast of Guadalcanal, about three miles north of Cape Esperance, after which, at 10.28 pm, he changed course to

head directly towards Savo Island and deployed into line ahead, with the destroyers *Farenholt*, *Duncan* and *Laffey* in the van, the cruisers *San Francisco* (flagship), *Boise*, *Salt Lake City* and *Helena* in the centre, and the destroyers *Buchanan* and *McCalla* astern; there was an average distance of 600 yards between each ship. At 11.8 pm Scott changed course to pass six miles west of Savo.

The cruiser *Helena* first contacted the enemy by radar at 11.25 pm, when they were fourteen miles away, but unfortunately she failed to report this to Admiral Scott for fifteen minutes. But having been told earlier by scout aircraft that the enemy force was approaching, Scott decided to continue patrolling the key stretch of water between Cape Esperance and Savo Island. This necessitated a turn to the south-west, and at 10.32 pm he signalled an order for his ships to reverse course in succession, but during this time-consuming manoeuvre he learned at last from the *Helena* that the enemy was only six miles away.

It was alarming news, for Captain Robert Tobin, the destroyer squadron commander,

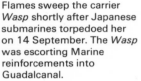

Flames sweep the carrier *Wasp* shortly after Japanese submarines torpedoed her on 14 September. The *Wasp* was escorting Marine reinforcements into Guadalcanal.

had carried out the turn in a separate movement ahead and north-east of the cruisers, intending then to move up and subsequently to take station at the head of the column. But when the turn was half complete, the centre destroyer, *Duncan*, had sighted the enemy on radar four miles off, assumed that the *Farenholt*, ahead, was closing them and rushed off at 30 knots to attack.

Soon Scott's battle line was dangerously disordered—and with a powerful enemy only about four miles north-west. His cruisers and the rear destroyers were in line, while the *Farenholt* and *Laffey* were between him and the enemy some 800 yards to starboard; the *Duncan* was closing the enemy alone. But Admiral Goto's force was approaching them supremely confident that it had not been detected and as unready for battle as the Americans had been at Savo Island in August.

The *Helena* fired first, at 11.47 pm, followed by the *Salt Lake City*. The night was suddenly lit by star shell as their projectiles slammed into the enemy cruisers; but the destroyers *Duncan* and *Laffey* were now in the line of fire. *Laffey* turned hard to try to move in behind the *Helena*, hitting the flagship *Aoba* with shells from three of her 5-inch guns as she did so.

In the confusion of gunfire, smoke and star shell, Admiral Scott thought that his cruisers were firing on the *Farenholt* and *Laffey*, and a minute after firing had begun ordered his cruisers to cease fire. But only the unfortunate *Duncan* was dangerously placed in the line of fire from both forces; shells hit her on both port and starboard sides, one plunging

Admiral Daniel J. Callaghan's flagship, the cruiser *San Francisco*, was severely damaged by enemy shells in the night action on 13 November in Ironbottom Sound, Callaghan being killed. Though fitted with radar, *San Francisco* failed to detect the approaching enemy force.

131

into the boiler room, others into an ammunition handling room, starting fires and crippling her.

By sheer good luck Scott had crossed the enemy's 'T' in the darkness, and as the American shells enfiladed the Japanese line Admiral Goto signalled a turn to the right in succession. In the event, some turned right, with the cruiser *Kinugasa* and a destroyer turning left, but as each ship reached the turning point they came under heavy fire, for the American cruisers had been slow to respond to Scott's order to cease fire. The *Aoba* was hit by some 40 shells, splinters from which struck down Admiral Goto; the *Fubuki* was sunk before she could finish the turn, and the cruiser *Furutaka* was set ablaze and sank shortly afterwards.

Four minutes after ordering the cease-fire Scott countermanded it, and at 11.55 pm he turned north-west to chase the Japanese, who were now in retreat. The *Aoba*, burning fiercely, but still firing, hit the cruiser *Boise* just before she was hit by 8-inch shells from the *Kinugasa*, which penetrated ammunition stores, tore No. 1 gun turret apart and incinerated the gun crews to a man. Only sea water flooding in through the torn hull saved the *Boise* from destruction by the fire which swept her.

Firing stopped at 12.20 am as the Japanese raced away to the north-west. They had paid for the battle with the loss of a cruiser and a destroyer (a second destroyer was sunk by carrier aircraft next day). They had also lost Admiral Goto, who lay dead in his cabin on the heavily damaged *Aoba*.

The American destroyer *Farenholt* survived, despite the shelling she had taken from both Japanese and American guns, but the *Duncan* had paid for her audacious dash alone

against the enemy line. One shell burst in the chart room, killing everyone there, splinters from another tore into every man on the bridge, while still more wrecked the radar, gunnery plotting and radio rooms, killing or wounding everyone present as fierce uncontrollable fires spread throughout the ship. She was abandoned at 2 am and 195 officers and men were picked up by the *McCalla*.

But while Admiral Goto's force had kept Scott's Task Force occupied, Admiral Joshima had landed two 150 mm howitzers, two field guns, an anti-aircraft gun, some 700 troops and assorted supplies at Tassafaronga, eastwards along the coast, and thus had accomplished the main objective of strengthening the Japanese army on Guadalcanal. The very next night, 12 October, these new guns were employed in a heavy bombardment of the hard-pressed Marines at Henderson Field. Both on land and at sea the crucial battles for Guadalcanal were yet to come.

The Battle of Santa Cruz, 25 October 1942

Admiral Yamamoto was still firmly resolved to throw the Americans off Guadalcanal. In September, at a conference with General Hyakutake and other army chiefs, and Admiral Kusaka, successor to Inoue as C-in-C of the South-Eastern Fleet, he had named 21 October 1942 as the date for an all-out combined attack. Out of the endless fighting ashore, afloat and in the air, three main actions were accordingly launched: the battle of Santa Cruz at sea and in the air on 25 October 1942, and the crucial battle ashore on 25–26 October. Meanwhile, every blow that the Japanese struck brought them a step nearer this crucial encounter.

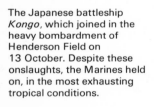

The Japanese battleship *Kongo*, which joined in the heavy bombardment of Henderson Field on 13 October. Despite these onslaughts, the Marines held on, in the most exhausting tropical conditions.

Henderson Field, the home of more than 90 of the bombers and fighters which had sunk or damaged Japanese ships and carriers, bore the weight of the first blows which were to herald the 25 October attack. From 13 to 17 October aircraft and warships pounded the Marines' defences and the airfield itself, supported by shells from the two big new howitzers.

On 13 October 24 bombers pounded the airfield, followed two hours later by a further fifteen. At 1am the battleships *Kongo* and *Haruna*, screened by a cruiser and five destroyers, fired several hundred 14-inch shells in earth-shaking salvoes which set ablaze fuel dumps and aircraft, shattered storehouses, command posts and flight control buildings. When they withdrew at 2.30am, almost all the aviation fuel there had been exploded, only 42 aircraft out of 90 were operational, 41 men had been killed and many others wounded. Two more air raids that day put Henderson Field out of action, except for a grass strip which only fighters could use. And on the night of 14–15 October two enemy cruisers slammed another 750 8-inch shells into the Field and its installations.

On 15 October six enemy transports were disembarking troops and supplies for General Hyakutake in broad daylight, screened by destroyers and protected by Zekes. Every available American aircraft in the region was hurled into an attack on the transports. Three of the transports were destroyed and beached, while three pulled off before they were fully unloaded.

The US Navy was stretched to the utmost at this time, while the Anglo-American landings in North Africa were in full swing and receiving priority. 'It now appears', declared Admiral Nimitz in a heartfelt report, 'that we are unable to control the sea in the Guadal-canal area. Thus our supply of the positions will only be done at great expense to us. The situation is not hopeless, but it is certainly critical'.

Changes followed quickly. On 18 October Vice-Admiral William F. Halsey took over from Vice-Admiral Ghormley as C-in-C of the South Pacific Fleet and the effects of his more aggressive leadership were soon felt. In addition, on President Roosevelt's insistence a task group which included the new battleship *Indiana* steamed down through the Panama Canal and proceeded at high speed to the South Pacific. As well as the *Indiana* the group included some 50 Army fighter aircraft, 24 B-17 Flying Fortresses, another 24 submarines, the carrier *Enterprise*, fully repaired after the battering she had taken on 24 August at the Eastern Solomons battle, and the US 25th Infantry Division.

Meanwhile, Halsey, still desperately short of aircraft carriers, reorganized his two available carriers into two task forces with one carrier in each, under the overall command of Rear-Admiral Thomas C. Kinkaid, who personally commanded the *Enterprise* group, Task Force 16, which included the battleship *South Dakota*, the heavy cruiser *Portland*, the anti-aircraft cruiser *San Juan* and eight destroyers; Rear-Admiral George D. Murray's Task Force 17 comprised the carrier *Hornet*, two heavy cruisers, two anti-aircraft cruisers and six destroyers.

Admiral Yamamoto's Combined Fleet consisted of an Advance Force, under Vice-Admiral Kondo, with two fast battleships, *Kongo* and *Haruna*, the carrier *Junyo* and 45 aircraft, six heavy cruisers and a destroyer squadron; and a Striking Force, under Nagumo, which included three carriers with 157 aircraft of the 3rd (Air) Fleet, four heavy

The Japanese battleship *Haruna*, which fired a stream of 14-inch shells into American positions on Henderson Field on the night of 13 October during another Japanese attempt to seize this vital position. Aviation fuel was exploded and only 42 aircraft were left undamaged.

cruisers and twelve destroyers. More than 220 aircraft were also available at Rabaul and a number of submarines took station where they could be most effective.

An order from Imperial Headquarters regulated the sequence of Japanese operations leading up to the battles of 25–26 October. This order, quoted in Morison's *History* stated: 'After reinforcement of Army forces has been completed, Army and Navy forces will combine and in one action attack and retake Guadalcanal Island airfield. During this operation the Navy will take all necessary action to halt the efforts of the enemy to augment his forces in the Solomons Area.'

The Japanese plans provided for the capture of Henderson Field by General Maruyama's troops by 22 October. On 19 October they attacked with tanks and infantry against the Marines' defensive positions around Henderson Field. The attack reached its climax in a fierce night encounter in the surrounding woods and jungle on 23–24 October. The Marines held fast, but in face of new attacks by reinforcements were forced to pull back temporarily to Lunga Ridge. Later they regained their position after hand-to-hand fighting in darkness and torrential rain. The failure of the Japanese to take Henderson Field was the peak of the fighting on land and thereafter it died down. The Japanese had lost 3,500 dead, but despite this failure a naval battle was inevitable.

Admiral Kinkaid's Task Forces 16 and 17 received news of two enemy carriers at midday on 25 October, when the Japanese were north-west of the Santa Cruz Islands and the American Task Forces were 360 miles away from them in a position west of the Islands. Kinkaid launched a strike force of 29 bombers and 12 search aircraft, but the strike failed to locate its target because the Japanese temporarily reversed course northward.

The 16-inch-gun *South Dakota*, which narrowly escaped destruction in the night battle of Guadalcanal on 14 November. A power failure closed down her radar, causing her to lose contact with her sister ships and steam within range of 14 enemy vessels, which put nearly all her gunnery control stations out of action before she was able to move away.

Kinkaid steamed north-west through the night of 25–26 October, keeping aircraft on the *Hornet* available for an immediate night strike, and at 6.50 am he received a report from search aircraft that Nagumo's carriers were barely 200 miles north-west. Fifty minutes later, at 7.40 am, two more search aircraft hit the carrier *Zuiho* with 500-lb bombs and holed the flight deck, but this carrier's aircraft had already flown off to attack Kinkaid's group.

Nagumo, resolved to be first to strike in an encounter in which every second counted, launched his first strike at 6.10 am and at once made ready for the next strike. Twenty minutes later, at 6.30 am, *Hornet* launched 29 dive-bombers, torpedo-bombers and fighters, and *Enterprise* launched another 19 half an hour later. The *Hornet*'s aircraft passed the enemy flight some 60 miles out at 17,000 feet, without fighters on either side interfering, but

when *Enterprise*'s aircraft appeared the Zekes attacked and shot down eight of them for the loss of two Zekes. It was an unfortunate beginning.

Radar location of the approaching Japanese aircraft was received on the American carriers at 8.57 am—the Japanese were 45 miles away and still at 17,000 feet. *Enterprise*, some ten miles away from *Hornet*, was hidden in a tropical rain storm and so escaped the strike; *Hornet*'s combat air patrol was flying at 22,000 feet, and was so near that in an attack on the enemy aircraft the Wildcats were likely to be hit by anti-aircraft fire from the cruisers and destroyers. At 9.10 am the enemy dive-bombers plummeted out of the high cumulus clouds in almost vertical dives through a curtain of shell bursts.

During the next sixty seconds, one bomb hit *Hornet*'s flight deck, a Kamikaze dive-bomber struck the smokestack and rico-chetted on to the flight deck, where its bombs exploded, and two torpedoes tore into her hull and burst in the engine room. Power and communications were lost, and as the stricken carrier slowed to a standstill in a cloud of smoke three more bombs tore deep into her and exploded, causing considerable damage. The enemy then pulled off, having lost 25 aircraft, but leaving the *Hornet* as good as finished. She was abandoned and later was sunk.

As this action ended, Lieutenant James E. Vose led eleven bombers of the American strike in an attack on the *Shokaku* which hit her with several 1,000-lb bombs, set her ablaze, crumpled and tore her flight deck, folded her aircraft hangars, but still failed to sink her. The rest of *Hornet*'s strike failed to locate the carriers, but damaged the cruiser *Chikuma* and unsuccessfully attacked the cruiser *Tone*.

Another enemy strike from *Zuikaku* and *Junyo* now located *Enterprise* and dived down for the kill through a barrage of anti-aircraft fire from the battleship *South Dakota* and other ships, which sent 26 Japanese aircraft down in flames. But three bombs hit the carrier, killing 44 and wounding 31 officers and men shortly before she successfully turned into the wakes of four torpedoes. Then for some 40 minutes crews of repairmen worked hard to clear the decks for her return-ing aircraft and *Hornet*'s. Her fate was still uncertain, for suddenly, at about 11.20, about twenty bombers from *Junyo* emerged from low cloud to loose bombs which just missed and slightly damaged the forward turret on the battleship *South Dakota*. The enemy then turned away, leaving another ten aircraft at the bottom of the sea. Later, an enemy sub-marine torpedoed the destroyer *Porter* and sent her to the bottom.

In this dramatic picture, taken in the Cape Esperance action off Guadalcanal on 12 October, one Japanese bomb has hit the carrier *Hornet*'s flight deck, two torpedoes have struck home deep inside her, and a suicide bomber dives down to hit and explode amidships. Minutes later, as she lay stationary, three more bombs tore through her decks. She sank with heavy losses early on 27 October.

Kinkaid, with one carrier lost, the other badly damaged and the firepower of a battleship reduced, ordered a general withdrawal. Attempts by two American destroyers to torpedo and sink *Hornet* after she had been abandoned failed, and at 1.35 am on 27 October enemy torpedoes blew the blazing hulk apart. Later that afternoon, the entire enemy force was ordered to retire to its base at Truk.

The fourth carrier battle in six months, the engagement at Santa Cruz was indecisive. The *Hornet* was lost, *Shokaku* and *Zuiho* had to return to Japan for several weeks for repairs, but worst of all for the Japanese was the loss of 100 bomber and fighter aircraft and their trained pilots. And they had to face these losses after an engagement the sole purpose of which was to exploit a victory by the army which never took place. It was a decisive setback to Japanese hopes and plans, but Imperial Headquarters still believed Japan could break the power of the United States Navy and planned to try again in November.

The Battle of Guadalcanal, 12–15 November 1942

Both the United States and Japan exerted themselves to the utmost in November to strengthen their forces ashore in the muddy and oppressive jungles, bracing themselves for the final battle for control of the island which both knew must come. Between 2 and 10 November 1942 the Japanese navy landed in western Guadalcanal troops from two cruisers and 65 destroyers—moreover, the well-equipped Hiroshima Division, intended for the overland attack on Port Moresby, New Guinea, was on its way to Guadalcanal, the

island of bitter deadlock. The Japanese hoped to land this division east of Cape Esperance so as to be able to launch a simultaneous attack from both sides of the island.

American reinforcements also reached Guadalcanal at the end of October and in early November. They included a regiment of 155 mm artillery on 30 October, four transports loaded with troops and three attack cargo ships bringing in more troops, ammunition and supplies, the last of which arrived just in time on 12 November.

Once again, the Japanese Combined Fleet would be at hand to support the landing of the Hiroshima Division, to exploit their expected successes ashore and to prevent interference by the United States Navy with the landings. Admiral Halsey was aware that this force probably consisted of two carriers, four battleships, five heavy cruisers, two light cruisers, thirty destroyers and the eleven transports of Rear-Admiral Raizo Tanaka's Reinforcement Group. Losses during the Guadalcanal campaign had cut the number of carrier-borne aircraft available to 95, but over 200 bombers, based at Rabaul, were ready.

As always in this campaign, Admiral Halsey could only field a smaller force, consisting of two new battleships, *South Dakota* and *Washington*, four heavy and four light cruisers, 22 destroyers and—if she was repaired in time—the carrier *Enterprise* and 78 aircraft. Much depended upon her arrival, but in case she failed to arrive, more land-based fighters, bombers and torpedo-bombers were made available at Guadalcanal, Fiji and Espiritu Santo. Under Admiral Halsey, the American naval forces were organized as four task forces.

The preliminary moves leading up to the battle began on 12 November, soon after American reinforcements in four transports, covered by Rear-Admiral Daniel J. Callaghan's Support Group of four heavy cruisers and ten destroyers, started disembarking at 5.40 am. Warning was given of an enemy air strike just after noon; the transports and cargo ships stopped unloading and made off in anti-aircraft formation. After the raid, in which Wildcats from Henderson Field shot down a number of enemy bombers, the transports returned to complete unloading. Then during the afternoon came reports of powerful enemy forces, including two carriers, two battleships or cruisers and a number of destroyers, approaching from 250 to 335 miles to the north-west on a course for Guadalcanal.

Admiral Kinkaid's Task Force 16—*Enterprise* and two battleships—was sailing for the island, but was clearly too far off to help. Callaghan therefore escorted the transports out to sea, leaving them with two destroyers to escort them on to comparative safety at Esperitu Santo, then calmly prepared for battle with the greatly superior Japanese force.

This was composed of eleven transports, bringing the 13,000 men of the Hiroshima Division, escorted by eleven destroyers; ahead of the transports steamed a powerful Raiding Group under Vice-Admiral Hiroaki Abe—two battleships, *Hiei* and *Kirishima*, the light cruiser *Nagara*, and fourteen destroyers assigned the task of bombarding and destroying Henderson Field in a lightning attack. On a calm sea and under a dark sky occasionally covered by cloud Abe's force approached Savo Island at midnight, anticipating that, as usual,

they would enjoy the freedom of the seas at night.

Admiral Callaghan, known to his men as 'Uncle Dan', had ordered his ships into line-ahead formation, with four destroyers in the van, followed by four cruisers—the anti-aircraft cruiser *Atlanta*, flagship of Rear-Admiral Norman Scott, plus two destroyers had been added to Callaghan's force—then another four destroyers astern. Callaghan evidently chose this formation because he believed it made communication simpler at night, but unfortunately the disposition of his ships neutralized his most important asset for a night encounter—radar. *Atlanta*, equipped with obsolete radar, preceded the cruisers and destroyers, which were equipped with longer-range search radar. Inevitably, this misuse of vital equipment, which the Japanese lacked altogether, would cost Scott dear.

At 1.30 am on 13 November 1942 the two opposing forces approached each other in Ironbottom Sound a few miles east of Cape Esperance at a combined speed of more than 40 knots, with about 14,000 yards between them. Callaghan, thanks to his radar, now had a supreme chance of quick victory. Properly applied it would have given him a precise indication of the enemy dispositions and position, so that his gunnery officers could unleash a stream of shells and torpedoes before the enemy were aware of their presence. But *San Francisco*, Callaghan's flagship, was in the van, equipped only with short-range, ineffectual radar; as a result Scott had to rely on the cruiser *Helena*, two ships behind him, for information from her long-range radar transmitted by voice radio—and on the same channel as that used for tactical control.

The *Washington*, one of America's newest battleships in 1942, sank the Japanese battleship *Kirishima* with nine 16-inch shells on 14 November, during the battle of Guadalcanal.

It was an absurd and regrettable situation. The outcome was that a great chance slipped by, and Callaghan's leading destroyer suddenly sighted two enemy destroyers leading the enemy line so as to cross the American 'T' barely 3,000 yards ahead. A confused and destructive action lasting 24 minutes followed this clumsy encounter.

Led by Lieutenant-Commander Parker in *Cushing*, the leading destroyer, the American line turned left to avoid colliding while the enemy ships at first continued on course; as a result they were placed on both the port and starboard bows of the American line. Enemy searchlights fell on *Atlanta* just after she opened fire. At once she became the main target of the leading enemy ships. Shells tore into her bridge, killing in this first salvo Admiral Scott and most of his staff. While *Atlanta* was still returning fire, two enemy torpedoes exploded in her vitals, crippled her and set her on fire.

In Morison's words, 'Japanese and American ships mingled like minnows in a bucket'. The destruction was appalling. The destroyer *Laffey*, almost blown apart by two point-blank salvoes from the battleship *Hiei*, was abandoned, but the *Hiei* herself was battered and set afire by a hail of 85 shells from the American ships. A torpedo tore into the cruiser *Portland*'s stern and blew part of it away. *San Francisco* was swept by shells from the enemy battleship *Kirishima* which killed Callaghan, Captain Young, and most of their staffs and damaged the engine and steering gear. The cruiser *Juneau* took a torpedo which blew up her forward stokehold, stopped her and put her out of action. The destroyer *Cushing* was crippled, *Barton* was blown to pieces, *Laffey* was sunk, *Sterret* and *O'Bannon* were damaged, and *Monssen* was abandoned when the blaze on board grew too fierce to handle.

At 2 am, as the action died away, Admiral Abe ordered his surviving ships to steam out of the action and thereafter the firing slowly petered out. The destruction of Henderson Field had been prevented, but the price was high—the lives of two American admirals, Scott and Callaghan, several hundred officers and men, three destroyers sunk, three badly damaged, and two cruisers crippled.

A grim sight presented itself to the noise-stunned survivors, noted Morison: 'Dotting the horizon were the dull red glows of smoldering hulls, now obscured by dense masses of smoke, now blazing up when uncontrolled fires reached new combustibles. The sea itself, fouled with oil and flotsam, tortured by underwater upheavals, rose in geysers from shell explosions.'

The enemy had lost two cruisers, *Yudachi* and *Akatsuki*, and the next morning torpedo-bombers from Kinkaid's carrier *Enterprise*, which had at last reached the area, hit and sank the battleship *Hiei*, near Tulagi. The *Cushing* and *Monssen* continued to burn, then sank during the afternoon, and the crippled *Atlanta* was scuttled in the evening. There was worse to come. The next morning, the cruiser *Juneau*, on her way to base at the New Hebrides with the *San Francisco* and three destroyers, was hit and sunk by an enemy torpedo. All but ten of her crew went down with her, nearly 700 officers and men. 'Friday the Bloody Thirteenth' was the name given by American sailors to this grim and costly night action.

Hopes of the defenders of Henderson Field, however, that the previous day's losses would discourage the enemy from further bombardments of the air strip were dashed. Under the cover of darkness, Vice-Admiral Mikawa's Support Group of cruisers and destroyers stealthily approached Savo Island just before midnight on 13 November. Mikawa patrolled

Japanese torpedo-bombers fly into the attack a few feet above the waves to avoid the furious screen of anti-aircraft fire put up by American warships.

west of Savo, while Rear-Admiral Nishimura's bombardment unit—two heavy cruisers, a light cruiser and four destroyers—blasted the airfield with 8-inch shells for about 37 minutes, destroying 17 fighters and a dive-bomber, and damaging another 32 fighters.

It was a grave setback, in view of the further enemy blows known to be on their way, but the balance of losses was evened at 8am on 14 November, when torpedo- and dive-bombers from *Enterprise* and Henderson Field attacked Mikawa's fleeing cruisers 140 miles north-west of Guadalcanal, holing the cruiser *Kinugasa*, and damaging the light cruiser *Isuzu*. *Kinugasa* was finally sunk two or three hours later, by Lieutenant-Commander James R. Lee's bombers.

The crucial period of the battle now neared. Rear-Admiral Raizo Tanaka's Reinforcement Group of twelve transports, packed with troops of the Hiroshima Division and escorted by twelve destroyers, was sighted approaching from the north-west. According to the Japanese plan, Henderson Field and every aircraft on it should by now have been destroyed by the battleship and cruiser bombardment. The Japanese were convinced that the *Enterprise* was still out of action and therefore did not anticipate the intervention of carrier aircraft.

Tanaka hoped to disembark these new troops west of the airfield for the encirclement operation that would finally crush the Americans, but at 11am bombers suddenly began attacks on his ships with 1,000-lb bombs. The attacks continued with little respite throughout the day, and by early evening Tanaka had lost seven transports with all their supplies, although he had managed to take off several hundred men from each on to his destroyers.

Despite these heavy losses, the Japanese were this time resolved not to flinch and turn back, but to press on and land their reinforcements at all costs. Vice-Admiral Kondo, with

the battleship *Kirishima*, two heavy and two light cruisers and a squadron of destroyers, raced south to support Tanaka's remaining transports and to pulverize Henderson Field, the mission in which Admiral Abe had failed.

But Rear-Admiral Augustus Lee's Task Force 64—the battleships *Washington* and *South Dakota* and four destroyers—which had been waiting about a hundred miles south-west of Guadalcanal for just this eventuality, now raced north-east to intercept Kondo. By the early evening of 14 November it was some nine miles west of the Guadalcanal coast, steaming in a flat calm sea in line ahead with the four destroyers leading the battleships *Washington* and the *South Dakota*, both of which were equipped with 16-inch guns.

The enemy cruiser *Sendai*, the leading ship in the Japanese force, sighted Lee's Task Force at 11.10pm as it was steaming into Ironbottom Sound, north of Savo Island. It headed towards the enemy with the *Shikinami*. Only a few minutes later the US force detected *Sendai* by radar, nine miles away to the north-west. Both *Washington* and *South Dakota* opened fire, but the *Sendai* escaped slowly in a smoke screen.

Once again American tactical control and use of radar was faulty, for not until six minutes later did they attack, and with guns instead of torpedoes. The enemy reacted quickly with both gunfire and torpedoes. Within minutes *Walke*, *Preston*, *Gwin* and *Benham*—all four US destroyers—were seriously damaged and put out of action without launching a single torpedo, while only one enemy destroyer was damaged.

The battle now turned into a joust between the two American battleships, with the *Washington* taking the principal part, and the fourteen enemy vessels. Owing to an electric power failure, the *South Dakota* lost track of the *Washington* and, temporarily lacking radar,

This dramatic photograph shows a Japanese torpedo-bomber hit by American anti-aircraft fire off Guadalcanal. The aircraft's torpedo falls in flames harmlessly into the sea.

closed on the enemy ships, at once receiving a hail of shells in her superstructure. This bombardment enabled *Washington* to detect the battleship *Kirishima*. Nine 16-inch shells out of 75 fired by *Washington* tore into *Kirishima*, damaging her steering gear and her engines, setting her ablaze and knocking her out of the action. She was abandoned and scuttled at 3.20 am.

While the *South Dakota*, with her gunnery control stations nearly all out of action, moved away at full speed to the south, *Washington* pursued the enemy to the north, until at 25 minutes after midnight Kondo ordered a general withdrawal. At about 4 am Tanaka, tenacious and crafty as ever, grounded his transports off Tassafaronga and managed to disembark 2,000 troops there.

The battle of Guadalcanal was decisive both in the struggle for control of the island and in the Pacific War as a whole. Japan had lost two battleships, *Hiei* and *Kirishima*, as well as eleven transports and several thousand trained infantry in their unsuccessful efforts to reinforce their army on the island. She had also lost heavily in aircraft, and although the United States had lost more fighting ships, she could replace them quickly and with relative ease compared to Japan.

The United States Navy, despite costly tactical errors in battle, had in fact won command of the seas in East Asia and, most important, her officers and men were convinced that they

had. Ashore, however, the Marines were still more or less under siege at Henderson Field, facing mortar fire from three sides and hanging on to their precarious hold as best they could. The Japanese, despite their failure to throw the Americans out of Guadalcanal, were not yet ready to withdraw from it themselves; therefore they were compelled to reinforce the garrison there. It led to the final encounter and their eventual withdrawal.

The Battle of Tassafaronga, 30 November 1942

Admiral Halsey had received information that Admiral Tanaka, with a force of eight destroyers escorting six transports, was likely to enter Ironbottom Sound during the night of 30 November. He ordered Rear-Admiral Carleton H. Wright, commander of Task Force 67, who, for reasons which are not entirely clear, had replaced the able and experienced Rear-Admiral Thomas Kinkaid as commander of the cruiser force which had been formed at Espiritu Santo, to intercept Tanaka's task force.

At 10.45 pm on 30 November, Wright's force cruised past Henderson Field towards Savo while Tanaka's steamed towards it in a southerly direction from the west. Wright had four destroyers ahead of his five cruisers —though not far enough ahead to be able to act as scouts and send him information—and two destroyers in the rear. Tanaka's force was

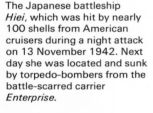

The Japanese battleship *Hiei*, which was hit by nearly 100 shells from American cruisers during a night attack on 13 November 1942. Next day she was located and sunk by torpedo-bombers from the battle-scarred carrier *Enterprise*.

simply eight destroyers carrying troops and supplies in line ahead, except for the *Takanami* on the port bow of his flagship, the destroyer *Naganami*. At fifteen minutes after midnight they were two miles off the coast, moving east at fourteen knots.

At 12.16pm Wright's leading destroyer, *Fletcher*, under Commander Cole, detected the Japanese by radar; they were to port, 7,000 yards away, and Cole asked permission to fire torpedoes. Now occurred a fatal delay, a tactical error disastrous in its effects. Instead of authorizing immediate independent torpedo firing at the approaching enemy, Wright hesitated and fumbled for four valuable minutes before giving the order, and thus lost the chance of destroying the still unsuspecting enemy.

He then ordered his ships, cruisers and destroyers to open fire. The flashes and noise of their guns at once alerted the enemy and Admiral Tanaka immediately ordered all his ships to carry out a reverse turn to the right at full speed, while firing torpedoes. The first in the line, *Takanami*, got her torpedoes away, but became the target for numerous American guns, was crippled, set afire and put out of action. The remaining seven enemy destroyers fired about twenty torpedoes altogether while turning, and at the same time cast overboard big drums of supplies destined for Japanese forces on Guadalcanal. It was a resolute and decisive manoeuvre.

Vice-Admiral Hiroki Abe commanded the formidable Raiding Group, including two battleships, which was assigned the role of destroying Henderson Field by bombardment during the battle of Guadalcanal, 13–15 November 1942.

In a few minutes the skilfully aimed torpedoes struck home. The American flagship, the heavy cruiser *Minneapolis*, was hit in the bows by two torpedoes which set her fuel tanks ablaze and cut power off from her gun turrets. *New Orleans*, the cruiser following her, was struck by a torpedo which slammed into her magazines, detonated explosives, blew off the bows and left her ablaze. A few minutes later a torpedo hit the *Pensacola* with destructive effect upon her engine-room and gun turrets. *Honolulu* escaped by skilful zig-zagging, but the *Northampton*, the last American cruiser in the line, was also hit simultaneously by two torpedoes which set her afire and caused her later to be abandoned.

Altogether 400 officers and men were killed in this defeat of a powerful radar-equipped American cruiser force by a destroyer force which had no radar but which was highly skilled in night fighting with torpedoes. Three of the American cruisers were ultimately saved, but they remained in dry dock for nearly twelve months.

Yet, despite this last brilliant victory, the Japanese resolved to evacuate Guadalcanal, the island which had cost them so much in men, ships and aircraft. Since the American landing they had lost nearly all their experienced pilots, five or six hundred aircraft, two battleships, an aircraft carrier, five cruisers, thirteen destroyers and six submarines, compared with American losses of two aircraft carriers, eight cruisers, seventeen destroyers, and many fewer aircraft.

Bitter fighting on land, in the air and between the rival squadrons of destroyers continued for weeks before the Japanese, during the night of 8 February 1943, managed to take off the last of their battered troops. For the United States it was a vital step forward in the campaign to clear the Western Pacific.

Philippine Sea
June 1944

The Battle of the Philippine Sea, 19 June 1944, dubbed by American sailors who took part 'The Great Marianas Turkey Shoot', cost the Japanese three aircraft carriers sunk and nearly all their trained pilots. For the Japanese it was a grave setback, but for the Americans it represented an important advance in their campaign to clear the West Central Pacific.

The battle was the outcome of the US invasion of the Mariana Islands, following the earlier seizure of the Marshalls in February 1944. The American attack on the Marianas provoked an all-out Japanese reaction because possession of the Marianas would give the United States naval and air bases only 1,500 miles away from the Home Islands; from these they would be able to hit the enemy's industrial base and cut Japanese communications with the Philippines and South-East Asia.

Admiral Soemu Toyoda, commander of the Combined Fleet, decided to deploy every available ship and aircraft in one big operation to destroy both the American amphibious invasion force and Admiral Spruance's protecting fleet. This was the first time the Japanese fleet had sought a major battle since the reverse at Guadalcanal in late 1942.

On 16 June Admiral Jisaburo Ozawa's 1st Mobile Fleet joined up with Admiral Matome Ugaki's Southern Force east of the Philippines. Their battle formation comprised four big and five small carriers, five battleships, including the giants *Yamato* and *Musashi*, eleven heavy and two light cruisers and 28 destroyers. Opposing them was Admiral Spruance's 5th Fleet of seven big and eight small carriers, seven battleships, eight heavy and thirteen light cruisers and 69 destroyers. Both sides had about 450 carrier aircraft, but the Japanese could also call upon another 500 based at Guam and Yap islands. They were about to launch the biggest series of air strikes against a surface fleet yet seen in the war.

Ozawa sighted the US fleet north of Guam at 8.30 am on 19 June and launched his first strike at once. He then launched another strike at 9 am, while at the same time US submarines torpedoed and sank the 33,000-ton carrier *Taiho*, his flagship, thus forcing him to move his flag and communications staff at a crucial moment in the battle.

An onslaught lasting eight hours then began against the US carriers. Most of the Japanese aircraft were located by radar, and by late afternoon some 400 of them had been shot down at ranges varying from 5 to 50 miles. It was a disaster for the Japanese, compounded when the 22,000-ton carrier *Shokaku* was torpedoed and sunk by the US submarine *Cavalla*.

Overnight, the Japanese fleet turned north-west, but during the afternoon of 20 June Spruance located it, launched powerful air strikes and sank the carrier *Hiyo* and two tankers, and damaged the *Junyo*. Twenty American pilots were shot down and 80 more ditched their aircraft in the sea (51 of them were rescued). The amphibious landings in the Marianas went ahead unhindered.

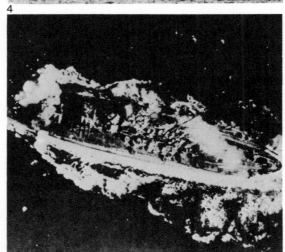

4

5

1. Admiral Toyoda, C-in-C of the Japanese Combined Fleet at the Battle of the Philippine Sea.

2. Admiral Ugaki, in command of the Japanese Southern Force.

3. The 22,000-ton aircraft carrier *Shokaku*, sunk by the US submarine *Cavalla*.

4. The super-battleship *Musashi*.

5. An aerial photograph of the *Musashi* under heavy attack from American bombers during the battle.

6. The Japanese aircraft carrier *Hiyo*.

7. The US submarine *Cavalla*, which sank the *Shokaku* with three torpedoes at a range of 1,500 yards.

8. The crew of the sinking Japanese carrier *Zuikaku* gather on her flight deck as she goes down off Cape Engano.

8

Leyte Gulfe
October 1944

By July 1944 US forces had completed their campaigns in the Mariana Islands and, together with the Australians, had driven the Japanese from the Solomons. By November 1944, after a stubbornly fought two-year campaign, the Japanese had been dislodged from New Guinea. Now the Americans were ready for the reconquest of the Philippines.

In September 1944, as the New Guinea struggle neared its end, there came two small but important moves considered essential to the Philippines campaign. General MacArthur's troops, the 31st Infantry Division, were put down on the beaches of the island of Morotai, which lies between New Guinea's western tip and the Philippines. Their seizure of the island was practically unopposed, and soon Australian engineer units had an airstrip ready, for Morotai was an essential base for Allied fighter and medium bomber aircraft in the forthcoming Philippines battle.

At the same time, Admiral Halsey, now Commander 3rd Fleet, seized Peleliu, one of the Palau group in the Central Pacific, thought to be a necessary staging-point in the Leyte battles. Halsey next used his carrier aircraft to carry out a series of air strikes against airfields on Mindanao in the southern Philippines, on Leyte and Samar in the central group, and on those in Luzon in the north.

These blows led to a total change in the Philippines invasion plans. Up till early September these were based on a campaign beginning with Mindanao and moving north; but when very little enemy opposition was encountered, it was decided to by-pass Mindanao and instead stage an immediate invasion of Leyte on 20 October 1944.

The first outcome of this dramatic decision was a series of strikes on airfields between the Philippines and Japan—Formosa, Okinawa and other islands of the Ryukyus group—in which from 10–17 October 1944 more than 500 Japanese aircraft were destroyed in furious air battles, about 20 cargo vessels were sunk and numerous ammunition and supply dumps bombed—at the small cost of 79 aircraft lost and 64 aircrew missing. By thus weakening the enemy air force these strikes were decisive in the outcome of Leyte battles, for not much more than 100 trained Japanese pilots were left to man their carrier-borne aircraft, a pitiful force to range against the Americans.

Admiral Chester Nimitz, Commander Pacific Fleet and Pacific Ocean Areas, had assembled the most formidable naval force ever seen up till that time, to transport General Walter Kreuger's 6th Army to Leyte beneath air cover supplied by carrier aircraft and General George Kenney's South-West Pacific Air Forces, in an attempt to inflict a final and crushing defeat upon the enemy's naval forces.

A feature of the command structure for the Leyte battles was the dual command exercised by General MacArthur, Supreme Allied Commander South-West Pacific, and Admiral Chester Nimitz. Under MacArthur, Vice-Admiral Kinkaid commanded the 7th Fleet, made up of a Northern Attack Force under Rear-Admiral Daniel E. Barbey, a Southern Attack Force under Vice-Admiral Theodore S. ('Ping') Wilkinson and an Escort Carrier Group under Rear-Admiral Thomas L. Sprague, altogether 6 battleships, 11 cruisers, 18 carriers and 86 destroyers.

Under Admiral Nimitz, Halsey commanded the 3rd Fleet's Fast Carrier Force of Task Force 38 (Vice-Admiral Marc A. Mitscher), comprising nine big and eight small carriers, five battleships, 17 cruisers, 64 destroyers and over 1,000 aircraft divided into four task groups. Including its minesweepers and smaller patrol craft, the two fleets added up to the most formidable naval force ever assembled, but dual command was to lead to losses and near disaster.

Kinkaid was assigned the task of transporting and landing General Walter Kreuger's 6th Army in its seizure and occupation of the Leyte area, while Halsey's 3rd Fleet was to cover the landings and attack and destroy the enemy fleet.

First moves in this great encounter began when the US Rangers occupied the small islands dominating the eastern approaches to Leyte Gulf. Rear-Admiral Jesse E. Oldendorf's

General MacArthur, who exercised a frequently uneasy dual command in the Pacific theatre of war with Admiral Nimitz.

A Japanese bomber falls in flames, narrowly missing an American aircraft carrier, after being hit by anti-aircraft fire.

gunfire support group then heavily shelled the landing beaches early on 20 October 1944, and in calm weather, with little opposition and no mines or underwater defences, Kreuger's troops were put ashore on the smooth, tropical beaches of Leyte's eastern coast. Before midnight 132,000 men were ashore, the principal enemy strongpoint had been seized hours earlier, and nearly 200,000 tons of equipment and supplies had been landed. This was the prelude to a bout of hard fighting in which some 70,000 Japanese soldiers and 15,000 American killed or wounded were to fall in a sharply fought campaign.

When Imperial Headquarters in Tokyo learned of MacArthur's plan to invade the Philippines, Admiral Soemu Toyoda, who had been appointed Combined Fleet C-in-C after Yamamoto's death in action, was ordered to put into action *Sho-1*, the plan for a decisive naval action off Leyte with the United States Fleet. After the US Fleet's presumed destruction, the American forces ashore would be cut off and vulnerable. The word *Sho* meant total victory, and its choice can be seen as a measure of the secret desperation then felt at Imperial Headquarters.

The Japanese plan was based once again on the traditional Samurai tactic of the feint attack to lure off the main part of the enemy force so that the remainder could then be quickly destroyed by another powerful naval force, which would afterwards join the feint attack force and finish off the enemy. Vice-Admiral Jisaburo Ozawa's Northern Force, made up of the four carriers *Zuikaku*, *Chiyoda*, *Chitose* and *Zuiho*, with the two battleship-carriers *Ise* and *Hyuga* (14-inch guns forward and flight decks aft), three cruisers and eight destroyers, was to steam south from Japan as the lure to draw Halsey's 3rd Fleet away to the north, and engage it in battle.

Ozawa, whose carriers possessed only a hundred inadequately trained pilots and whose

battleship-carriers possessed none at all, was thus ordered to sacrifice his fleet to Halsey's formidable Fast Carrier Task Force—the elements of which have already been described. Ozawa revealed later that he bowed to this order to sacrifice his fleet in the certainty that the final outcome would be disaster.

The second, but most important part of the plan provided for Vice-Admiral Kurita's Striking Force to race out from its station in the Lingga Roads, near Singapore, to attack Kinkaid's 7th Fleet, which was protecting the American landings, and then destroy Kreuger's invasion forces. Kurita's Striking Force, which included the giant 18-inch-gun battleships *Musashi* and *Yamato*, was to be reinforced by Vice-Admiral Kiyohide Shima's 2nd Striking Force from Formosa, consisting of two heavy cruisers, a light cruiser, and seven destroyers. While these forces concentrated on the destruction of the invasion fleet, Vice-Admiral Fukudome's 2nd Air Fleet, reinforced by what were the fighting remnants of the 1st Air Fleet, was also to attempt to wipe out Halsey's carriers.

The forces of the United States Navy and the Imperial Japanese Navy were both readied now for the battles in which each hoped to destroy the other: the battle of Surigao Strait, the battle of Cape Engano and the battle of Samar, called collectively the battle of Leyte Gulf.

Vice-Admiral Takijiro Onishi, the new naval commander of the 1st Air Fleet in Manila, made a personal appeal to Zeke fighter pilots to help offset the crucial shortage of fighter cover for the surface ships by Kamikaze—suicide dive-bombing attacks with 550-lb bombs against the enemy carriers and battleships. According to Masatake Okuyima, an air staff officer with the navy general staff, Onishi formed a Divine Wind Special Attack Squad—*Kamikaze Tokubatsu Kogekitai*—from volunteers among those pilots willing to

Admiral Jisaburo Ozawa, whose Northern Force of four carriers, two battleships, three cruisers and eight destroyers was intended to lure the US 3rd Fleet away from Leyte to the north, so as to split the American naval force.

Vice-Admiral Takeo Kurita, whose Striking Force raced out from its station near Singapore to attack Admiral Kinkaid's 7th Fleet and try to destroy the American invasion forces. Kurita's force included the world's biggest battleships, the 18-inch-gun *Musashi* and *Yamato*.

The Japanese battleship *Ise*, part of Admiral Ozawa's Northern Force, possessed a main armament of four 14-inch guns forward and a launching deck for fighter or dive-bomber aircraft aft. A novel concept, its drawback seems to have been an inability to land aircraft on the short flight deck once they were catapulted into the air.

sacrifice their lives in this way.

Admiral Ozawa's unfortunate carrier force —the lure—sailed from Japan's Inland Sea on 20 October 1944. On 18 October 1944, two days before the initial American landings on Leyte, Admiral Kurita's 1st Striking Force, with its two 74,000-ton super-battleships, had refuelled at Brunei, North Borneo, and set course for Leyte. On 22 October his Centre Force steamed for the Sibuyan Sea and the San Bernadino Strait, so as to enter Leyte Gulf via Samar and the north, while at the same time the Southern Force, under Admiral Shoji Nishimura and Admiral Kiyohide Shima, steamed through the Mindanao Sea to reach Leyte Gulf through the Surigao Strait. Their orders were to attack the enemy's amphibious forces in Leyte Gulf at 6.30 am on 25 October 1944, paving the way for a heavier attack by Kurita's force that day at 8.30 am.

But first blood went to the United States. The submarines *Darter*, under Commander David McClintock, and *Dace*, under Commander B. D. Claggert, sighted Kurita's Centre Force west of the dagger-shaped island of Palawan, between North Borneo and Mindoro, early on 23 October. Having reported the event by radio to Admiral Halsey, they manoeuvred to attack, and at 6.30 am *Darter* fired two torpedoes accurately into the cruiser *Atago*, Kurita's flagship, and two into the cruiser *Takao*, sinking the first and crippling the second. *Dace* then hit and sank the cruiser *Maya* with well-aimed torpedoes. Kurita's weakened Centre Force resolutely steamed on towards the Sibuyan Sea and to its next encounter, Kurita having transferred his flag to the *Yamato*.

On 24 October the battles reached their climax. Halsey's carrier aircraft—alerted by *Darter*'s warning—sighted Kurita's super-battleship fleet in the Sibuyan Sea, but this time the Japanese struck first. Seventy-six aircraft from Ozawa's Northern Force—the lure —attacked Admiral Frederick Sherman's Tank Group 38.3 (part of Task Force 38) and, defying the curtain of anti-aircraft fire, sank the light carrier *Princeton* at a cost of 56 aircraft. The cruiser *Birmingham* was badly damaged when *Princeton*'s torpedoes all blew up at once with a tremendous blast as she came alongside to help the stricken carrier.

But during this engagement another much more violent and crucial action was fought out. The carriers of Admiral Mitscher's Task Force 38 launched one air strike after another in the Sibuyan Sea on Kurita's already battered Centre Force which, without any air cover, was more or less defenceless.

Skilled now, after more than two years of sea-air warfare against the enemy, the American pilots aimed their bombs and torpedoes with accuracy, unhindered by enemy aircraft. During attacks lasting an entire day, the world's greatest battleship, *Musashi*, absorbed blows from no less than 21 torpedoes and more than 30 bombs before she capsized and sank in the early evening's tropical darkness, with the loss of over half of her ship's company of 2,200 men. Kurita's flagship, *Yamato*, was also hit by bombs which slowed, but failed to stop her. The Admiral's other ships were also hit, but continued on their course, except the cruiser *Myoko*, which was crippled and withdrew with a destroyer escort.

The delay caused by this encounter in the Sibuyan Sea had done more than seriously weaken Kurita's force. It had also ruined the most vital part of the timetable upon which the Japanese plan was based, for Kurita was now unable to join Admirals Nishimura and Shima in their Leyte Gulf attack next day at 8.30 am. Protesting bitterly about lack of air cover Kurita turned back westwards, feeling that he could thus avoid daylight air attacks and later, under cover of darkness, once more advance. He was encouraged to do so by a message from Admiral Toyoda ordering him,

Vice-Admiral Thomas C. Kinkaid, commander of the US 7th Fleet, which was part of General Douglas MacArthur's South-West Pacific Command. Kinkaid's task was to transport and land General Walter Kreuger's 6th Army on Leyte.

The 18-inch-gun battleship *Yamato*, pride of the Japanese navy, played an ineffectual role in the naval engagements at Leyte Gulf. She was sunk on 7 April 1945 by US carrier aircraft at the battle of Okinawa.

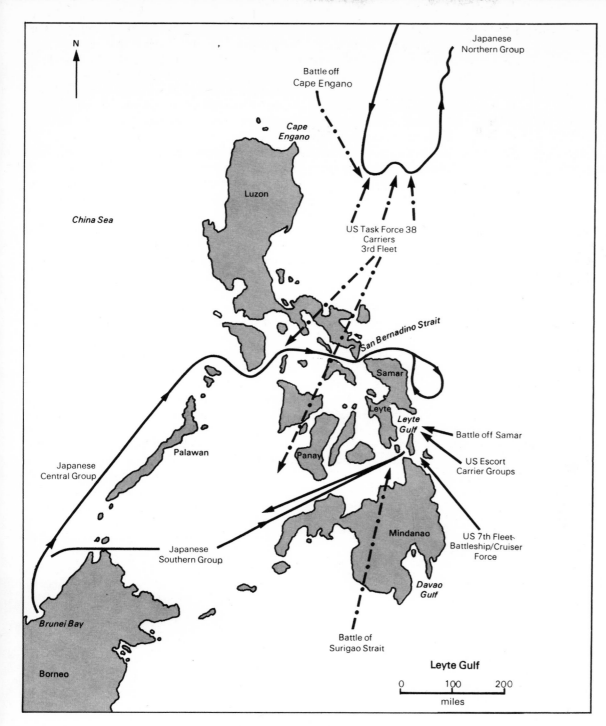

Japanese
Northern Group

Battle off
Cape Engano

Cape
Engano

Luzon

China Sea

US Task Force 38
Carriers
3rd Fleet

San Bernadino Strait

Samar

Leyte

Leyte
Gulf

Battle off Samar

US Escort
Carrier Groups

Palawan

Panay

Japanese
Central Group

Mindanao

US 7th Fleet
Battleship/Cruiser
Force

Japanese
Southern Group

Davao
Gulf

Brunei Bay

Battle of
Surigao Strait

Borneo

Leyte Gulf

0   100   200

miles

'counting on divine aid', to continue on course towards the San Bernadino Strait.

By the afternoon of 24 October 1944 the complex movements of the enemy forces as they presented themselves to the two key American Admirals, Kinkaid and Halsey, were as follows: Kurita's Central Force and Nishimura's Southern Force were approaching Leyte from the San Bernadino Strait and the Surigao Strait respectively. Halsey was aware that Kinkaid had more than enough firepower to drive off or destroy Nishimura's Southern Force, while Kurita's Central Force, lacking any carriers, had been so weakened that, according to Halsey's latest information, it had turned back towards the west.

There was still the possibility that Kurita

would reverse again, steam out from the San Bernadino Strait, and race southwards past Samar to pound the transports and cargo vessels at Leyte while Kinkaid's force was in battle with Nishimura's Southern Force. But Halsey considered this a lesser danger than the approach of Admiral Ozawa's Northern Force of carriers and battleship-carriers, whose aircraft apparently had attacked him during the morning and had sunk the *Princeton*. Halsey considered that this decoy force presented the greatest danger, for he could not know that Ozawa now had only 29 aircraft aboard his carriers.

Halsey therefore decided against taking his carriers north without an escort for air strikes against Ozawa, leaving his battleships in

station ready to pound Kurita's force; nor would he mass his entire fleet for a crushing blow against Kurita. Instead, he decided to race north with the 17 fleet carriers, 6 battleships, 17 cruisers and 64 destroyers of his four task groups to deal an annihilating blow against what he imagined was Ozawa's powerful carrier striking force bearing down from the north. He issued the orders and Task Force 38 raced north that afternoon.

With all the eagerness of a hungry trout, Halsey had leaped for the bait the Japanese had dangled before him. He had dangerously exposed MacArthur's invasion forces and put the entire operation in jeopardy, for now there was no American force ready to stop Kurita attacking the invasion fleet at Leyte. The system of dual command between MacArthur and Nimitz, two competing warlords, was beginning to scatter sand in the works of America's great war machine, for not even President Roosevelt had felt himself able to promote one as supreme commander over the head of the other.

The drama of Leyte advanced to its climax. Vice-Admiral Kinkaid, commanding the 7th Fleet, was informed of Nishimura's approach with his Southern Force towards the Surigao Strait around noon on 24 October; he assigned

A Japanese dive-bomber makes a suicide dive at an American warship during the Leyte Gulf battle. American naval personnel in the foreground duck for shelter.

An ungraceful but safe landing for a Grumman Hellcat on the deck of a US carrier.

150

to Rear-Admiral Oldendorf the task of intercepting them with the powerful gunfire support group which had been supporting the Leyte landings.

Two or three hours later he received a copy of Halsey's orders to his fleet to steam away north. However, he supposed that Halsey would not have done so without having left behind a force strong enough to stop Kurita. He therefore made no changes in his dispositions.

Well before midnight on 24 October Oldendorf had deployed his force of six battleships, four heavy cruisers—including the *Shropshire*, of the Royal Australian Navy—and four light cruisers so as to dominate the fifteen-mile-wide stretch of water between Leyte and Hibuson Island into which, if he got that far, Nishimura would debouch from the Surigao Strait. For Oldendorf had also assigned to two destroyer divisions the task of steaming down the Strait to meet the enemy with torpedo attacks; and a force of 39 torpedo-boats was patrolling the entire Strait with orders to send back radio reports of all vessels sighted and then to proceed to the attack at once.

The Japanese Southern Force steamed at some 25 knots towards the entrance to the Strait in two separate groups, first Nishimura in line ahead, with Shima following two hours behind. Four destroyers were in Nishimura's van, then the battleship *Yamashiro*, his flagship; then at intervals of about 900 yards the battleship *Fuso* and the cruiser *Mogami*. Shortly after midnight they were sighted by the torpedo-boats, which reported their position and then went into

Four Japanese cruisers sank the American light carrier *Gambier Bay* on 25 October 1944 near Samar Island at about 9 am, only a few minutes before Admiral Kurita ordered the general withdrawal of his fleet.

The cruiser *Atago*, Admiral Kurita's flagship, sank quickly when hit by two torpedoes fired by the American submarine *Darter* in the early stages of the battle.

Pilots and crewmen of the US carrier *Enterprise* prepare to launch a reconnaissance patrol of the powerful new Grumman Hellcat fighter-bomber two or three days before the first landings on Leyte, in the Philippines. Another American carrier is visible in the background.

The St Lo, an American escort carrier (right), sinks in flames shortly after being hit by a Japanese suicide dive-bomber heavily loaded with explosive at Leyte on 25 October 1944. To the left, an American destroyer is also hit and erupts in flame and smoke while more bombs burst alongside, an enemy aircraft falls in flames and another zooms down to attack.

The crew of this American aircraft carrier at Leyte Gulf spring for cover as a Japanese suicide pilot slams into the hull and another swoops down in his death dive.

the attack. But they were unsuccessful and sustained losses at the hands of the enemy destroyers.

Then at 3 am, while Nishimura pressed on, torpedoes fired by the American destroyers from a distance of between 8,200 and 9,300 yards hit the battleship *Fuso* and three destroyers, leaving them burning or sinking. Twice the battleship *Yamashiro* was hit, but she continued on her course, her only companions now being the cruiser *Mogami* and the destroyer *Shigura*.

Nishimura was now steaming into an overwhelming concentration of artillery from Oldendorf's force, deployed across the entrance to the Surigao Strait at right angles to his line in the classic 'T' situation. Desperately he signalled *Fuso* to come up fast, but that vessel was by then sinking. A few seconds after 3.53 am a storm of 14-inch shells, followed by torpedoes, hit the Japanese vessels in such quick succession that they could do little to return fire with any accuracy. *Yamashiro* was soon aflame; *Nogamo* was struck

by a salvo on the bridge which wiped out her captain and staff; the destroyer *Shigura*, almost unscathed, turned south to escape. The end for *Yamashiro* came soon after Oldendorf had ordered a temporary cease-fire to avoid striking his own ships. Two torpedoes hit her as she turned south and she sank at about 4.20 am, taking with her Admiral Nishimura and all of her crew but four.

Admiral Shima's force entered the Strait soon after 4 am. Promptly, an American torpedo-boat, PT-137, shot a torpedo into the light cruiser *Abukima* and crippled her. Soon afterwards, having fired eight torpedoes unsuccessfully at distant enemy ships, Shima gave the order to turn about and retire. At this moment his flagship, *Nachi*, collided with the cruiser *Mogami*, which was running from Oldendorf's shellfire. The pursuit phase of the encounter ended at about 6.20 am, after the destroyer *Asagumo* had been sunk, and Oldendorf had ordered withdrawal.

The United States lost only 39 men killed and 114 wounded—mostly in one destroyer—

in this battle of Surigao Strait. This engagement is celebrated as the last occasion in the Second World War—and no doubt the last in the history of naval warfare—in which the classic centuries-old line-of-battle tactics came into play.

While Oldendorf's ships were disposing of the enemy's Southern Force, Admiral Halsey, who had raced northwards with the formidable Task Force 38 (minus Task Group 38.1, which was refuelling in the south) had sighted Ozawa's Northern Force about 200 miles north-east of Cape Engano, Luzon, at 2.20 am on 25 October. Halsey could put no less than 401 fighters, 214 dive-bombers and 171 torpedo-bombers into the air, compared with Ozawa's 29.

At 8 am, in the first strike, the carrier *Chitose* and a destroyer were sunk, while Ozawa's flagship *Zuikaku* was hit by a torpedo which destroyed her entire communications system and forced the Admiral to transfer to a light cruiser, the *Oyodo*. In the next strike, at 9.45 am, dive-bombers set the

Ohiyoda ablaze; in the third strike the veteran carrier *Zuikaku* was hit simultaneously by three torpedoes which tore her apart and put her quickly beneath the waves; in the fourth strike the *Zuiho* was sunk after a succession of heavy blows. The two final strikes were strangely unsuccessful, especially in their efforts to sink the converted battleship *Ise*. Four carriers and a destroyer, all lacking air cover, was Halsey's final score. But with over three hundred dive-bomber and torpedo-bomber sorties flown after his dramatic overnight dash, this was by no means remarkable.

Soon Halsey had cause to wonder if he had not acted rashly in taking Task Force 38's ships north, leaving Kinkaid's invasion fleet open to attack. Admiral Kurita's still-powerful force had passed through the San Bernadino Strait soon after midnight, had raced south down Samar Island's east coast towards Leyte, and at 7 am his battleships had opened fire on Kinkaid's escort carriers.

Rear-Admiral Sprague was suddenly surprised to find this force, Taffy 3, of six escort carriers, three destroyers and four destroyer escorts, engaged by Kurita's four battleships, six heavy cruisers and ten destroyers. Calls for help began to reach Halsey. Immediately he ordered Admiral McCain to finish refuelling his Task Group 38.1 near San Bernadino and hurry to the aid of Admiral Sprague's Taffy 3, engaged in trying to beat off Kurita's attack. Two hours later he ordered south a force of battleships and cruisers under Admiral Lee, but neither of these forces could reach Sprague for a few hours.

It seemed that Kurita held the trump card, for his guns were already firing on Admiral Sprague's force off the coast of Samar Island. However, the weather gave Sprague a slight advantage. The wind enabled his carriers to steam as fast as possible away from Kurita's approaching ships while at the same time launching aircraft to attack them. Unfortunately, these same aircraft were armed for operations ashore and could not do much against Kurita's warships. Then a rain squall, added to the prevailing smoke from the carriers, gave them fifteen minutes respite while his three destroyers went boldly into

The Japanese carrier *Zuiho*, an element of Admiral Ozawa's Northern Force, carried out evasion tactics to try to avoid aerial attack by torpedo-bombers from the carrier *Enterprise* during the Leyte Gulf actions. This remarkable picture was taken by a torpedo-bomber seconds after its torpedo had struck home aft, where smoke and flame can be seen. The *Zuiho* finally went down later on 25 October 1944. Camouflage simulating a battleship covers her decks.

the fray against Kurita's battleships and cruisers.

Destroyer *Johnston* launched torpedoes at 10,000 yards and hit the cruiser *Kumano*, but within minutes was overwhelmed and sunk by a storm of shells. At the same time torpedoes from the destroyer *Hermann* heading for the 18-inch gun battleship *Yamato* caused her to turn away and reverse course for ten valuable minutes in which she was unable to bring her guns to bear. *Hoel*, the third destroyer, was hit by enemy shells more than 40 times before she capsized and went down in this fight against impossible odds. For the American destroyer crews it was an encounter at once tragic and heroic.

During this hectic engagement, aircraft from Sprague's own carriers and every other available carrier within range attacked the enemy battleships and cruisers with bombs and torpedoes, causing them to adopt drastic evasion tactics, swinging in wide arcs and sometimes reversing course. Sprague's carriers, chugging along at their maximum speed of $17\frac{1}{2}$ knots, thus managed to prevent the battleships from closing the range to less than about 18,000 yards, but four fast enemy cruisers closed at about 9 am and sank carrier *Gambier Bay* a few minutes later. Four of the carrier dive-bombers replied by hitting the cruiser *Chokai* with ten bombs, sending her to the bottom. She was followed within a few minutes by the cruiser *Chikuma*, after another successful dive-bombing attack.

This effective air attack from the small enemy force demoralized Kurita, for suddenly at 9.11 am when the defenceless transports were almost within his reach at Leyte, he ordered a general withdrawal. He then reformed his fleet, intending to set course for the north, away from the vital centre of action, to join Admiral Ozawa's battered remnants, but changed his mind and turned back into the San Bernadino Strait, intending to head for Japan. Halsey returned to the area too late to intervene, but next day his and MacArthur's land-based aircraft sighted Kurita and sank one more of his cruisers and two destroyers. Another of Sprague's carriers, the *St Lo*, was destroyed by a Kamikaze suicide attack on 25 October.

The battles of Leyte Gulf had ended. For the Japanese navy it had been a moment of destiny, for the Americans had broken its power decisively, sinking in five days three battleships, four carriers, six heavy and four light cruisers, nine destroyers and one submarine, as well as destroying several hundred aircraft. The Americans themselves had lost one light fleet carrier, two escort carriers, three destroyers, a submarine and a number of aircraft. Their losses in men were also small compared with the heavy casualties of the enemy.

But, as the battle of Coral Sea first demonstrated, the carrier-borne aircraft had become the decisive factor in naval warfare, and thus in sea power, though not for long. Within two or three decades guided missile cruisers and vertical take-off aircraft like the British Harrier were challenging the all-too-vulnerable carriers in the struggle for sea power.

In this picture the aircraft carrier *St Lo* is seen at the moment a Kamikaze suicide dive-bomber explodes on her flight deck during the Leyte Gulf action off Samar Island.

157

Bibliography

Admiralty. *Naval Attachés' Despatches, Russo-Japanese War*
R. Bacon. *The Jutland Scandal*
G. Bennett. *Naval Battles of the First World War*
B. Bingham. *Falklands, Jutland and the Bight*
W. S. Chalmers. *The Life and Letters of David Beatty, Admiral of the Fleet*
W. S. Churchill. *The World Crisis, 1914–1918*
J. Creswell. *Naval Warfare*
E. A. Falk. *Togo and the Rise of Japanese Sea Power*
T. G. Frothingham. *The Naval History of the World War*
W. Goodenough. *A Rough Record*
J. E. Harper. *The Truth About Jutland*
G. von Hase. *Kiel and Jutland*
L. Hirst. *Coronel and After*
R. Hough. *The Fleet that had to Die*
J. Irvine. *The Smokescreen of Jutland*
J. Irving. *Coronel and the Falklands*
R. Keyes. *Naval Memoirs*

D. Macintyre. *Jutland*
B. Milne. *The Flight of the Goeben and Breslau*
A. Novikoff-Priboy. *Tsushima*
H. Pochhammer. *Admiral Spee's Last Voyage*
V. Semenoff. *The Battle of Tsushima*
K. Toyo. *Naval Battles of the Russo-Japanese War*

The Pacific War
W. S. Churchill. *The Second World War* (Vols 1–6)
J. Horikoshi and O. Masatake. *Zero*
S. E. Morison. *History of the United States Naval Operations in World War II* (Vols 1–12)
The Two-Ocean War
C. Nimitz and E. B. Potter. *Triumph in the Pacific: The Navy's Struggle against Japan*
W. D. Puleston. *The Influence of Sea Power in World War II*
P. Young. *World War, 1939–45*

Acknowledgments

The publishers would like to thank the following for the use of the photographs indicated.

Associated Press 126 bottom; Barnaby's Picture Library 23 top, 37, 50/51, 66/67; Central Press Photos 84/85 centre, 85 lower centre, 117 upper centre and bottom, 126 top; Fujiphotos 8 top, 11 top, 12, 14 top, 18, 91, 105 bottom, 106 top, 107 top, 130/131, 139, 141, 142 top centre, 142/143 centre and bottom, 143 upper centre, lower centre and bottom, 146 right, 147 top, 150 top, 157; Imperial War Museum endpapers, 16 bottom, 22/23 centre, 24, 29 bottom, 31 top, 32, 40, 43, 44/45, 46, 48, 49, 52, 60/61 bottom, 71 top and bottom, 73 top and bottom, 74, 76, 77, 79, 81 top, 84/85 bottom, 85 upper centre, 90 bottom, 98/99 top, 99 top, 100, 103 bottom, 106 bottom, 112/113, 116/117 top, 117 top, 118, 124, 125, 128/129, 132, 133, 140/141, 143 top, 146 left, 147 bottom, 148 bottom, 151 bottom; Keystone Press Agency 89, 102, 107 bottom, 111, 116 top, 117 lower centre; Kyodo Photo Service 108 top; Mansell Collection 64 top; Österreichische Nationalbibliothek 9 bottom, 26; Popperfoto 38/39, 83 top, 85 bottom, 94, 98/99 bottom, 116/117 centre and bottom, 120 top, 150 bottom; Radio Times Hulton Picture Library title page, 11 bottom, 14 bottom, 17, 28, 29 top, 36, 38 top, 47, 53 bottom, 54/55, 80 bottom, 82 top, 84 top; Photo Science Museum, London 85 top; Senshi-Shitsu 142 top right; Staatsbibliothek Berlin 6, 30 top and bottom, 42, 58, 59, 60 top, 61 top, 64 bottom; Süddeutscher Verlag 27 top and bottom, 34, 34/35, 36/37, 39 top, 53 top, 57, 60/61 top and centre, 61 centre and bottom, 64 centre, 66, 68 top and bottom, 74/75, 78/79, 80 top, 82 bottom, 83 bottom, 96/97, 108 bottom, 113, 121 top, 136, 138, 154, 154/155; Ullstein 10 top and bottom, 15, 16 top, 19, 22 top, 22/23 top and bottom, 23 centre and bottom, 31 bottom, 33, 72; US Department of the Navy contents page, 86, 88, 90 top, 92, 92/93, 95, 103 top, 104 top and bottom, 105 top, 112, 114/115, 120/121, 134/135, 137, 144, 147 centre, 148 top, 152/153, 156; US National Archives 122, 123, 127, 131, 151 top; US Office of War Information 110; Roger Viollet 8 bottom, 9 top, 20/21.

George Allen and Unwin Ltd:
From *Tsushima* by A. Novikoff-Priboy
Reprinted by permission

Cassell and Company Ltd and Houghton Mifflin Co:
From *The Second World War* (Vol. 4) by Winston Churchill
Reprinted by permission

Little, Brown and Company:
From *History of the United States Operations in World War II* by S. E. Morison
Reprinted by permission

Laurence Pollinger Ltd:
From *Zero* by Martin Caiden, J. Horikoshi and O. Masatake
Reprinted by permission

Index